T0304081

ROUTLEDGE LIBRARY EDITIONS:
EXCHANGE RATE ECONOMICS

Volume 1

THE EXCHANGE RATE ENVIRONMENT

THE EXCHANGE RATE ENVIRONMENT

SIMON BROOKS, KEITH CUTHBERTSON AND
DAVID G. MAYES

Routledge
Taylor & Francis Group

LONDON AND NEW YORK

First published in 1986 by Croom Helm

This edition first published in 2017
by Routledge
2 Park Square, Milton Park, Abingdon, Oxon OX14 4RN

and by Routledge
711 Third Avenue, New York, NY 10017

Routledge is an imprint of the Taylor & Francis Group, an informa business

British Library Cataloguing in Publication Data
A catalogue record for this book is available from the British Library

ISBN: 978-0-415-79325-4 (Set)
ISBN: 978-1-315-21117-6 (Set) (ebk)
ISBN: 978-1-138-72302-3 (Volume 1) (hbk)
ISBN: 978-1-315-19325-0 (Volume 1) (ebk)

Publisher's Note
The publisher has gone to great lengths to ensure the quality of this reprint but
points out that some imperfections in the original copies may be apparent.

Disclaimer
The publisher has made every effort to trace copyright holders and would welcome
correspondence from those they have been unable to trace.

THE
EXCHANGE
RATE
ENVIRONMENT

**SIMON BROOKS, KEITH CUTHBERTSON
AND DAVID G. MAYES**

CROOM HELM
London • Sydney • Wolfeboro, New Hampshire

© 1986 Simon Brooks, Keith Cuthbertson and David G. Mayes
Croom Helm Ltd, Provident House, Burrell Row,
Beckenham, Kent BR3 1AT
Croom Helm Australia Pty Ltd, Suite 4, 6th Floor,
64–76 Kippax Street, Surry Hills, NSW 2010, Australia

British Library Cataloguing in Publication Data

Brooks, Simon
    The exchange rate environment.
    1. Foreign exchange
    I. Title II. Cuthbertson, Keith III. Mayes,
    David G.
    332.4'56   HG3851
    ISBN 0–7099–1762–7

Croom Helm US, 27 South Main Street,
Wolfeboro, New Hampshire 03894-2069

Library of Congress Cataloging-in-Publication Data

Brooks, Simon.
    The exchange rate environment.

    Includes bibliographies and index.
    1. Foreign exchange. I. Cuthbertson, Keith. II. Mayes, David G.
III. Title.
HG3851.B75 1986   338.4'56   86-16768
ISBN 0-7099-1762-7

Photosetting by Mayhew Typesetting
Printed and bound in Great Britain

CONTENTS

ABBREVIATIONS

BOF   balance of official financing
CAM   current account monetary models
CAN   current account news
CID   covered interest differential
CYN   cyclical news
DC   domestic credit
EC   European Community
ECU   European Currency Unit
EFTA   European Free Trade Association
EMCF   European Monetary Cooperation Fund
EMH   efficient market hypothesis
EMS   European Monetary System
EUA   European Unit of Account
IMF   International Monetary Fund
IMM   imternational monetary models
IV   instrumental variables
KAM   capital account monetary models
LBS   London Business School
NBPS   non-bank private sector
NEDO   National Economic Development Office
NIESR   National Institute for Economic and Social Research
OECD   Organisation for Economic Cooperation and Development
OEEC   Organisation for European Economic Cooperation
OLS   ordinary least squares
OPEC   Organisation of Petroleum Exporting Countries
PPP   purchasing power parity
PSBR   Public Sector Borrowing Requirement
RE   rational expectations
REH   Rational Expectations Hypothesis
SDR   special drawing right
2SLS   two stage least squares
VB   visible balance

ABOUT THE AUTHORS

All three are practising applied economists with wide experience of macroeconomic forecasting. Brooks worked for six years at the National Institute for Economic and Social Research, specialising in overseas trade of the UK, macroeconomic model building and forecasting. He has recently moved to HM Treasury. Cuthbertson moved from HM Treasury to the National Institute with a period of lecturing at Thames Polytechnic intervening. He is currently working at the University of Newcastle. His main interests are monetary economics, applied econometrics and macroeconomic forecasting and analysis. Mayes was a lecturer in statistics at the University of Exeter before becoming the editor of the National Institute Economic Review in 1981. Since 1983 he has been Head of Statistics Division at the National Economic Development Office.

FOREWORD

We first considered the idea for this book when we were all three at the National Institute of Economic and Social Research in London during 1981. To a large extent it was stimulated by the difficulties in providing satisfactory forecasts of the exchange rate. A lot of effort went into modelling this sector and the work of others was examined with great care in case some major ideas were being missed. It was no satisfaction to us to see that other forecasters were having a similar lack of success. It was of course a much more serious matter for those whose business depended upon satisfactory foreign exchange decisions.

The main problem had been to predict when the rise in sterling would peak. Industry was finding it more and more difficult to compete. As sales at home and abroad fell and the volume of trade moved more and more against the UK, people wondered how long the rise in North Sea oil production and high interest rates would offset the growing imbalance in activity. It was not until we forecast that the down turn was *not* likely over the next few months (after having said the opposite on several consecutive occasions) that the peak was reached.

Over the ensuing years it has become a little easier to sort out the determinants of exchange rates although forecasting is still a very hit-and-miss task. We thought it would be helpful to try to set out what appears to make exchange rates change and to show how these various factors contribute to an explanation of the past.

However, the problem for the future remains. We therefore set out the main types of method that are used for forecasting and outline their relative drawbacks. Some of these methods can be pursued by anyone with relatively little expertise in this field; while the results of others are widely available. There is however no certain way forward. Anyone who speculates in exchange rates can come seriously unstuck. We emphasise how it is possible to minimise exposure to risk by hedging. However, some of these opportunities are often not available to the small trader or individual at reasonable cost and he will need to know as much as possible about the risks he faces.

Much of the talk about exchange rates in the press and in political debate treats the rate of exchange as if it were a single thing. Anyone undertaking a particular transaction is facing the exchange rate with only one particular currency, not some weighted average. Discussions of the position which are appropriate to the US dollar may be totally at variance with those which should be applied to the Swiss franc. However, all these rates are interdependent. The concerns of any one company may be very different from those of government.

Although many of the worries expressed, particularly at the beginning of the 1980s, were about the levels of exchange rates, similar concern is evident about the way exchange rates seem to fluctuate, moving to values which seem to be 'too low' or 'too high' relative to the prices of the two countries and the balance of trade. The view has been widely expressed that this must be a failing of the current flexible exchange rate system. Could we not do better, say, by joining the exchange rate mechanism of the European Monetary System (EMS)?

We have therefore decided to look in some detail at why these fluctuations, which may appear excessive, occur. We thought we should also consider what other systems were available and look at them in some detail. It is ironic that during the period of fixed exchange rates under the Bretton Woods system there were complaints about the lack of flexibility and the distortions fixity placed on economic behaviour. Now we have flexibility there is pressure for fixity because of the difficulty unexpected changes pose for undertaking transactions. In particular we wanted to look at whether full participation in all aspects of the EMS might be a way out.

There are no simple recipes for success but the more countries wish to control exchange rates while leaving the market free, the more they must co-ordinate other policies to prevent the pressures which lead to short- and long-run fluctuations in rates. Possibly this is a way forward — and international organisations such as the Organisation for Economic Co-operation and Development (OECD) like to think so. However, as things stand the exchange rate environment is still one of great uncertainty and complexity.

We hope in this book that we have managed to explain how the system operates, what it would be like if it changed and how people can best act in the face of uncertainty. We have chosen to present the empirical, theoretical and policy issues in a firm economic framework so that the book will be of value to students of macroeconomics, applied economics and international economics in mainstream academic courses. This same firm foundation is designed to help those who actually have to use foreign exchange markets to understand their workings and the actions they can take. We have stood back from the jargon and second-to-second manipulations of the foreign exchange dealers to try to explain the market in which they operate and have not considered how they undertake their work as such; our concern has been with the determinants of the flow of business they transact.

We have enjoyed writing this book and we apologise to those in our immediate circle who have suffered from our attention to this work. We acknowledge our debt to those who have helped, sometimes inadvertently, in making comments and criticisms. We single out particularly the editor who stimulated us into writing the book in the first place, and who thereafter put up with all the delays stoically; the publisher's academic advisers; and the army of typists, including ourselves, who struggled with various versions, especially Irmela Stegemann who struggled with the job of putting our various notes together in the final stage. Neither the Treasury nor NEDO are in any way to be implicated in the views expressed here, which are our own personal ideas; we are however grateful to them for allowing us to undertake the work; as indeed we are to the National Institute, which also has no responsibility for the outcome.

Mayes is grateful to NEDO for allowing him to undertake the work; Brooks and Cuthbertson look forward to Sundays not spent thinking and writing about exchange rates. Cuthbertson is grateful for the opportunity provided by a Hallsworth Fellowship at the University of Manchester to complete part of his contribution to the book and for comments from Ronnie MacDonald. Although this book is a private venture and in no sense necessarily reflects the views of our past and present employers, we must acknowledge our debt to the National Institute where we were first confronted by the problems posed by the need to forecast the exchange rate.

Simon Brooks
Keith Cuthbertson
David G. Mayes

1 INTRODUCTION

The Structure of the Book

The purpose of this book is to offer an explanation of the role that exchange rates play in the economic system, to examine how they are determined in the variety of exchange regimes which exists now, and to look at the developments in such regimes since the Second World War. The book focuses on the empirical evidence and evaluates the pitfalls in exchange rate forecasting.

Part 1

The book begins with a discussion of the prevailing floating exchange rate world in which the major Western world countries operate. In countries with developed capital markets it is international short-term investment decisions which dominate the day-to-day movements in exchange rates. The central part of Chapter 2 explains how such decisions are thought to be made and the way in which spot and forward markets appear to work. Since the operators in these markets are very well informed it is necessary to view these transactions within the framework of 'efficient' markets, in which current trading takes full account of the consequences of correctly anticipated future events. In such markets there will be no effect on spot rates when the correctly anticipated event takes place — say a change in interest rates — but the same change will have an effect if it occurs unexpectedly.

However, these short-run capital flows form only part of the set of transactions which affect exchange rates. Chapter 2 also sets out the nature of the transactions which take place between countries and explains their likely determinants. This exposition covers not merely exports and imports of goods, but also services and current transfers, portfolio and direct investment and monetary movements.

Two main types of transaction in the foreign exchange market can be distinguished: *arbitrage*, where the purchaser or seller hedges his transaction against risk of loss from unexpected changes in the exchange rate; and *speculation*, where the person holds an open position, taking a risk in order to try to make a gain on the transaction. This ability to hedge is extremely important in considering the difficulties posed by floating exchange rates since it allows buyers and sellers to avoid losses despite the fluctuations. The forward rate and the spot rate are closely linked through the process of hedging.

Chapter 3 continues with an exposition of what has come to be known as 'the modern theory of the forward rate' and it is this which forms the heart of exchange rate determination. Speculation in the forward market will take place if people's expectation of the spot rate in the future does not correspond with the current forward rate. Such speculation will itself tend to eliminate the gap as it will affect the forward rate. The chapter contains a survey of such empirical evidence as there is about the determination of the forward exchange rate according to this hypothesis and about the relative importance of speculation and arbitrage transactions. It is concluded by a study of an alternative explanation of exchange rates known as the Cambist approach, as this also has considerable correspondence with the data available.

The role of expectations in exchange rate formation is crucial. Because of the particular nature of the transactions, which are undertaken by well informed professionals in banks rapidly and almost continuously throughout the day the market can adjust quickly and completely to the fluctuation in supply, demand and their determinants. Their understanding of the working of the market and the information available to them is such that it is not implausible to suggest that expectations are formed in a 'rational' manner, where this is taken to mean that on average expectations are correct and are formed as if the people actually knew what determined exchange rates. This, coupled with the 'efficient' trading of the market, which tends to eliminate all opportunities for profit over and above normal margins and transaction costs, makes exchange rate determination one of the most interesting areas of modern economics.

Chapter 4 looks mainly at the way in which exchange rates have fluctuated round what might be thought of as equilibrium values, of which PPP is an example. The chapter examines the hypothesis of 'overshooting' mainly in the context of a model developed by Dornbusch. The basis of the explanation is that when the international economic system gets out of equilibrium because of an unexpected shock, the foreign exchange market can adjust to the new circumstances rapidly — much more rapidly than the product and labour markets can, where the period of adjustment may take years. The exchange rate thus may adjust more in the short run than it needs to finally when all the other markets have adjusted as well. It thus 'overshoots' its equilibrium value. However, it is not clear that overshooting is all-pervasive and the chapter also considers circumstances where the exchange rate may 'undershoot'.

Chapter 4 therefore tackles one of the major questionmarks which lies over the system of exchange rates, namely that of instability. Evidence to the House of Lords Select Committee on Overseas Trade has indicated that while high levels of the exchange rate may present problems for firms, they can adjust to them; what they find much more difficult to cope with is *fluctuations* in rates, particularly when they are unexpected.

In Chapter 5 we examine specifically the phenomenon of unexpected events and their impact on the exchange rate. Estimation of the determinants of the exchange rate is made particularly difficult because of the important role of two factors: *expectations*, on the one hand, which are only indirectly measurable; and *unexpected events*, or 'news' on the other which, by their very nature, are unpredictable. The various economic theories which have been advanced to explain exchange rates, among them purchasing power parity, interest rate parity and the 'modern' theory of forward exchange are placed in their empirical context by explaining estimates which have been made of recent exchange rate behaviour and examining the path of some of the major currencies.

Part 2

Using the theory developed in Part 1, Part 2 goes on to consider alternative exchange rate regimes which operate currently or have been in widespread use in the recent past. Chapter 6 describes the historical development of exchange rate regimes since the Second World War. Some of the particular regimes are then discussed in detail starting with fixed rate systems, concentrating primarily on the system which prevailed from Bretton Woods up to 1971. The second major regime, considered in Chapter 7, is the European Monetary System, looking at its origins with the 'snake', and examining its role in payments in the European Communities. Possible future developments in this system are discussed, as is the concept of optimum currency areas. Chapter 8 examines dual exchange rates, considering first of all the investment currency market which prevailed in the United Kingdom up to 1980 and the French and Belgian franc systems, concluding with the effects of exchange controls and the regimes frequently employed by developing countries. This exposition includes a consideration of the dollar premium and interest equalisation tax. The discussion then moves on to crawling peg and other similar moving exchange rates, such as that employed by New Zealand. The last section of this chapter examines commodity exchange with Eastern bloc countries, in particular looking at the effects of the agreements between Finland and the USSR, where price rises in imported oil have stimulated rather than depressed the Finnish economy.

Part 3

Having set out the empirical background it is then possible in Part 3 to discuss the many policy issues which arise from the effects upon the economy of changes in exchange rates, whether or not intended as a result of deliberate policy. In order to highlight the policy consideration we begin in Chapter 9 by looking at the effects of a devaluation under fixed exchange rates, examining the appropriate domestic policies which have to accompany it. This introduces a discussion of the transmission mechanism and the contrasts between the monetarist and Keynesian views of the working world. The J-curve effect on the balance of payments can then be explained as can the impact on the inflationary wage–price spiral. The exchange rate is thus shown both as an instrument of policy and as a policy objective, particularly in regard to UK policy over the last few years, where the most important feature in the reduction in the rate of inflation in 1980 was the rise in the exchange rate.

The relation between interest rate and exchange rate policy is set out in Chapter 10 with a discussion of the linkage between the foreign sector and the domestic money supply. Further policy measures, such as controls, tariffs, quotas, intervention and sterilisation, are also considered, so that a full picture of the importance of exchange rates in the operation of the economy is developed in Chapter 11. We take as a particular issue in Chapter 12 the impact of North Sea oil on the sterling exchange rate and the experience of countries in the 1974 and 1979 oil crises, showing how the reactions to a similar problem were different in the two cases, with a generally more expansionary reaction to the first crisis including a fall in real interest rates, while in the second case, the imposition of strict monetary policies led to a bidding up of international interest rates in an effort to prevent adverse movements in exchange rates from further worsening the high rates of price inflation.

Chapter 11 also considers the complex process of short-run adjustment to changes in monetary policy which is widely thought to lead to overshooting and exchange rate volatility under the current flexible system. Furthermore, in the light of the current vigorous debate over the merits of the management of trade both within the United Kingdom and in the world as a whole, the chapter discusses the role of the exchange rates as a means of protecting export and import competing industries in both the short and the long run.

Part 4

The last chapter, Chapter 13, brings us to the most important facet of exchange rate behaviour from the point of view of all those who have to plan transactions in foreign currencies — from spending on holidays to the financing of major development projects — namely, forecasting the future. We examine the success, or rather lack of success, of various models in forecasting exchange rates in the past and draw on this experience to suggest the factors which have to be borne in mind in forming a view about the future.

One of the major problems is the modelling and forecasting of expectations, which play such an important role in the determination of short-run investment flows and can result not just in exchange rate volatility, but in substantial and sustained departures from what might be regarded as 'equilibrium' exchange rates under theories such as purchasing power parity. The pound has been subject to these pressures, as have many currencies, and the experiences of the Japanese yen and the Swiss franc are considered as well.

Nevertheless a view has to be formed even if it amounts to nothing more than saying that it is not worth going to the trouble of investigating likely movements. In such a case the judgement is that the losses from an incorrect strategy are likely to be less than the costs of seeking a better one and hence foreign exchange transactions are only undertaken as and when they are needed for payments purposes. This chapter seeks to show how more active strategies could pay off by at least restricting losses.

Why Exchange Markets are Intrinsically Complicated

Exchange rate forecasting is an area in which large sums of money are made and lost within very short periods of time. Currency transactions can be undertaken rapidly in large volumes by very well-informed traders. In the current world of floating exchange rates between the major Western countries it is market forces which determine the outcome. It is the purpose of this book to explain what those market forces are and how they operate.

Despite the wealth of information available to currency traders all transactions are undertaken in the face of considerable uncertainty. While the framework of exchange rate determination may be understood, the actual outcomes in the future are forecast with considerable inaccuracy even by those whose livelihood depends upon it. The essential characteristic of foreign exchange transactions which makes them so uncertain is time.

Many transactions are related to the financing of trade and the payment of bills between purchasers in one country and suppliers in another.

Within a single country the process of relative price determination is well known and the general price level can be forecast quite accurately over relatively short periods of time, such as three months. Thus a supplier can predict quite well what the real value of payments made to him by purchasers will be relative to his own costs. Some contracts may allow variations in price from time to time but they are rarely indexed to the movements in some other price on a day-to-day basis. More often than not contracts are for a fixed price for a given delivery time or period. Nonetheless, given the ease of predicting the domestic price level, a supplier can estimate the probability for his transactions with local customers reasonably accurately. When conducting transactions between countries the same level of certainty does not apply. If the seller denominates his price in his customer's currency then the real value of the payment in his own currency is uncertain. As the seller's exchange rate rises or falls, his revenues fall or rise. The seller thus faces the problem, should he wait until the money is due and then sell his foreign exchange at the rate prevailing at that date — which is unknown — or should he borrow foreign currency and exchange it now at the known rate, leaving his debt to be covered by the forthcoming payment.

If the seller's exchange rate rises then he should have followed the first strategy and sold his foreign exchange at the outset, if it falls then the second strategy is correct. However, this description is simplistic as it ignores the costs of holding money in the form of interest payments. If exchange rates remain unchanged between signing a contract and payment then the seller would be better off on the day of payment if he adopts the borrowing strategy when the domestic rate of interest exceeds the foreign rate. This is because when he exchanges foreign currency in today's market he can invest the proceeds at the domestic rate of interest until the day of payment.

Even this, however, is too simple because there is a market not just for foreign exchange to be delivered immediately, the 'spot' market, but a market for exchange contracts in the future, the 'forward' market. Thus there is a price for foreign exchange to be delivered in the future which will be in the form of a premium or discount over the spot rate. At first blush one might think that the existence of a premium or discount in the forward market merely represented the buyers' and sellers' opinions of which way the currency would move between now and the future date for delivery after taking account of a small margin for the cost of undertaking the transaction. In practice it will, however, be more complicated as the forward price will also take into account the differential between domestic and foreign rates of interest.

There are three major aspects to the determination of exchange rates. The first relates to the general factors which determine the basic supply and demand for a currency relating to trading patterns and the relation between the prices of goods between the two countries. Secondly there are complexities in the relation stemming from different rates of interest. But overall the most important effect on movements in exchange rates in the short run is people's expectations of future exchange rates. In the chapters which follow we try to distinguish these aspects in the determination of exchange rates, explaining the factors which affect supply and demand, the way in which the market works and in particular how expectations are formed.

The Genesis of Exchange Rate Systems

The current sophisticated system reflects the need for arrangements which will facilitate transactions to the satisfaction of all those involved at reasonable cost. Elementary systems are carried out by means of *ad hoc* bartering. One trader arrives with a set of goods to exchange with those of another country — food for clothing, for example. As time passes accepted quantitative exchange rates will become established. Then as the system becomes more sophisticated an intermediate, readily transportable means of payment is introduced which has value both in the country of the seller and in the country of the purchaser, such as precious metal or stones.

If each transaction is balanced in terms of goods there is no need for a separate unit of exchange. Even when each transaction is not balanced it may be possible to use the currencies of the two countries involved in the transactions without some internationally acceptable medium of exchange if the traders who are selling more than they are buying and hence accumulating the foreign currency can match themselves with other traders who are buying more than they are selling and hence need the foreign currency. In such a way markets in foreign currencies can be set up.

There are many ways such systems could operate, but they will tend to be organised centrally both to try to match sellers and buyers easily and quickly and to minimise the stocks of non-interest-bearing currency which are held. At one extreme all holdings of foreign exchange have to be surrendered to the central authority at a rate fixed by it in terms of the domestic currency and foreign exchange requirements will only be met with its agreement, again at a fixed rate. This is the case with several Eastern bloc regimes. Under these circumstances the central authority controls both prices and quantities (not surprisingly encouraging the formation of black markets in foreign exchange) and can therefore prevent there being any significant undesired mismatch between the supply and demand for the foreign currency in the domestic economy. Without the control over quantities, any attempt to fix exchange rates will require the central authority to hold a stock or reserve of foreign currencies in order to smooth out any mismatch between supply and demand at the desired rate. Any enduring excess demand will lead to exhaustion of the reserve while excess supply will lead to an ever increasing reserve.

The Bretton Woods system of 'fixed' exchange rates established after the war differed from the Gold Standard where each currency had a rate of exchange with gold and hence in effect with each other. Exchange rates were fixed in effect with respect to the US dollar which in turn had a fixed rate of exchange with respect to gold of $35 per ounce. Limited day-to-day fluctuations were permitted round the 'fixed' rates to allow orderly trading in foreign exchange markets and central authorities supplemented use of their reserves with quantitative controls on foreign currency holdings. Nevertheless because they were committed to try to maintain fixed rates of exchange and because they wished neither to exhaust their reserves nor add to them without limit, the authorities had to influence the factors affecting the demand and supply of foreign currencies by domestic residents. In effect this was primarily through the demand for exports and imports and the level of interest rates relative to those in foreign countries (principally the United States).

In crude terms the main determinants of both exports and imports are the level of activity in the consuming country and the relative price of the traded product or service to those of the products or services with which it has to compete, although other aspects of non-price competitiveness such as quality and delivery lag are also very important. Thus in the case of imports, the main determinants are domestic activity and the price of imports relative to the domestic price level; and in the case of exports, they are the sum of activity in each export market and the price of exports relative to the price of products from all other exporting countries as well as those of the domestic product in the foreign importing countries.

In a system of fixed exchange rates the domestic central authority can only affect domestic activity, domestic prices, export prices and import prices. Foreign activity and prices are beyond its control. Thus unless exports are also restricted by shortage of production capacity, as they were in most countries after the war, the only means of increasing the demand for them is through their price — by trying to influence domestic costs and by export subsidies — supplemented by non-price improvements in competitiveness. Imports, however, can be affected both through their price by tariffs and other restrictions or by adjusting the price of domestic output, and by managing the level of domestic demand.

In the period of fixed exchange rates international agreements limited the use of tariffs and subsidies and so countries tended to meet foreign exchange deficits by deflating the domestic economy hence reducing the rate of expansion of domestic activity relative to that abroad and thereby directly trying to reduce the rate of increase in domestic and export costs. In most countries monetary methods of control were secondary but the demand and supply of foreign exchange would also be influenced by changes in interest rates — higher interest rates leading foreigners to deposit their money and lower interest rates to remove it.

The Fixed but Adjustable System

In the extreme case, a country may not be able to maintain its rate of exchange despite the maximum feasible amount of domestic deflation, cost restraining measures or rising interest rates. Under these circumstances, in the 'fixed' rate system, the usual resort was not to allow the rate to fall on its own (*depreciate*) according to market pressures but to fix a new (lower) rate and move directly to it (*devalue*). Obviously the choice of such a new level has to be made with great care and skill. If the change is too small it does not solve the problem and if it is too large then other countries will be inclined to institute devaluations of their own leading to a smaller relative devaluation of the first country's currency than was intended or might have been achieved had the initial step not been so large.

A devaluation makes a country's exports cheaper and its imports more expensive and in the short run it has the ironic effect of worsening the balance of trade. Demand for both exports and imports cannot respond immediately to a change in price — indeed it has been argued that it may take as long as four years for the full effect of a relative price change to filter through to UK exports of manufactures (Brooks, 1981). Thus, with roughly unchanged volumes, export prices and values fall and import prices and values rise. Thus the balance of payments deteriorates. As demand adjusts to the relative price change this effect is usually fairly substantially reversed. The whole process is normally known as the *J-*

curve, reflecting the shape of the movement in the balance of trade over time. However this favourable outcome will occur only if trade is sufficiently elastic with respect to price; if it is inelastic — the sum of the price elasticities of demand for imports and exports is less than unity, (the Marshall–Lerner condition) — then a *revaluation* and not a devaluation is required to improve the balance of trade.

There is also considerable debate about how long the favourable effects from a devaluation endure, and indeed whether devaluation is a particularly useful policy tool at all as the rising import prices it generates contribute to the rate of domestic price inflation.

Exchange Rate Policy under Floating Exchange Rates

The role the exchange rate plays as a policy instrument clearly depends on the type of exchange rate regime that prevails. In a freely floating world it is not an instrument at all although government policies affect its value. Even in other regimes a government must have a degree of control over currency markets if it is to pursue a successful exchange rate policy.

In a simple world one might expect that the exchange rate system provided the numerical relationship to translate the amount of money required to pay for the generality of goods in one country to the amount of money in other currencies required to buy the same group of goods in the other countries. In so far as that relation did not exist and international trade was unhindered then by purchasing in other countries one could exploit such discrepancies and, by the normal operation of these interdependent markets, eliminate them. This process is called 'commodity arbitrage'. However such elimination would not be total even in a simple world as there are costs of transport between countries which would permit differences. The relative prices of goods will differ between countries because of differences in tastes, climate and resources, thus making possible apparent differences in the cost of purchasing the same group of goods.

In the real world there are further constraints — trade is not free. Although tariffs may have been eliminated on trade in manufactured goods among the European Community (EC) and European Free Trade Association (EFTA) countries and generally reduced to low levels between them and the other major Western industrial countries, there are many non-tariff restraints on traded manufactures and more particularly on agricultural products. Indeed, as has been widely noted, these restraints have been increasing steadily over recent years in the form of piecemeal quotas and 'voluntary' agreements, such as those for Japanese cars. Some goods and services are not traded at all, either because of weight or perishability or for reasons of sheer impracticability — in the case of haircuts and restaurant meals, for example. Thus divergences in general price levels after allowing for exchange rates are quite possible between countries. It is a matter of very considerable difficulty to provide a satisfactory explanation of the levels that exchange rates hold at any particular time, let alone to forecast them into the future.

Currency Flows Arise for other Reasons than the Financing of Trade

It is simplistic to think of foreign exchange transactions wholly in terms of the financing of trade. The range of transactions is much larger. Trivially we must also consider current account transactions which relate to transfers between different countries. Residents in one country may have incomes earned in another country from employment, property or financial assets, they may receive gifts or pensions from abroad and the pattern of such flows will be outward as well as inward. Companies will also have a complex network of transactions across borders with subsidiaries and in respect of holdings of foreign assets. Governments will have similar requirements relating, for example, to armed forces stationed abroad, embassies and trade missions. However, their requirements for foreign exchange and foreigners' demands for their domestic currencies will be similar in general concept to those relating to the financing of trade.

The major distinction comes with capital flows, which can be subdivided into four main groups for ease of analysis. In the first place there is straightforward direct investment abroad: for example, a company wishes to set up manufacturing or distribution facilities abroad by the purchase of buildings, plant and machinery. Here the motivation will tend to be rather more complex than that for trade. In setting up a foreign plant a company can serve the foreign market from the inside, avoiding the restraints which affect trade in the form of tariffs and quotas, for example. Profits will occur locally, in the foreign currency, and the firm will have to choose between re-investment abroad and repatriation (in so far as this is not covered by restrictions imposed by the foreign government). Thus the firm has to weigh up the relative rates of return on investment in the two countries, allowing for the vagaries of exchange rate fluctuations over the future. Even if exchange rates remain fixed, an improvement in domestic production costs relative to those abroad would lead to a preference for exporting rather than direct foreign investment.

More directly relevant to the short-run determination of exchange rates is portfolio investment, particularly in short-term assets, which, as we noted earlier, could be used as a hedge against exchange rate losses on trade flows. Most wealth holders and financial institutions in particular will wish to hold diversified portfolios in which foreign assets will form a significant role. At the time of writing there has been a considerable run of purchases of foreign assets by UK institutions following the abolition of exchange controls in 1979. A large proportion of funds is held in short-term assets which can be traded at short notice with relatively small transactions costs. It is the management of these funds which makes a major contribution to short-run fluctuations in exchange rates. They respond not just to obvious changes such as movements in interest rates, where the effects of the change in the uncovered interest rate differential will tend to be offset by movements in the rate of exchange as people try to take advantage of the differential, but also to changes in expectations, whose generation may be merely rumour. Some times signals are explicit such as James Callaghan's famous reply in the House of Commons that he would neither confirm nor deny that the rate of exchange was to be changed, shortly before the 1967 devaluation of the pound. (One of the authors, in common with many other people, although then an undergraduate, managed to convert the then £50 maximum permitted into Deutschmarks and make over 10 per cent on the transaction within a week despite double transaction costs. The ability to gain or lose rapidly in such transactions is emphasised by the fact that others chose less felicitously and converted their pounds into currencies which were devalued by more than the pound such as the peseta.)

Finally we come to consider the government or central authority. If it wishes to manage the exchange rate then, when all the other transactions are taken into account, it has to balance the transactions — by running down reserves if the demand for foreign exchange exceeds the supply or accumulating them if the reverse occurs. It can of course trade on its own account and as a trader with substantial assets it can have a significant effect on exchange rates. If the rate of exchange is beginning to fall the central authority can step in and purchase its own currency with its reserves thus keeping the rate up. While such intervention is required under the rules of the fixed exchange rate system, central authorities often also intervene under flexible exchange rates to smooth the operation of the market and prevent the more extreme fluctuations in transactions from causing instability.

Is There More to Exchange Rate Theory than PPP?

In traditional models of the exchange rate it was thought that, since the exchange rate was the means of converting between expenditures in one country and the money of another, a given sum of money, when converted at the going rate, would buy about the same quantity of goods in all countries. This theory, known as 'purchasing power parity' (PPP) has considerable elementary appeal — although obviously it cannot be expected to fit exactly when not all goods and services are fully tradeable.

Figure 1.1: Pound-dollar Exchange Rate and Purchasing Power Parity 1977–1984

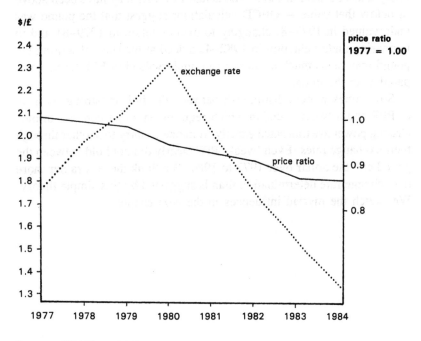

Source: IMF Financial Statistics

In practice there are long and substantial departures of exchange rates from PPP. So much so that those wishing to make comparisons of standards of living between countries re-compute their own PPP exchange rates because actual rates are so misleading.

A quick look at the recent history of the exchange rate between the pound and the dollar will illustrate the extent to which there can be divergences from PPP. In Figure 1.1 the dotted line shows the path of the pound/dollar exchange rate over the years 1977 to 1984, using annual average values to eliminate short-run variations. It is clear that the dollar fell (pound rose) by a quarter between 1977 and 1980. Since 1980 the value of the dollar relative to the pound has risen by two-thirds totally eliminating the depreciation of the early years. In the mean time, however, PPP has only drifted down by a little over 10 per cent, reflecting the somewhat faster price inflation in the UK. To match this the dollar also ought to have risen by about 10 per cent over the period. However it must be borne in mind that 1977 is an arbitrary origin. It does *not* imply that PPP held in 1977. The actual PPP rate may have been above or below that value — OECD calculations suggest that the pound was undervalued in 1977–8, changing to overvaluation in 1979–81 and to increasing undervaluation in 1982–4; indeed at the time of writing the pound may be as much as 40 per cent undervalued in PPP terms compared with the dollar.

Sometimes writers distinguish between the full or 'strong' version of PPP and a 'weak' version which requires only that *changes* in purchasing power are translated exactly from one country to another through their exchange rates. Even 'weak' PPP clearly did not hold between the pound and the dollar over 1977 to 1984. We think there is rather more to exchange rate determination than is suggested by this simple theory. We sketch the myriad influences in the next chapter.

PART 1

EXCHANGE RATE DETERMINATION: THEORY AND EVIDENCE

2 THE SPOT MARKET, THE FORWARD MARKET AND THE CAPITAL ACCOUNT

Introduction

In this chapter we discuss the relationship between capital flows, spot and forward exchange rates. In so doing we hope to throw some light on why exchange rates are volatile over the short run and also to assess the scope for government intervention in influencing the spot rate.

If a domestic resident who does not currently own any foreign currency wishes to buy a foreign asset he will have to purchase a suitable sum of that foreign currency in the 'spot' market in order to be able to buy the asset. Commonly he will wish to convert back the proceeds of the sale of that asset into his own currency when the asset matures. However, there is a risk that when the proceeds are converted back the exchange rate will have changed and the asset holder could make a loss. These demands for purchase and sale of foreign currency will affect the spot rate of exchange. If the domestic resident wishes to remove any risk associated with the future value of the spot rate when his foreign investment matures, then he can agree *today* to sell his foreign currency proceeds which are to be paid in, say, three months' time, for a *known amount* of domestic currency (which he will also receive in three month's time). The rate of exchange agreed today at which the contract will be completed in three month's time is known as the 3-month forward rate. This whole transaction of purchasing spot and selling forward is referred to as *covered arbitrage*. The extent to which arbitrage transactions in the spot market influence the spot exchange rate depend in part on movements in the forward rate. Thus we need to understand the behaviour of the forward market before we can fully understand the behaviour of the spot exchange rate.

An alternative strategy for a domestic resident when investing in foreign assets is to take a risk on the amount of domestic currency he will obtain when the foreign asset matures. To do so, one forms an expectation of the *future* spot rate, hence undertakes a *speculative* spot transaction. One might use this strategy if one's expectation of the future spot rate of the domestic currency were greater than the forward rate that one could currently obtain in the market.

Whether one acts as an arbitrageur and incurs no risk, or as a

17

speculator, the relative interest return on domestic and foreign assets will influence the decision as to whether to invest in domestic or foreign assets. Domestic monetary policy is frequently used to influence domestic interest rates and hence may influence capital flows and the spot exchange rate.

In the previous chapter we discussed whether the spot exchange rate responded to relative price differentials between the domestic and foreign country. The purchasing power parity (PPP) view of exchange rate determination fails to explain short-run changes in the spot exchange rate (say quarter to quarter) adequately because short-run movements in prices tend to be *relatively* small, while exchange rate changes are large and highly volatile. However, capital flows respond to change in interest rates and the expected exchange rate and since these variables are highly volatile they may provide an 'explanation' of short-run volatile changes in the spot rate.

To understand the forces that impinge on the spot exchange rate because of short-term capital flows we have to examine the behaviour of arbitrageurs and speculators in the spot market. Since arbitrage activity in the spot market is always accompanied by a counterpart transaction in the forward market we also need to explain the behaviour of the forward rate of exchange. By analysing the spot and forward market we hope to explain the volatile movements in the exchange rate (or capital flows under a 'fixed' exchange rate regime) and to assess the scope for policy intervention to alter the spot exchange rate.

Discussions of the capital account tend to involve a large number of technical terms. In this chapter we present a simple account of the concepts used and relate them to the possible determinants of capital flows. We spend very little time discussing what are known as long-term capital flows or direct investment since we are interested in forces that cause volatile short-run changes in the exchange rate, and these are believed to be largely due to actual or potential changes in portfolio investment (i.e. changes in holdings of *financial* assets). The short-term nature of our analysis also enables us to ignore influences on the spot rate that arise from current account transactions. In any case, it could be argued, given the extensive diversification of holdings of financial assets among different countries, that the potential influence of capital flows on the exchange rate far outweighs current account effects, except in the very long run when the latter lead to a net accumulation or decumulation in wealth.

We begin the chapter with a brief exposition of the definitions used in the balance of payments accounts together with an account of a 'perfect market'. This is followed by an introduction to the forward market which involves arbitrage and hedging activity. The determinants of the demand for spot currency by arbitrageurs and hedgers are presented. Next we discuss the behaviour of *speculators* in the spot market and end with a brief account of possible determinants of direct investment. We are then able to isolate the proximate determinants of the spot rate which are relative interest rates, the expected spot rate and the forward rate. The main aim in this chapter is therefore to provide the basic concepts needed to understand the analysis of the capital account, forward market and the efficient markets hypothesis which are presented later in the book.

Definitions and Notation

The Balance of Payments: An Overview

The balance of payments accounts record transactions between domestic and foreign residents, of both the private and government sectors. The account is divided into a number of sub-accounts. The *trade account* deals with transactions in real tangible goods. The *invisibles account* records transactions dealing with services (e.g. insurance, and foreign travel), transfers abroad (e.g. government payments to foreign agencies such as the EEC) and 'property income' (i.e. flows of interest, dividends and rent on investments held in other countries).

The *net* balance in any account is the difference between receipts earned by domestic residents from sales of goods or assets to foreigners and expenditure incurred by domestic residents on purchases from foreigners. Although receipts and disbursements involve foreign currency, the accounts are usually presented in the domestic currency using the appropriate bilateral exchange rate. The difference between export receipts and sales of goods and import payments on goods is given by the trade balance (sometimes called the visibles balance). The trade balance plus the invisibles balance yields the current account balance. The various balances for the UK are recorded in Table 2.1.

If the domestic economy has a current account surplus then domestic residents must be accumulating assets or reducing their liabilities to the rest of the world. In the simplest case one could view a current account surplus of the UK with the USA as involving an increased dollar deposit (asset) in a New York bank held by a UK 'export firm' or a reduction in the UK export firm's dollar bank advance (liability) held at the New York bank. A current account surplus increases the (nominal) wealth of domestic residents.

Table 2.1: The UK Balance of Payments (in £ millions)

	1974	1975	1976	1977	1978	1979	1980	1981	1982	1983
Current account										
Visible balance	−5,351	−3,333	−3,929	−2,284	−1,542	−3,449	+1,513	+3,652	+2,384	− 716
Services balance	+1,075	+1,515	+2,503	+3,350	+3,858	+4,155	+4,356	+4,458	+3,706	+3,902
Interest profits and dividends balance	+1,415	+ 763	+1,355	+ 97	+ 623	+1,034	− 61	+1,056	+1,165	+1,948
Transfers balance	− 417	− 468	− 775	−1,116	−1,777	−2,265	−2,079	−1,945	−2,049	−2,218
Invisible balance	+2,073	+1,810	+3,083	+2,337	+2,704	+2,924	+2,116	+3,569	+2,822	+3,632
Current balance	−3,278	−1,523	− 846	+ 53	−1,162	+ 525	+3,629	+7,221	+5,206	+2,916
Financial account										
Capital transfers	− 75	—	—	—	—	—	—	—	—	—
Direct investment	− 721	− 556	−1,346	− 559	−1,449	−1,295	− 776	−4,154	−1,445	− 152
Portfolio investment	− 402	+ 141	+ 528	+1,865	−1,158	+ 344	−2,299	−3,582	−5,760	−4,470
Oil and miscellaneous investment	−1,222	− 117	+ 605	+ 670	− 120	−1,568	+ 248	+ 534	+ 94	+ 493
Trade credit	− 722	− 518	− 992	− 355	− 630	− 792	−1,156	− 839	−1,385	−1,157
Foreign currency borrowing or lending abroad by UK banks	− 295	+ 253	+ 108	+ 367	+ 434	+1,622	+2,054	+1,462	+4,271	+1,167
Changes in external sterling liabilities	+1,588	− 66	−1,145	+1,471	+ 180	+3,336	+3,820	+2,756	+4,250	+4,133
External sterling lending by UK banks	+ 53	+ 96	+ 350	+ 58	− 504	+ 205	−2,500	−2,954	−3,299	−1,386

Table 2.1 (continued)

Other capital transactions	− 48	+ 242	− 204	+ 559	− 149	− 18	− 841	− 576	+ 5	− 930
Total investment and other capital transactions	+1,602	+ 154	−2,977	+4,169	−4,264	+1,834	−1,450	−7,353	−3,187	−3,648
Allocation of SDRs	—	—	—	—	—	+ 195	+ 180	+ 158	—	—
Official financing	+1,646	+1,465	+3,629	−7,361	+1,126	−1,905	−1,372	+ 687	+1,284	+ 816
Total financing account	+3,175	+1,619	+ 652	−3,192	−3,138	+ 124	−2,642	−6,508	−1,903	−2,832
Balancing item	− 105	− 96	+ 194	+3,139	+1,976	+ 401	+ 987	+ 713	−3,303	+ 84

Source: *United Kingdom Balance of Payments*, 1984.

Broadly speaking the capital or 'financial' account deals with purchases of assets between countries. Portfolio investment is the purchase or sale of *financial* assets or a change in financial liabilities between domestic and overseas residents. For example, if a domestic resident purchases a security from a foreign resident this is a capital *outflow* since the domestic resident has to purchase foreign currency to undertake the transaction. There is an inflow of an asset (*security*) but an outflow of foreign currency: the situation parallels the import and payment for goods by domestic residents in foreign currency.

In our previous example, the UK exporter of goods used his dollar receipts to 'purchase' a dollar deposit in a New York bank: a current account surplus was *accommodated* by a capital outflow. However, autonomous shifts of domestic assets (currency) into foreign assets may also occur on a very large scale. These are often colourfully referred to as 'hot money' or speculative capital flows.

A surplus on the current account leads to gain in (net) foreign assets without any reduction in domestic assets. Payment for the foreign asset is in the form of goods and hence the stock of financial wealth held by domestic residents increases. In the case of *autonomous* capital account transactions domestic residents swap domestic currency for foreign assets; the stock of wealth remains unchanged, only its composition changes. However, wealth will increase in the future as interest receipts on the foreign asset accrue and these are correctly recorded in the current account. The effect of interest receipts on the current account (and hence on the exchange rate) will not normally be considered in our analysis in this chapter since it renders a number of models of exchange rate determination rather complicated and intractable.

Returning now to portfolio investment on the capital account, an increase in bank loans to domestic residents by a foreign bank, that is, an increase in foreign liabilities, involves a *potential* source of foreign currency and therefore constitutes a capital inflow.

Direct investment is the purchase (or sale) by domestic residents of tangible (real) assets held by overseas residents. For example, the purchase of the Dorchester Hotel in the UK by a foreign consortium is an inflow of *direct* investment since foreign currency is initially obtained by UK residents. Similarly the purchase of any UK-owned firm by overseas residents constitutes an inflow of direct investment into the UK. In official statistics many of the capital account figures are usually recorded as *net* transactions between residents and non-residents as in Table 2.1.

We shall deal here with the final major item in the balance of payments accounts, the balance of official financing, in a straightforward manner. The joint balance on current and capital account we shall call the *balance of payments* position (i.e. the sum of the current account balance and total investment and other capital transactions shown in Table 2.1). A balance of payments surplus involves a net demand for foreign currency by domestic residents (and an equal net supply of domestic currency). This excess demand for foreign currency may be met by the domestic monetary authorities either by running down their foreign exchange reserves or by borrowing from foreign official agencies including the International Monetary Fund (IMF). The amount of foreign exchange supplied by the domestic authorities from this source is called the balance of official financing (BOF) in the UK. (In the USA it is known as the 'official settlements' balance.) It follows that arithmetically the sum of the balance of payments position plus the BOF is always zero.[1]

In this arithmetic sense 'the balance of payments always balances': an excess demand by the private sector is met by an increase in supply by the authorities.

This can be seen from the last column of Table 2.1 which shows the position for the UK in 1983. In that year there was a deficit of £716 million on visible trade which was substantially outweighed by a surplus on invisible trade of £3,632 million to give an overall surplus of £2,916 million. There was a net outflow of both portfolio and direct investment from the UK (£4,470 million and £152 million) which when added to all the other capital transactions gave a net outflow of £3,648 for the 'Total investment and other capital transactions'. The sum of this and the current account surplus gives a balance of payments position of £732 million for 'Official financing' (actual 'Official financing' was £816 million as there was a residual error or balancing item of $(-)$£84 million in the accounts on that occasion).

If the excess demand for foreign currency is not met by the authorities, that is, if there is a policy decision of no intervention in the foreign exchange market, there will be a tendency for the price of foreign currency to rise (i.e. a depreciation of the home currency) until the excess demand is eliminated. Thus, broadly speaking, under a freely floating exchange rate the BOF is zero: a non-zero BOF tends to indicate government intervention in the foreign exchange market.

In the real world any agents operating in the foreign exchange market may be involved in both current and capital account transactions. For example, companies engage in trade in the domestic currency (e.g. home sales), in foreign currency (e.g. sales and purchase of goods from abroad) and hold domestic as well as foreign currency assets. In addition, governments deal in a wide range of current and capital account transactions and in particular may purchase or sell foreign assets including foreign currency on the foreign exchange market thus influencing the exchange rate and simultaneously altering the level of the foreign exchange reserves.

For analytic purposes we tend to separate the capital from current account transactions even though actual transactions involve both 'accounts'. For example, a UK importer who has to pay for goods imported from the US in three months time may enter the spot market and purchase a US commercial bill today which matures in three months. Alternatively the UK importer may wait three months and then switch from sterling to dollars if he feels the spot rate might then be more favourable. A current account transaction, therefore, may imply a capital account flow. However, as we shall see, the considerations involved in such a decision are the same as those for a 'pure capital account' transaction (i.e. disregarding any flow of goods).

Summary. The published (*ex post*) balance of payments accounts always balance: the sum of current and capital account balances and the BOF is zero. However, the (*ex ante*) desired *net demand* for foreign currency by private agents may not sum to zero. Without intervention by the authorities excess demand (supply) may lead to changes in the exchange rate to 'clear' the foreign exchange market.

Exchange Rates

Exchange rates may be measured in units of foreign currency per unit of domestic currency or vice versa: this is purely a matter of convenience. For example if we take the UK as the domestic economy and the US as the foreign or overseas economy the spot rate for sterling may be expressed as 1.3 dollars per pound sterling (i.e. foreign per unit of domestic currency) or equivalently 76.9 pence (£0.769) per dollar (i.e. domestic per unit of foreign currency). In Part 1 we have chosen to measure the exchange rate, S, in units of the domestic currency per unit of the foreign currency (i.e. sterling per dollar in our examples). Thus an appreciation of the spot rate for sterling (against the dollar) will involve a *fall* in S. To see this, note that an appreciation of sterling implies a move from say 1.3 to 1.4 dollars per pound which is a *fall* from $S = 0.769$ to $S = 0.714$ pounds per dollar. It follows that an *increase* in S is a depreciation of sterling (and an appreciation of the dollar). 'Depreciation' and 'appreciation' refer to the domestic currency unless otherwise stated.

Notation in Part 1

Generally speaking upper case letters denote variables (e.g. S = exchange rate) and their natural logarithm is given in lower case letters (e.g. s = ln S = log$_e$ S) but there are exceptions to this convention. *Percentage* changes (expressed as a decimal) are denoted by a dot over the variable and absolute changes by Δ. For example $\Delta S = S - S_{t-1}$; $\dot{S} = (S - S_{t-1})/S_{t-1}$. For small changes, the absolute first difference of the logarithm of a variable is approximately equal to its percentage change: i.e. $\Delta s \simeq \dot{S} \equiv (S - S_{t-1})/S_{t-1}$. (For Parts 3 and 4 notational conventions are given on page 164.)

Perfect Market: Perfect Capital Mobility

To complete this section, we should explain a widely used concept in economics, namely what would happen if the system worked 'perfectly'. The real world is, of course, imperfect in many respects but is more clearly viewed as a set of departures from perfection than without such a paradigm. Before proceeding further we therefore outline our definition of a 'perfect goods' market, its relation to 'perfect substitutes', a 'perfect capital market' and 'perfect capital mobility'.

Two 'goods' are perfect substitutes when, from the point of view of demand, they are considered homogeneous (identical). Perfect substitutes have infinite elasticities of demand: a small change in the price of one of the 'goods' leads to an increase in demand for the 'other' homogeneous goods sufficient to ensure that only it is purchased. 'Goods' here include both commodities and financial assets (bonds) and liabilities. Clearly for perfect substitutes there is a *tendency* for the prices of the two goods to be equal because of the potential effect of switches in demand. However, equality between prices is only achieved when there is *perfect mobility*. We define the latter as entailing that:

(a) 'goods' are perfect substitutes;
(b) transactions costs are negligible;
(c) access to information is freely available and the costs of processing the information are negligible;
(d) there are no constraints on voluntary exchange (and goods are perfectly divisible);
(e) individuals are rational and hence seek to purchase homogeneous goods at the lowest possible price.

Conditions (a) to (e) imply market clearing: prices are flexible and alter instantaneously in response to perceived or actual excess demand.

If there is perfect mobility then prices of homogeneous goods will be equal in all markets at all times. When the 'goods' being compared are domestic and foreign *assets* and (a) to (e) are satisfied, then we have *perfect capital mobility*. We shall use the terms 'perfect mobility' and 'perfect market' synonymously, although the reader should note that the latter term may require additional conditions when used by other economists (e.g. Minford and Peel, 1983). A perfect market is more likely to hold in asset markets than in the market for commodities or labour. In Chapter 5 we shall meet the term 'efficient market', a concept closely allied to our definition of a perfect market.

The *process* by which prices are equalised in a perfect market relies on the view that actual or perceived excess demand leads to a change in relative prices. Notice that prices may be equalised without any trading (exchange) actually taking place. It could be the *threat* of large flows that leads traders to set prices at equilibrium instantaneously. The process by which prices are equalised is known as 'arbitrage'. Perfect (goods) mobility is frequently referred to as perfect (goods) arbitrage. Since perfect arbitrage does not require actual trading to take place, the size of the *measured* elasticities of demand for goods reveals little about whether one has a perfect (goods) market.

If there is a perfect market in *tradeable goods* then potential switches in demand instantaneously equalise prices expressed in a common currency. Using the superscript * to denote variables relating to the foreign country and hence measured in the foreign currency we have for example a foreign goods price level of P^*. Foreign goods have a price in domestic currency of P^*S and perfect commodity arbitrage ensures instantaneous equality with the price of domestic goods, P, hence

$$P = P^*S.$$

This implies PPP (Purchasing Power Parity) through commodity arbitrage. In testing it is recognised that the existence of market imperfections such as the degree of monopoly, transport costs, etc., may imply that only a weak form of PPP holds (i.e. only price *changes* are equalised and not necessarily price levels as well). Also, slow adjustment in commodity prices (for whatever reason) means that one might expect PPP due to commodity arbitrage to hold only in the long run.

The assumption of perfect capital mobility in asset markets results in the equalisation of returns to domestic and overseas investment: we discuss this below.

Forward Markets

Forward contracts are commonplace in business and everyday life. For example, the purchaser of a new house agrees to pay, and the seller agrees to relinquish his legal title to the house at a specified date in the future (the 'completion date'). Similarly, mail order firms and households undertake an implicit forward contract when they agree on 'cash-on-delivery'. Some forward contracts take the form of gentlemen's agreements and others are backed by explicit legal contracts.

In some markets the purchase and sale today for delivery in the future is highly organised. Examples of such markets for 'real' tangible commodities include those for crude oil and raw materials. Usually, thriving futures markets arise where the commodities to be traded are homogeneous and easily classified (e.g. crude oil, or tin of a particular quality). Prices are quoted and transactions usually take place in a common currency, regardless of the country in which the market is situated — the US dollar being the currency used most frequently as the numeraire and means of payment. Spot transactions, that is the exchange today for delivery today, also takes place in such markets. Usually a spot transaction is for delivery in the near future (e.g. the time it takes the oil tanker to reach port) — spot transactions are therefore usually forward contracts of short maturity.

Spot and forward transactions *in different currencies* take place mainly through the dealing rooms of large commercial banks. Banks act as brokers who quote the buying and selling prices of currencies for delivery spot (actually in two days time) or for delivery in the future. The forward contract can be made for different maturity dates; one month, three month and six month contracts in the major currencies being the most prevalent. In practice, forward contracts for periods in excess of one year are rare.

For each maturity and each major currency the bank quotes a rate today at which it will buy or sell at a specific date in the future. Exchange rates are all quoted against the dollar from which cross rates may easily be inferred. At each maturity the rate at which the bank is willing to buy a currency is lower than the rate at which it sells it: this 'profit margin' or 'bid–ask spread' as it is known in the jargon covers transactions costs (e.g. computer time and personnel) of running the dealing room. For reasons to be explained below the forward rate for a particular maturity may be above or below the current spot rate (i.e. the currency may be at a forward discount or premium).

The forward market has two main functions. First it eliminates exchange risk on future transactions and second the forward market may be used for speculative purposes. Consider first the elimination of exchange risk. Suppose a UK importer has to pay $1m in three months' time for delivery of goods from the US, and he wishes to *hedge* against possible future changes in the spot exchange rate. The UK importer asks his bank to provide $1m in three months time and the bank quotes a three month forward rate of say 1.1 $/£ (0.91 £/$). The UK importer knows he has to provide £910,000 in three months. The forward contract is an IOU and no funds change hands today. The UK importer has used the forward market to hedge against any exchange risk since he knows exactly how much sterling he must provide in three months' time to meet his dollar debt.

The bank may itself incur no exchange risk on the deal if it has another customer, say a US importer, who has to pay for goods from the UK in sterling in three months' time. The US importer will supply dollars and demand sterling from the bank in three months. Thus for a large number of transactions the bank, acting as broker or 'middleman' may be able to *match* the supply and demand for funds in the forward market.

The bank may not have a matching transaction and may take an *open position* in the forward market by speculating on the value of the spot rate in three months' time. Non-banks may also act as speculators in the forward market. Suppose today's three month forward rate is 1.1 $/£ (i.e. 0.91 £/$) and a speculator *expects* the spot rate in three months' time to be 1.0 $/£. Then if he agrees today to provide £100 in three months he will receive $110 from the bank in three months. However if he has correctly guessed the future spot rate he can sell the $110 for £110 and hence make £10 on the deal. Note that there are no interest rate complications to worry about here since the actual exchange of currencies all take place at the same time. On occasions a bank may itself take an open forward position and hence act as a speculator.

Considering the hedger again, it is important to explain that the use of the forward market is not the only way one can eliminate exchange risk. For example our UK importer could sell spot sterling in exchange for dollars and invest the proceeds in a dollar asset which matures in three months and yields $1m. Whether it is cheaper for the hedger to use the spot or the forward market depends on the interest rate in the two countries, and the spot and forward rates. This constitutes the 'covered interest differential' which we explain further below.

As well as the hedger trying to minimise the cost of eliminating exchange risk we need also to consider agents (including banks) who try to earn a *riskless* profit by investing in foreign assets. By selling domestic currency spot, purchasing a three month foreign asset and selling the proceeds *today* in the three month forward market one is guaranteed a known return in domestic currency. This *covered arbitrage* return may exceed the yield on three month domestic securities. If covered arbitrage into foreign assets is profitable then it turns out that the hedger should cover his exchange risk by spot purchases of foreign currency rather than using the forward market. Hence hedgers and covered interest arbitrageurs both respond in a similar fashion and analytically we can consider them as a single group.

We have discussed speculation in the *forward* market. Speculation may also take place in the spot market. Agents, banks included, may undertake the same type of transaction as the covered arbitrageur except for one crucial difference. The spot speculator does not sell the foreign currency forward but instead forms an expectation of what the spot rate might be in three months' time when his foreign asset matures. He therefore undertakes an open or risky transaction.

Covered Interest Arbitrage and the Demand for Spot Currency

The forward market allows some agents, namely those involved in covered interest arbitrage, to make a riskless profit from capital movements. Take sterling (£) as the domestic currency and the dollar ($) as the foreign currency. Consider a UK company that is deciding whether it is more profitable over a three month period to invest in a UK sterling bank deposit at a three month interest rate r or in a dollar deposit in a New York bank at an interest rate of r^*. If the company invests £Z in a UK bank deposit then at the end of three months it will receive £$(1 + r)Z$. If the UK company treasurer invests in the US market then he will convert £Z into Z/S dollars in the spot market which after three months will have accrued to $(1 + r^*)(Z/S)$. If the company treasurer contracts *today* to sell his $(1 + r^*)(Z/S)$ dollars for sterling in the forward market at a rate F (sterling per dollar) then he is assured of receiving £$F[(1 + r^*)(Z/S)]$ in three months' time. He will therefore invest in the US rather than the UK if

$$F[(1 + r^*)(Z/S)] > (1 + r)Z \tag{2.1}$$

i.e. if

$$F > [(1 + r)/(1 + r^*)]S = F^* \tag{2.2}$$

F^* as defined in equation (2.2) above is sometimes known as the *interest* *parity forward rate.* Thus a covered interest arbitrageur would switch assets from the UK to the US if the forward rate on the dollar exceeded its interest parity forward rate. There is a more usual and useful way of expressing the covered interest arbitrage condition by re-arranging equation (2.2) to give an expression for the covered interest differential (CID) in favour of the dollar. In logarithmic terms:

$$
\begin{aligned}
\text{CID} &= f - f^* \\
&= f - (r - r^* + s) \\
&= r^* - r + f - s \\
&\approx r^* - r + (F - S)/S > 0
\end{aligned}
\qquad (2.3)
$$

if $\ln(1 + r)$ and $\ln(1 + r^*)$ are approximated by r and r^*. $r^* - r$ is the *un*covered interest differential in favour of the dollar. The term $f - s \approx (F - S)/S$ is the *forward premium* on the foreign currency. If $F > S$, the amount of sterling received per dollar 'spent' in the forward market exceeds that obtainable in the spot market: the dollar is said to be at a 'forward premium' against sterling (and sterling is at a forward discount against the dollar). $f - s$ is also referred to as the cost of forward cover.

It is worth noting in equation (2.3) that the forward premium (on the dollar) $(f - s)$ is a form of 'interest cost' in using the forward market which is then compared with the foreign interest differential. If F is the three month forward rate then the interest rates must also be three month rates (i.e. a quarter of the annual rates). A word of caution: different authors may define the *forward premium* in different ways, particularly, when F and S are measured in different units to those used here. To avoid confusion we shall refrain from using the term whenever possible.

Consider a numerical example. With $r = 0.02$ (2 per cent per quarter), £100 (= Z) invested in UK securities yields £102 (= $(1 + r)Z$) after three months. If $S = 0.7143$ £/$ (1.4 $/£), £100 sold on the spot market yields \$140 [=(Z/S)]. \$140 invested at foreign interest rate $r^* = 0.019$ (1.9 per cent per quarter) yields \$142.66 [= $(1 + r^*)(Z/S)$] after three months. If the three month forward rate $F = 0.7168$ £/$ (1.395 $/£) then \$142.66 sold *today* will yield £102.26 (= $0.7168 \times 142.66 =$ £$F[(1 + r^*)Z/S)]$ also payable in three months. The net gain to the arbitrageur in investing £100 in the US as opposed to the UK is £0.25 (= £(102.25 - 102)). To check our formula note that the uncovered differential against the dollar is $r^* - r = -0.001$ (0.1 per cent). However $F = 0.7168 > S = 0.7143$ and each dollar sold earns relatively more sterling in the forward market (than it costs in the spot market). The percentage forward premium on the dollar is $(F - S)/S = 0.0035$ which exceeds the interest differential against the dollar $r^* - r = -0.001$. Hence CID $= r^* - r + (F - S)/S = 0.0025$ (0.25 per cent) and our formula of equation (2.3) indicates that the CID is in favour of investment in the US rather than the UK. In practice transactions costs might mean that such a small CID remains unexploited.

The demand for *spot* sterling by *covered interest arbitrageurs* will be higher the higher foreign interest rates relative to domestic rates, the higher is the forward rate F, and the lower is S. The lower is S (£/$) the more spot dollars one receives for each spot pound 'sold' and therefore the greater the value of US securities one can purchase for a given sterling outlay. On anticipating the dollar receipts at the end of three months (from investing in the US) the higher is the forward rate for the dollar the more sterling one receives per dollar surrendered in the (forward) foreign exchange market.

If there is a CID in favour of a UK resident investing in US securities then there is also an incentive for all other holders of UK securities to sell them and use the proceeds to invest in US securities. There is therefore a net demand for dollars on the spot foreign exchange market and a net supply of sterling.

Hedgers may also respond in their payments habits to the return to covered interest arbitrage. Consider our earlier example of a UK importer who expects delivery of goods from the US in three months' time to the value of Y dollars, and wishes to minimise his sterling costs. He can use his sterling funds to invest in a UK security, and sell the sterling proceeds today (for Y dollars) in the forward market. Alternatively he can switch from sterling to dollars in the spot market and invest in a US security, which on maturity will yield Y dollars. If the CID is in favour of the dollar then he will minimise his costs by entering the spot market and investing in a US asset as did the 'pure arbitrageur' above.[2]

In covered interest arbitrage transactions there is no risk of loss from unforseen changes in 'asset prices' (including exchange rates). Interest rates are known and assets held to maturity.[3] The only risks are 'default' risks (e.g. the New York bank becomes bankrupt) or sovereign risk (risk of government default, e.g. by the imposition of exchange controls which prevent repatriation of the proceeds of the overseas investment).

Market Equilibrium: Covered Interest Parity

If a CID in favour of the US should emerge (i.e. CID > 0) market forces will tend to eliminate it. The increase in the *demand* for spot dollars and the increase in the sale (supply) of forward dollars will tend to lead to an appreciation of the dollar in the spot market (i.e. S increases) and a depreciation in the forward market (i.e. F falls), $f - s$ therefore falls 'pushing' the CID towards zero. The net sale of UK assets will tend to cause an increase in the UK interest rate on the former and a fall in the US interest rate[4] thus reducing the interest differential in favour of the US.

Since covered interest arbitrage involves a 'riskless return' we might expect market forces to keep the CID close to zero at all times or equivalently the forward rate equal to the interest parity forward rate: $F = [(1 + r)/(1 + r^*)]S = F^*$. The latter condition is also referred to as *covered interest parity*.

There are several reasons why the measured CID might not always be zero. First there are transaction costs (i.e. brokerage fees) involved in the purchase and sale of assets and currencies which are not represented in equation (2.3). Second there is a risk of default or of the imposition of exchange controls. Third there are potential measurement problems. Spot market transactions are for delivery two days hence (i.e. are a short forward transaction) and there are bid–ask spreads in both the forward and spot markets so the rate stated by the researcher as being representative for a given foreign exchange transaction at a particular time may not be the one actually used in the transaction. The exact yield on a given purchase or sale of assets is not known, only average yields (e.g. *average daily yields*) are published. Fourthly, wealth or the liquidity position of arbitrageurs may provide constraints on their activities. Fifthly, and perhaps most importantly, covered arbitrage requires speculators to provide foreign exchange in the *forward market* and the supply of speculative funds might not be infinitely elastic thus preventing some profitable arbitrage transactions. In the extreme, speculators may not provide any funds to arbitrageurs (see Chapter 3, on the Cambist and modern theory of the forward market). If the CID is always zero then

$$f = s + r - r^*.$$

However this equation should not be taken to imply that s, r and r^* determine the forward rate, in any unidirectional causal sense: the three endogenous domestic variables s, r and f are determined simultaneously (whilst r^* is exogenous given our small country consumption).

Arbitrageurs' Demand for Spot Currency

If we subsume the effects of transaction costs, etc., referred to above in a catch-all variable Z_A we may represent arbitrageurs' (net) *desired stock* demand[5] for spot dollars $AD\$$ or supply of spot sterling $AS\pounds$, as:

$$AD\$ \ (= AS\pounds) = a[r^* - r + (f - s)] + Z_A \qquad (2.4)$$

where a is a constant measuring the responsiveness of arbitrageurs to a change in the CID and Z_A is likely to be negative. Since arbitrage transactions are free of exchange risk and $AD\$$ represents *desired* (rather than realised) demand we expect a to be large. Even if the CID is only small we might still expect substantial arbitrage flows. On the other hand if the foreign exchange market is a perfect market, instantaneous arbitrage might keep CID = 0 without any flows taking place. Actual as opposed to desired flows require a supply of speculative funds and the influence of the latter is discussed in Chapter 3 under the modern theory of the forward rate.

It is perhaps worth noting at this point that an increase in the net demand for spot dollars by arbitrageurs implies an equal increase in net *supply* of *forward* dollars since an arbitrage transaction (by definition) involves a simultaneous sale and purchase of currency. Equation (2.4) may therefore be applied to the forward market and in Chapter 3 we demonstrate how this is used in developing the 'modern theory' of the forward rate.

Speculative Capital Flows in the Spot Market

Rather than using the forward market, economic agents might take a view about the value of the exchange rate in three months' time. The *expected* exchange rate then plays a similar role in the decision about whether to invest in the UK or the US as did the forward rate for the covered interest arbitrageur. Thus 'speculators' in the *spot* market will wish to invest in the US rather than the UK if the uncovered interest differential in favour of the dollar $(r^* - r)$ exceeds the expected depreciation of the dollar $_t s^e_{t+1} - s < 0$. The variable $_t s^e_{t+1}$ is the (logarithm of the) expected spot rate for time $t + 1$, formed on the basis of information known at time t. Where no ambiguity is likely to arise we shall simply write this without the subscripts, that is, as s^e. Speculators' stock demand for spot dollars (supply of spot sterling) is given by:

$$SS\pounds = c(s^e - s + r^* - r) + Z_S \qquad (2.5)$$

where Z_S represents other possible influences on speculators' demand such as wealth and transactions costs. Notice that for speculators operating in the spot market there is not a corresponding forward transaction and hence no limit in principle (other than total wealth) on the size of c, the response coefficient of speculators. The term $(s^e - s + r^* - r)$ is sometimes referred to as the 'speculative return' or the 'uncovered return'.

What factors are likely to influence the size of c? Speculators (by definition) undertake a risky transaction. They could end up as gainers or losers in absolute terms as well as relative to the return on the safe domestic asset, depending upon movements in the one unknown; the expected spot rate. We might expect speculators' utility to depend positively on the expected return from speculation; negatively on the perceived disutility from risk and negatively on the degree of risk incurred. The degree of risk depends directly upon the variance of the exchange rate: the higher this variance the lower we might expect c to be. Hence the response coefficient, c, is larger as: (a) the perceived variance (riskiness) in the exchange rate becomes smaller; (b) the marginal utility from the expected yield is larger; and (c) the marginal disutility from increased risk approaches zero.

Perfect Capital Mobility: Uncovered Interest Parity

If c is very large there is a tendency for the speculative return to be zero at all times. Suppose $(s^e - s + r^* - r)$ differs from zero due to a sudden unexpected increase in r^*. There may then be a massive capital outflow leading to a depreciation in the domestic currency (rise in s), a rise in domestic interest rates (as domestic assets are sold to purchase foreign assets) or a rise in the expected exchange rate s^e (that is an *expected* appreciation in the domestic currency). Alternatively the mere *threat* of a capital outflow may lead market participants in the foreign exchange market to 'mark up' the spot exchange rate of the domestic currency immediately (a fall in s) to eliminate the speculative return. This may have immediate repercussions on s^e and r but further 'price' changes would eliminate the possibility of any uncovered speculative returns. *Perfect capital mobility and the absence of risk aversion* therefore ensures that the speculative return is zero at all times; it is known as the *uncovered* or *open* arbitrage, or *uncovered interest parity* condition:

$$r^* - r + s^e - s = 0 \tag{2.6}$$

Under our assumptions, Equation (2.6) is an equilibrium relationship that must hold if there are to be no speculative capital flows, that is for domestic and foreign asset holdings to be in equilibrium. Equation (2.6) does not imply unidirectional causation. s, s^e and r are determined simultaneously (r^* is exogenous). Equation (2.6), however, provides a restriction on the relative movements of the endogenous variables s, s^e

and r. To complete the system we need *at least* two other equations to determine any two of s, s^e and r leaving the 'third variable' to be determined by Equation (2.6). We investigate more elaborate models incorporating Equation (2.6) in Chapter 4 when we discuss capital account monetary models (e.g. Dornbusch (1976) overshooting model).

Speculation and the Spot Exchange Rate

Even if c is small, large volatile capital flows and changes in the spot rate might ensue if substantial and frequent changes in expectations take place. The foreign exchange market is a 'spot auction market' and 'prices' can change very quickly. Volatile movements in s^e may be caused by the arrival of new information ('news') which alters people's perceptions of the future course of the exchange rate. We investigate this issue further in Chapter 5.

Domestic monetary and fiscal policies may influence domestic interest rates, capital flows and hence the current spot rate: this mechanism appears in the Dornbusch model. If inflationary *expectations* are incorporated in nominal interest rates (the Fisher effect) then the former may also influence the current spot rate. Further, inflationary expectations might *directly influence* the *expected change* in the current spot exchange rate. The latter mechanism is the basis of the Frankel (1979b) real interest rate model of the spot rate discussed in Chapter 4.

World monetary and fiscal conditions may influence r^* and hence the current spot rate: for a given s^e, a rise in r^* is likely to be accompanied by a depreciation in the spot rate of the domestic currency or a rise in the domestic interest rate. If s responds quickly to changes in r^* but goods prices are sticky in the short run, the real exchange may change. Changes in r^* may then be transmitted to the real domestic economy via relative prices and the trade balance. Hence under flexible exchange rates, the level of domestic output is not totally insulated from the world economy at least in the short run.

Direct Investment

Direct investment, the purchase or sale of real assets between residents and non-residents involves complex long-run considerations of relative profitability. We do not wish to dwell on such issues here and for analytic convenience we assume that *flows* of direct investment depend upon the relative *real* return to investment in the two countries. We assume that agents consider returns in terms of the purchasing power, in the country in which the investment is undertaken. The real return to investment in the domestic economy is measured by $(r - \pi^e)$ where π^e is the expected rate of inflation in the domestic currency. The real return to investment in the foreign country as perceived by domestic residents is $(r^* - \pi^{*e})$: the latter is measured in terms of purchasing power over foreign (and not domestic) goods. For simplicity we ignore the repatriation of any profits from the venture.[6] The demand for the domestic currency spot, due to inward direct investment is

$$D\pounds = d[(r - \pi^e) - (r^* - \pi^{*e})]. \tag{2.7}$$

The search and transaction costs of direct investment are much greater than for portfolio investment and hence the former is likely to be determined by very long-term considerations about relative rates of return. If funds are to be repatriated then direct investment also requires one to form a view of the spot rate. Decisions are unlikely to be taken on the basis of short-run changes in the spot rate. As we are primarily interested in explaining movements in the exchange rate over a fairly short horizon we have not considered direct investment in the analysis which follows. It is also the case that 'country risk' which involves an analysis of socio-political factors plays an important part in decisions over direct investment such as setting up a subsidiary in a foreign country. Unfortunately space limitations preclude discussion of these aspects of the problem.

Summary and Conclusions

In this chapter we introduced the terminology required to understand discussions and analysis of behaviour in the spot and forward markets. In so doing, we have noted that the covered interest differential and the uncovered speculative return determine arbitrageurs' and speculators' demand for *spot* currency, respectively. In a 'perfect market' agents equalise the expected returns to 'investing' in domestic and foreign assets and this gives rise to the covered and uncovered interest parity conditions (the latter also requires the assumption of 'risk neutrality'). Finally, because capital flows are determined by 'flex-price' or 'jump variables' such as interest rates and expectations concerning the future spot rate this may (in principle at least) account for the observed volatility in the spot rate.

Notes

1. There is also a residual error in the accounts called the 'balancing item', shown as the last item in Table 2.1, as not all flows are measured accurately. It can sometimes be substantial, but we have excluded it from our discussion for ease of exposition.

2. To obtain $Y at the end of three months by investing in the US one needs to purchase $Y/(1 + r^*)$ in US securities and this requires a sale of £$S[Y/(1 + r^*)]$ in the spot market. To obtain $Y in the forward market one has to have £FY available in three months' time, which in turn requires an investment today *in UK securities* of £$FY/(1 + r)$. Hence one invests in the US security if the sterling costs of obtaining $Y (in three months' time) by investing in the UK, namely $FY/(1 + r)$ are greater than the sterling one has to give up to invest in US securities, namely £$SY/(1 + r^*)$. Taking logarithms yields, after rearranging: invest in the US to minimise cost if $f - s + r^* - r > 0$ which is the same as Equation (2.3) in the text.

3. We do not deal explicitly with the choice of non-capital certain assets (e.g. investment in long-term bonds) which are not held to maturity and therefore have uncertain asset prices denominated in their own currency. In this case the 'yield' would include expected capital gains. We also leave on one side considerations of the real (i.e. inflation adjusted) returns on the assets: an acceptable assumption for investment over a short time horizon.

4. This is perhaps easier to see when the assets involved are short-term 'marketable' assets such as commercial or Treasury bills. But faced with a withdrawal of (wholesale) deposits banks may also raise interest rates in order to retain their funds.

5. We assume that a given covered differential leads to a desired *stock* of assets and therefore individuals do not continuously add to their assets (stock) if the differential remains positive. For a detailed discussion of stock-flow concepts in the context of the foreign exchange market see Beenstock (1978).

6. The definition of direct investment used in the UK includes all profits retained overseas. Thus direct investment relates to the accumulation of real assets overseas and does not necessarily imply that any foreign exchange transaction has taken place to enable it.

3 THEORIES OF THE DETERMINATION OF THE FORWARD RATE AND SPOT CAPITAL FLOWS

Introduction

In principle government policy may influence the spot rate by altering domestic interest rates or by influencing the expected spot rate or the forward rate. However, we can greatly enhance our knowledge of the impact of monetary policy on the spot exchange rate by analysing the 'modern theory' and Cambist views of the forward rate. In the 'modern theory' the forward rate is a weighted average of the interest parity forward rate and the expected spot rate. It turns out that if the response of arbitrageurs to the (riskless) return to investing in foreign assets is high, then government intervention in the *forward market* will lead to substantial capital flows in the *spot market*. Hence, forward intervention is useful under a fixed exchange rate regime to stem a capital outflow. On the other hand, if the arbitrage response is large, a rise in domestic interest rates will not lead to large *arbitrage* spot capital flows. Large *speculative* flows in the spot market are then required to stem any capital outflow. The forward market is not simply interesting *per se*, but because of the possible use of forward intervention by the authorities to support the spot rate. This method of support for the spot rate does not require a rise in domestic interest rates and was frequently used by deficit countries under the Bretton Woods system when they faced a speculative outflow on the capital account. In the final part of the chapter we discuss the bankers' or Cambist view of the forward market. This analysis suggests that non-bank covered arbitrage transactions do not lead to net capital flows in the *spot* market and the latter therefore result purely from speculative activity.

To anticipate our main conclusions we find that the evidence, on balance, supports the view that arbitrage transactions are highly elastic and hence intervention in the forward market by the authorities may influence spot capital flows and the spot exchange rate. The evidence on the size of speculative flows indicates that these appear to be relatively inelastic which is indicative of a substantial degree of risk aversion on the part of speculators. However, we have reservations about the robustness of these results. The efficient markets hypothesis discussed in Chapter 5 provides further evidence on this issue and we reserve judgement on the matter until then.

Outline

The rest of the chapter is organised as follows. First we discuss the modern theory of the determination of the forward rate. In order to test the theory we need to measure the unobservable expected spot rate and we therefore briefly describe how the rational expectations hypothesis can be of use in this context. We then present illustrative results of tests of the 'modern theory' and then move on to tests of the determinants of spot capital flows (the theoretical aspects of which we introduced in the previous chapter). It turns out that empirical evidence from both forward rate and capital flows equations yield complementary evidence on the size of the arbitrage and speculative response on the capital account. We then examine the policy implications of these empirical results. Next we turn to an alternative view of the working of the forward market namely the Cambist or 'bankers' view'. Finally we present a summary and conclusions.

The Modern Theory of the Forward Rate

Covered interest arbitrage involves a simultaneous purchase (sale) of foreign currency in the *spot* market and its sale (purchase) in the forward market. The demand for *spot* currency by arbitrageurs provides an equal supply of the currency in the forward market. To obtain an equilibrium in the forward market the supply of a particular currency by arbitrageurs must be voluntarily matched by an equal demand for the forward currency by other agents. These 'other agents' are speculators in the *forward* market (and must not be confused with speculators in the *spot* market, discussed in Chapter 2). The return to speculation in the forward market depends upon the differential between today's forward rate, f, and the spot rate expected to prevail at the time of maturity of the forward contract, s_{t+1}^e. Equilibrium in the forward market for foreign exchange provides a constraint on the relationship between foreign and domestic interest rates, the spot rate, the expected spot rate and the forward rate. This so called 'modern theory' of the forward market allows the forward rate to be viewed as a weighted average of the expected spot rate s_{t+1}^e and the interest parity forward rate, $f^* = s + r - r^*$. As the elasticity of the speculative schedule for forward foreign exchange approaches infinity the current forward rate f, is equal to the expected future spot rate, s_{t+1}^e. The latter relationship has been investigated in a different strand of the literature known as the 'efficient markets hypothesis' (EMH). We discuss this in Chapter 5.

In our examples we continue to take sterling (£) as the domestic currency and the dollar ($) as the foreign currency. The reader might like to refresh his memory of covered interest arbitrage in Chapter 2 where it is shown that arbitrageurs' *spot* demand for foreign currency, $AD\$$, is given by $AD\$ = a(r^* - r + f - s)$, where $(r^* - r + f - s)$ is the covered interest differential, CID. The arbitrageurs' supply of *forward* foreign currency $ASF\$$ is equal to $AD\$$; hence:

$$ASF\$ = a(r^* - r + f - s) = a(f - f^*) \qquad (3.1)$$

where f^* is the interest parity forward rate; $f^* = r - r^* + s$. The larger the CID the greater is the amount of foreign currency offered for sale on the forward market: arbitrageurs wish to sell foreign currency forward and purchase domestic currency, forward.

Under what conditions would 'speculators' purchase (demand) foreign currency ($) from the arbitrageurs and sell domestic currency (£) to them in three months' time? Suppose $F = 0.769$ £/$ (= 1.3 $/£). For each dollar the speculator agrees to purchase in three months' time he must also agree to provide £0.769. If the spot rate the speculator expects to prevail in three months' time is $S_{t+1}^e = 0.833$ £/$ (= 1.2 $/£), then for each dollar received from the arbitrageur he expects to obtain £0.833 in spot market in three months' time. Under these conditions the speculator expects to obtain 0.833 £/$ but only has to pay out 0.769 £/$: he expects to make a profit of £0.064 on each dollar of the deal. When the uncovered speculative return in the *forward* market (S_{t+1}^e/F) is greater than unity, speculators will buy foreign currency in the forward market and supply domestic currency forward. If $S_{t+1}^e > F_t$, that is $S_{t+1}^e/F > 1$, then, taking logarithms, $s_{t+1}^e - f > 0$.

Speculators' demand for foreign currency ($) in the forward market $SDF\$$, is given by:

$$SDF\$ = c_f(s_{t+1}^e - f) \qquad (3.2)$$

c_f is the responsiveness (loosely speaking, the elasticity) of the speculative demand for forward currency to the return to forward speculation $(s_{t+1}^e - f)$. c_f depends upon the individual's taste for risk and return and the perceived variability of the risk he faces.

Equilibrium in the forward market occurs when the supply of forward currency equals demand:

$$a(f - f^*) = c_f(s^e_{t+1} - f) + G_f + Z_f \qquad (3.3)$$

where G_f measures any net intervention in the forward market by the monetary authorities and Z_f is a set of variables other than $(f - f^*)$ and $(s^e_{t+1} - f)$ that might influence arbitrageurs' or speculators' demands for forward currency (e.g. their liquidity position). Re-arranging (3.3) we obtain the modern theory of the forward rate, namely, that the forward rate is a weighted average of the interest parity forward rate and the expected spot rate, given G_f and Z_f

$$f = \delta s^e_{t+1} + (1 - \delta)f^* + \gamma_0(G_f + Z_f) \qquad (3.4)$$

where $\delta = c_f/(c_f + a)$ and $(1 - \delta) = a/(c_f + a)$, $\gamma_0 = 1/(c_f + a)$.

A test of the 'modern theory' requires either estimation of the asset demand/supply equations (3.1) and (3.2) to determine a and c_f or estimation of the forward rate equation (3.4). The former is not possible since data on asset stocks and flows in the *forward* market are not available.

Estimates of δ give the relative weights of arbitrage and speculative activity in determining f, (i.e. $\delta/(1 - \delta) = c_f/a$). However, separate estimates of c_f and a cannot be obtained (i.e. c_f and a are not 'identified, in the terminology of econometrics) from the forward rate equation unless data on G_f or Z_f are available. If figures on government intervention in the forward market are available the estimate of γ_0 gives an additional equation in c_f and a, namely $\gamma_0 = 1/(c_f + a)$. This enables a and c_f to be 'identified' in terms of the estimated coefficients (i.e. $\hat{a} = (1 - \hat{\delta})/\hat{\gamma}_0$ and $\hat{c}_f = \hat{\delta}/\hat{\gamma}_0$, where $\char`\^$ denotes an estimate).

According to the 'modern theory' the greater the elasticity of the speculative schedule relative to the arbitrage schedule the larger is the coefficient on the expected spot rate $\delta = c_f/(c_f + a)$ as compared with that on the interest parity forward rate. The testable predictions of the theory are that δ is significantly greater than zero and that the sum of the coefficients on s^e_{t+1} and f^* is unity.

The forward market equation (3.4), although having f as the dependent variable, should not be interpreted as implying that s^e_{t+1} and f^* determine f in a unidirectional causal sense. Equation (3.4) is a relationship between the variables which must hold if there is to be equilibrium in the forward market: causation may run in any direction, including from s^e_{t+1} to f^*, the so-called independent variables of the equation. In the equation, f, f^*, s^e_{t+1} (as well as G_f) are jointly determined and the modern theory by no means provides a *complete* description of the behaviour of the forward exchange market. An econometric implication of the above discussion is that the forward market equation should be estimated using a simultaneous equation technique such as two stage least squares (2SLS) or instrumental variables (IV), rather than ordinary least squares (OLS).

Tests of the forward market equation require data or proxy variables for the expected one period ahead spot rate s_{t+1}^e. Estimation of the demand function for speculative funds in the *spot* market, discussed in Chapter 2, also requires 'data' on s_{t+1}^e. Survey data of foreign exchange dealers' expectations about future spot exchange rates are not generally available and hence researchers have had to apply models of expectation formation. Although there are many different ways in which individuals might form their expectations, many researchers have applied the concept of rational expectations (RE) to behaviour in the foreign exchange market.

Rational Expectations Hypothesis (REH): An Introduction

Survey data on exchange rate expectations are not available and hence to model capital flows we need some method of measuring the 'unobservable' *expected* exchange rate. The REH provides two useful methods of obtaining such proxy variables.

According to the REH individuals use all relevant available information when forming their expectations. In its strongest form (Muth, 1961) it is assumed that agents act *as if* they use the 'true' model of the economy when forming their expectations of the future. It is also assumed that the actual out-turn differs from that expected, only by a zero mean random error, i.e. that the 'true' model has only (additive) zero mean random errors. This is the property of the RE known as *unbiasedness* which allows one to use the actual ex-post value recorded for a variable as an unbiased measure of what its expected value was. Thus, if we invoke RE we immediately have a proxy variable for the 'unobservable' (one period ahead) expected exchange rate namely, the actual out-turn value in the next period. (However, use of this ex-post value requires a special but straightforward estimation technique known as instrumental variables; see McCallum, 1976.)

The REH assumes that foreign exchange speculators act *as if* they use the correct model of the foreign exchange market when forming their expectations. If we know the determinants of the *actual* one period ahead exchange rate we can use this relationship to *predict* the *future* exchange rate. Such forecasts provide a data series for the expected exchange rate. A simple example will clarify the point. Suppose our theory of exchange rate determination leads us to believe that the *actual* spot rate is governed by purchasing power parity *in the long run*. Under PPP, $S_t = (P/P^*)_t$.

Let us assume that PPP only applies after a lag of one quarter and that there is a random disturbance to the relation:

$$S_{t+1} = b_0(P/P^*)_t + b_1(P/P^*)_{t-1} + u_t \tag{3.5}$$

where $b_0 + b_1 = 1$ and u_t is a zero mean random error (i.e. 'white noise'). We have limited the lagged price effect to one quarter (for ease of exposition) and imposed PPP in the 'long run' (i.e. $b_0 + b_1 = 1$). Since we have data on all the variables in Equation (3.5) we can obtain regression estimates of b_0 and b_1. Faced with information on current and past prices our 'best' forecast of next periods exchange rate S^e_{t+1} is given by:

$$S^e_{t+1} = \hat{b}_0(P/P^*)_t + \hat{b}_1(P/P^*)_{t-1} \tag{3.6}$$

where $\hat{b}_0$ and $\hat{b}_1$ are the estimated values of the parameters.

The *estimated* equation (Equation 3.6) may therefore be used to generate a data series for the expected spot rate. Notice that since $\hat{b}_0$ and $\hat{b}_1$ are unbiased estimates of the 'true' values b_0 and b_1 on average, then S^e_{t+1} differs from the actual out-turn S_{t+1} only by the random error, u_t which has a mean of zero.

Thus by invoking the REH we are able to obtain a data series for the expected exchange rate over the past, by two different routes. We can either use the ex-post one period ahead rate S_{t+1} (together with an instrumental variable estimation method), or use the *predictions* from a relationship of the form given by Equation (3.6). In the latter case it may be wise to try several types of equation and hence obtain several alternative forecast series S^e_{t+1}. We may then check the sensitivity of our results to the form of 'expectations equation' chosen. Having outlined how the REH may be invoked to yield estimates of the expected exchange rate we are now in a position to examine the determinants of capital flows and the forward exchange rate empirically. Both capital flow equations and the forward rate equation, yield estimates of the relative size of arbitrage and speculative flows (on the spot and forward markets) and hence of the scope for government policy towards the exchange rate.

Testing the Modern Theory of the Forward Exchange Rate

In the previous section, we arrived at the result, based on an equilibrium model of the forward market, that the forward rate could be expressed as a weighted average of the interest parity forward rate f^*, and the one period ahead expected spot rate, s^e_{t+1}. The weights or coefficients on these two variables sum to unity, and the ratio of the two coefficients gives the size of the arbitrage elasticity relative to that for the speculative demand for forward currency. The forward rate also depends on 'other' variables Z_f, that might influence the arbitrage or speculative demand schedules for forward currency and on the amount of government intervention in the forward market, G_f. Data on the latter two variables enable one to 'identify' the *absolute* values of the elasticities of the demand for arbitrage and speculative funds (rather than their relative size). In this section we test the validity of the 'modern' theory and obtain estimates of the arbitrage-speculative response in the forward market.

The forward rate equation derived above (Equation 3.4) is:

$$f = \delta s_{t+1}^e + (1 - \delta)f^* + \gamma_0(G_f + Z_f) + u_t \tag{3.7}$$

where $\delta = c_f/(c_f + a)$, $(1 - \delta) = a/(c_f + a)$, $\gamma_0 = 1/(c_f + a)$, u_t is an error term, a and c_f are defined in Equations (3.1) and (3.2) and our estimating equation is:

$$f = \hat{\alpha}_0 + \hat{\alpha}_1 s_{t+1}^e + \hat{\alpha}_2 f^* + \hat{\gamma}_0(G_f + Z_f). \tag{3.8}$$

If the modern theory is correct we expect $\hat{\alpha}_1 + \hat{\alpha}_2 = 1$; $\hat{\alpha}_2/\hat{\gamma}_0 = [a/(c_f + a)]/[1/(c_f + a)] = \hat{a}$ and hence gives an estimate of the absolute value of the arbitrage elasticity. Similarly $\hat{\alpha}_1/\hat{\gamma}_0 = \hat{c}_f$, the elasticity of the speculative schedule. Without data on G_f or Z_f we can only obtain an estimate of the ratio of the arbitrage to the speculative schedule $\hat{\alpha}_2/\hat{\alpha}_1 = \hat{a}/\hat{c}_f$. If either Z_f or G_f is excluded from the equation and these variables are reasonably constant over the sample period of estimation this may produce a statistically significant constant term. If the theory is correct we expect u_t to be 'white noise'[1]. To estimate the forward rate equation we need to provide a data series for the expected spot rate, s^e, and rational expectations can be employed here.

The rational expectations hypothesis (REH) predicts that the expected spot rate is determined endogenously by variables that influence the actual spot rate. Different researchers assume different models for the determination of the spot rate and hence use different series for s_{t+1}^e: this accounts for some divergence in the results presented below. In the REH, expectations are unbiased, and therefore the *actual* one period ahead spot rate s_{t+1} provides an unbiased predictor of the *expected* spot rate. Although there are some additional estimation problems posed by using the actual one period ahead spot rate as a proxy variable for the expected rate, it has nevertheless proved popular amongst researchers in this area.

For clarity of exposition we shall present a schematic overview of the empirical work. For example, we assume that all the results quoted use variables as they appear in Equation (3.8): although not factually correct, this does not alter the arguments or conclusions reached. The studies we discuss are illustrative rather than wholly representative or exhaustive.

Beenstock and Bell (1979) and Beenstock (1978) used unpublished data on the UK government's intervention in the forward market for a number of currencies against sterling and were therefore able to estimate the absolute size of the arbitrage and speculative schedules. In general they take what could be described as a 'current account' view of the way expectations about the spot rate are formed: they assume that the latter depends upon lagged values of the terms of trade τ (relative prices) and the visible balance (VB).

We can represent this relationship as:

$$s^e_{t+1} = X\beta_t \tag{3.9}$$

where β is a (vector) of parameters and X represents the (vector of) relative price and visible balance variables. Substituting (3.9) in (3.8) we obtain:

$$f = \alpha_0 + \alpha_2 f^* + \gamma_0 G_f + \alpha_1(X\beta), \tag{3.10}$$

there being no terms in Z_f.

They estimate the following equation:

$$f = \alpha_0 + \alpha_2 f^* + \gamma_0 G_f + X\alpha^*. \tag{3.11}$$

From our estimate of $\hat{\alpha}_2$ we obtain an estimate of $\hat{\alpha}_1 = (1 - \hat{\alpha}_2)$. Using the estimate of $\hat{\alpha}^*$ we may derive $\beta = \hat{\alpha}^*/\hat{\alpha}_1$ and hence obtain an explicit equation for s^e. A representative equation from Beenstock and Bell for the three months sterling-dollar forward rate is:

$$f = 0.947\, f^* + 0.00049\ G_f + \text{terms in } \tau \text{ and VB (current and lagged).}$$
$$\quad (11.2) \qquad\qquad (2.2) \tag{3.12}$$

$R^2 = 0.9$; dw $= 1.77$; data period: 1966 (1) – 1974 (3) quarterly.

(Instrumental variables used for s in f^*; numbers in parenthesis are t-statistics.

The 'weight' of arbitrage in determining f is large at 0.95. The absolute value of the arbitrage response indicates that a one percentage point change in the arbitrage return yields a capital flow of about $2,000m but the speculative response is a mere $100m. When the implicit equation for s^e is derived it is found that a one per cent change in relative prices generates a one per cent change in the expected spot rate: a plausible result since we know that PPP holds approximately over this data period. The parameter estimates quoted are subject to fairly wide margins of error since the coefficient of G which is required to determine a and c_f is not particularly well determined.

Results in Beenstock (1978) for the three month forward rates of the Canadian dollar, the French franc and the Deutschmark, against sterling give broadly similar results: the 'weight' of arbitrage in determining the forward rate is in excess of 80 per cent.

Using a similar approach, Ormerod (1980) employs alternative proxy variables for the unexpected spot rate. He invokes the unbiasedness property of the REH and uses the actual future spot rate in place of s_{t+1}^e (this requires estimation by instrumental variables (IV) to avoid 'errors in variable bias'). This approach is generally unrewarding. The actual future spot rate is insignificant for most currencies reported; the weight of arbitrage is nearly unity and the equation has acute autocorrelation in the residuals (i.e. the residuals are not white noise). In a second attempt to provide proxy variables for s_{t+1}^e, following earlier work, he assumes that s_{t+1}^e is determined by *lagged* values of the interest parity forward rate f^*, the actual spot rate s, and the visible balance, that is $X = (f^*, s, \text{VB})$. He substitutes these variables in the forward rate equation in place of s_{t+1}^e and is also able to obtain an estimate of $\hat{\beta}$ in the manner described above. Knowing $\hat{\beta}$ and X, Ormerod generates a series for $\hat{s}_{t+1}^e = X\hat{\beta}$, and then uses this series directly in the forward rate Equation (3.7) with $\gamma_0 = 0$. For the sterling-dollar forward rate he obtains:

$$f = 0.42f^* + 0.58\hat{s}_{t+1}^e \qquad\qquad (3.13)$$
$$ (0.22) \quad\ (0.25)$$

IV, Aug. 72–July 75, SE = 0.7(%), dw = 2.3.

In this equation speculation and arbitrage now have approximately equal weight in determining f, in marked contrast to the results using the actual future spot rate.

In many of the studies of the forward rate equation the correlation between f^* and s_{t+1}^e (usually regardless of the particular proxy variable used) is high. Such 'multicollinearity' masks the separate influence of f^* and s_{t+1}^e in determining the forward rate. This may be due to the fact that speculators form their expectations of the future spot rate based on the interest parity forward rate $s_{t+1}^e = f^*$; all the variables in f^* are known at the time expectations are formed. This would account for the high degree of multicollinearity and high standard errors on the f^* and s_{t+1}^e variables (or the variables that determine the latter). In such circumstances it is virtually impossible to place a precise estimate on the relative impact of arbitrage and speculations in determining the forward rate. Nevertheless the results available tend to favour marginally the view that the arbitrage schedule is more elastic than the speculative schedule, at least for the late 1960s and early 1970s for many major currencies against sterling.

It is of interest to note here that, since the speculative schedule appears to be far from being infinitely elastic, the forward rate is not an unbiased predictor of the expected spot rate: the interest parity forward rate also has a (major) influence in determining f. This has a bearing on our later discussion of the efficient markets hypothesis (EMH) which implies that $s_{t+1}^e = f$ (plus a white noise error).

Other studies for the UK forward exchange rate equation (Table 3.1) give a wide variety of estimates for the relative weights of arbitrage and speculative activity in determining the forward rate. These results are not directly comparable since they cover different estimation periods and use different proxy variables for the expected spot rate. However in broad terms we feel that the evidence suggests that arbitrage has a higher weight than speculative activity.

Table 3.1: The Ratio of Arbitrage to Total Forward Market Activity

Hutton (1977)	0.24
Minford (1978)	0.493
Argy and Hodjera (1973)	0.91
Beenstock (1978)	0.95
Ormerod (1980)	0.42–0.95

The reader may recall from Chapter 2 that arbitrageurs deal simultaneously in the spot as well as the forward market, and also that speculation takes place in the spot market because of uncovered investment overseas. We can obtain alternative estimates of the elasticity of the arbitrage and speculative demands for *spot* currency since data on spot capital flows are readily available.

Capital Flows in the Spot Market: Empirical Tests

In Chapter 2 we found that arbitrage demand responds to the covered interest differential (Equation 2.4) while speculative demand in the *spot* market responds to the uncovered (or speculative) return (Equation 2.5). The arbitrage supply of spot sterling (the domestic currency) $AS\pounds$ and the speculative supply of spot sterling $SS\pounds$ are given by:

$$AS\pounds = a(r^* - r + f - s) + Z_A \tag{3.14}$$

$$SS\pounds = c(s_{t+1}^e - s + r^* - r) + Z_s. \tag{3.15}$$

In general data on *stocks* of foreign assets are not available but data on capital *flows*, particularly net capital flows are readily available for most industrialised countries. To utilise such data we need to re-cast our theory of desired asset stocks given by Equations (3.14) and (3.15) into a theory about the flow demand (or supply) for currencies.

It is generally accepted that there are three phases in the adjustment to long-run equilibrium in the capital account. Consider an increase in the domestic interest rate. There is an immediate stock adjustment as arbitrageurs and (spot) speculators attempt to switch existing assets into the domestic currency. In subsequent periods there may be further lagged adjustments as some agents react slowly (this is the basis of the so-called partial adjustment mechanism). Finally there will be a small but continuous adjustment due to the growth in total wealth as a higher domestic interest rate (*ceteris paribus*) leads to a greater proportion of *additional* wealth being placed in domestic assets.[2]

In practice, these three phases of the adjustment process are difficult to disentangle and many researchers in this area have assumed instantaneous adjustment (within the data period of observation). In this case the short term capital *in-flow* into the domestic economy is given by:

$$\begin{aligned}
STC &= -(\Delta AS\pounds + \Delta SS\pounds) \\
&= a\Delta(r - r^* + s - f) + c\Delta(r - r^* + s - s_{t+1}^e) - \Delta(Z_A + Z_s) \\
&= a\Delta CID + c\Delta UD + \Delta(s - s_{t+1}^e) - \Delta(Z_A + Z_s) \tag{3.16}
\end{aligned}$$

where *CID* and *UD* are the covered and uncovered interest differentials respectively.

There are several major problems in attempting to estimate capital flows equations. The unobservable expected spot rate s_{t+1}^e could in principle be estimated in a number of ways. As with the forward rate equation we could invoke the unbiasedness property of the REH and use the actual one period ahead spot rate s_{t+1} or estimate a separate equation to generate a series for s_{t+1}^e using the predictions from an estimated equation $\hat{s}_{t+1} = X\beta_t$, where X is a set of (pre-determined) variables thought to influence s_{t+1}^e. Alternatively many researchers have used the series $\hat{s}_{t+1}^e$ generated from estimates of the forward rate equation, as discussed in the previous section. Another device often used is to measure large changes in expectations by 'crisis' dummy variables. This, of course, is a rather arbitrary procedure but it is only recently that 'news' or 'unexpected' events have been more adequately modelled, and these more recent technical innovations have yet to pervade this area of the literature.

Constraints on capital flows or access to credit may mean that *actual* data on capital flows do not correspond to *desired* flows as given by the theory. In such disequilibrium situations a change in interest rates may not be expected to induce capital flows. However the modelling of situations in which individuals are 'off' their (notional or desired) demand curves has not been extensively applied to studies of capital flows. Perceived differences in risk between two countries may influence capital flows (the Z variables) but are rarely modelled explicitly and generally dummy variables are used.

Perhaps the most damning *a priori* reasons for viewing the results from studies of capital flows somewhat sceptically is that 'prices' in asset markets (e.g. s, r and f) may adjust quickly to eliminate any profitable returns. The covered and uncovered returns may therefore be very close to zero for most time periods. (This is the efficient markets hypothesis which we discuss in Chapter 5.) If there is little variation in the independent variables of the capital flows equation we cannot hope to obtain precise estimates of the arbitrage and speculative responses. A near zero estimated response in the capital flows equation would not therefore necessarily imply that spot speculators and arbitrageurs were unresponsive to changes in relative yields. On the contrary it is the *threat* of large capital flows rather than actual flows (on which we have data) which produce near zero changes in the respective returns.

The final problem in estimating capital flows equations is connected with our last point. If international financial markets are near 'perfect markets' then a change in any independent variable in the capital flows equation, say, an increase in the foreign (US) interest rate, r^*, will quickly lead to changes in other variables which have been treated as exogenous, say domestic (UK) interest rates r (or the current spot or forward rate or even changes in the expected spot rate). This simultaneity requires the use of instrumental variable (IV) estimation techniques such as two stage least squares (2SLS) rather than ordinary least squares (OLS).

Perhaps we should balance our sceptical remarks a little. During the Bretton Woods fixed exchange rate period of the 1950s and 1960s (for which we have data on capital flows) there may be data periods within our estimation sample period where the covered and uncovered returns show substantial changes which are not considered during 'crisis' periods. These, possibly limited, data periods may be sufficient to provide plausible and reasonably precise estimates of the response of arbitrage and speculative flows across the spot exchange market. Again our examples below are meant to be illustrative of the methods used and do not provide a comprehensive survey of results.

Beenstock (1978) provides a useful illustrative example of an equation for short term capital *in-flows* into the UK over the period 1964–74.

$$STC = 54 + 300 \, \Delta CID + 48 \, \Delta UD + 6 \, \Delta s^e - 935 \, CRIS + u_t \qquad (3.17)$$
$$ (5.8) \qquad (5.8) \qquad (5.8) \qquad (3.8)$$

$R^2 = 0.76$; $SE = £190m$; $dw = 1.8$.
Data period: 1964 (2) – 1973 (4), quarterly.

CRIS represents a series of dummy variables to pick up speculative 'runs' of the pound. s^e is the series derived from the forward rate equation as discussed above. When the theoretically correct term $\Delta(s^e - s)$ is used it fails to be significant under any circumstances; hence only Δs^e is included. Multicollinearity amongst the rates of return (ΔCID, ΔUD and Δs^e) is a severe problem and these variables are weighted to give the best fit for the equation (in terms of minimising its standard error). Instrumental variable *IV* estimates are used for the covered interest differential but not for the uncovered differential. The errors in the equation, u_t, are autocorrelated (but this is taken account of in the estimation method used).

The estimated arbitrage response is £300m (about $800m) for a one percentage point change in the covered differential and £48m for a one percentage point change in the uncovered differential. The relatively riskless arbitrage response is therefore greater than the 'risky' speculative response in the spot market, as one might expect (assuming that is, that speculators in the *forward* market supply forward currency to arbitrageurs). We cannot directly compare the estimated speculative response in the spot market with that estimated (from the forward rate equation) for speculators who operate in the *forward* market, since these may be different, agents or people may hold different perceptions of 'risk' in the two markets. However, we can directly compare our estimates of *a* from the forward rate equation estimated by Beenstock, namely $2,000m, with that from the capital flows equation of $800m. Although the divergence is large, which is worrying, Beenstock argues that the biases in the two measures imply that the 'true' estimate lies somewhere between the two. Other estimates of the arbitrage response from capital flows equations for the UK are:

£ *million*

Hodjera (1971)	921
Branson and Hill (1971)	140
Minford (1978)	91
Hutton (1977)	96

showing a range very similar to the equivalent values in Table 3.1.

Policy Implications

We have examined some illustrative empirical results for the forward rate equation and for short-term capital flows and in both cases we have been able to throw some light on the size of the response of arbitrageurs and speculators to changes in their respective returns to investing overseas. We now examine some of the broad policy implications of alternative views concerning the strength of arbitrage and speculative activity.

Under the Bretton Woods 'fixed' exchange rate system of the 1950s and 1960s countries that found themselves in temporary balance of payments deficit on current account often resorted to increases in domestic interest rates to attract a temporary capital in-flow and hence stem the drain on foreign exchange reserves and preserve the exchange rate at its 'fixed' parity. To achieve the same ends, governments often purchased the domestic currency in the *forward* market to push the domestic currency to a (forward) discount and encourage inward arbitrage demand for spot currency. It is generally thought that governments did not deal extensively in the spot market to support the currency. Day-to-day fluctuations might be met by spot intervention by the authorities but that is all. (It is difficult to ascertain whether the authorities did deal extensively in the spot market since the figures are not published.) An immediate policy question that arises is whether domestic interest rate increases and intervention in the forward market do have a substantial influence on capital flows.

Our forward rate equation and the short-term capital flows equation are:

$$\Delta f = [c_f/(c_f + a)]\Delta s_{t+1}^e + [a/(c_f + a)]\Delta(r - r^* + s)$$
$$+ [1/(c_f + a)\Delta G] \tag{3.18}$$

$$STC = a\Delta(r - r^* + s - f) + c\Delta(r - r^* + s - s_{t+1}^e) \tag{3.19}$$

where we have set 'other' influences equal to zero, that is,

$$Z_A = Z_s = Z_f = 0 \text{ (see Equations 2.4 and 2.5).}$$

For the moment let us assume that speculative flows in the *spot* market are zero ($c = 0$) as we wish to concentrate on the interrelationship between the forward rate and short-term capital flows. An increase in the domestic interest rate r is unlikely to affect r^* if the domestic economy is 'small', an assumption frequently made for the UK. Given Beenstock's (1978) estimates for the UK, a one percentage point increase in r, leads to an arbitrage in-flow of about \$2,000m if we take the estimate of a from the forward rate equation. However this estimate assumes that the other elements that make up the covered interest differential in the capital flows equation (Equation 3.19) namely $s - f$ remain constant. The forward rate equation (Equation 3.18) indicates that f will move in the same direction as r in order to preserve equilibrium in the market for *forward* currency. Further, the greater is the relative weight of arbitrage activity in determining the forward rate, the larger is the offsetting induced change in f consequent on the change in the domestic interest rate. Beenstock (1978) finds that the offset effect may be as high as 95 per cent. Thus an initial change in the domestic interest rate of one percentage point only increases the *covered* interest differential by 0.05 per cent and the consequent *arbitrage* short-term capital in-flow is reduced to \$100m. Given this evidence (and our assumption to ignore speculative *spot* flows) it would appear that, for the UK, a policy of altering domestic interest rates to attract a capital in-flow was unlikely to be very effective in the period 1964–71. The reason for this is that the supply of speculative funds in the *forward* market to arbitrageurs was very inelastic and this therefore limited arbitrage transactions in the *spot* market. Algebraic-ally this result can be derived by substituting the forward market equa-tion (Equation 3.18) in the short-term capital flows equation (Equation 3.19) and re-arranging:

$$STC = \left[\frac{ac_f}{a + c_f} + c \right] \Delta(r - r^* + s - s^e) + \frac{a}{a + c_f} \Delta G. \quad (3.20)$$

Ignoring speculative *spot* flows for the moment (i.e. let $c = 0$), the 'reduced form' coefficient on the uncovered differential ($r - r^*$) may be written as $c_f/(1 + c_f/a)$.

In the limit as a approaches infinity this coefficient is equal to c_f, the elasticity of forward cover provided by speculators (in the forward market): here c_f provides the upper bound for the response of arbitrage capital flows to a change in the uncovered differential.

Next consider government intervention in the forward market as a means of influencing capital flows. From the forward rate equation (Equation 3.18) we see that a change in G leads to a change in the forward rate which in turn causes a change in the covered interest differential and in short-term capital flows. The coefficient on G in the reduced form equation (Equation 3.20) is $a/(c_f + a)$ which Beenstock (1978) estimates to be 0.95. Hence government intervention of \$100m in the forward market induces a \$95m short-term capital in-flow: a powerful effect. In other words, government intervention in the forward market has a powerful influence on spot arbitrage transactions because it supplements the inelastic supply of speculative forward funds provided by private agents. In the limit as a approaches infinity the response of short-term flows to government intervention in the forward market is one for one $(1/(c_f/a + 1) \rightarrow 1$ as $a \rightarrow \infty)$. In contrast, if the elasticity of *forward* speculation is infinite, that is $c_f \rightarrow \infty$, then according to Equation (3.20) the response of short-term capital flows to government intervention in the *forward* market is zero. The reason for this is to be found in the forward rate equation (Equation 3.18). If $c_f \rightarrow \infty$ then the forward rate is determined entirely by the expected spot rate and cannot therefore be influenced by forward intervention (unless the latter were to influence the expected spot rate directly or indirectly). We investigate the relationship $f = s_{t+1}^e$ in the section on the efficient markets hypothesis.

Finally let us consider the influence of the elasticity of spot speculative activity, the parameter c. The larger c, the larger any capital in-flow after a change in the uncovered interest differential (or the spot or expected spot rate) will be. Uncovered spot transactions do not require forward cover and hence the coefficients in the forward rate equation have no influence on uncovered spot transactions. Nevertheless, if Beenstock's (1978) result for the UK that c is equal to about £48m (\$150m at the then prevailing exchange rate) is correct then such spot speculative flows are unlikely to have been large. However we have already expressed our misgivings about accepting this estimate.

It is worth briefly recalling the case where the speculative demand for spot currency c is infinite. Under *fixed* exchange rates any attempt at sterilising capital flows by open market sales of government debt to the domestic non-bank private sector will be thwarted by further capital flows: an independent monetary policy under fixed exchange rates becomes impossible (and the predictions of the CAM model under fixed exchange rates discussed in the next chapter are validated). However, the results of Beenstock and others for the UK suggest that the speculative response in the spot market is rather low and hence sterilisation is possible. We discuss the speculative response in the section on the efficient market hypothesis.

An important point concerning the policy implications discussed above needs to be made. In discussing the response of capital flows to changes in the domestic interest rate and government intervention in the forward market we implicitly assumed that the spot rate and the expected spot rate remained unchanged. For fairly obvious reasons, most notably the simultaneity involved, this is unlikely to be the case. However the system of two equations (Equations 3.18 and 3.19) can only determine two endogenous variables which are taken to be f and STC. We need a more complete model to determine s and s^e but generally this area of the literature does not deal with this aspect. Therefore we have used severe *ceteris paribus* assumptions when discussing the policy implications of the effect of r and G_f on f and STC and this must be always borne in mind.

The Forward Market, Bank Arbitrage and Transactions Costs

There is an alternative model of the working of the forward market to the 'modern view' discussed at the beginning of this chapter. This alternative approach is known as the 'bankers' view' or the *Cambist approach*. The Cambist view focuses on the way in which banks act as brokers in the foreign exchange market, and it is argued that this implies that the forward rate does not deviate from the interest parity rate (or equivalently, that the covered differential is always zero). Covered interest arbitrage by *non-banks* does not therefore result in a *net* capital movement into a currency. Net capital movements can only arise as a result of *speculative spot* transactions by non-banks, or as a result of banks' automatic spot transactions, in response to non-bank *forward market speculation*. Thus, in the Cambist approach, it is speculative transactions which influence the spot rate: covered arbitrage does not. However, the Cambist approach applies to homogeneous assets (e.g. eurocurrency assets) and the 'modern theory' may still be applicable for *non-bank* covered arbitrage between heterogeneous assets (e.g. the euro-Deutschmark market and US commercial bills).

If the Cambist approach is correct and the covered differential is always zero then there is no cost advantage to hedgers in using the forward rather than the spot market. In such circumstances the reason the forward market exists at all is presumably due to transactions costs or brokerage fees which differ when using each market. It is easy to see how this might arise since using the spot market to 'cover' one's exchange risk requires a purchase and sale of a domestic and a foreign asset and a 'spot currency' transaction while covering in the forward market requires only a single transaction.

The Cambist view alters our perception of the *mechanisms* involved in the forward market but it does not alter our broad policy conclusions that domestic interest rates and forward intervention may in principle be used to influence capital flows and the spot exchange rate.

Banking Mechanisms and the Forward Rate: the Cambist Approach

The Cambist approach, in contrast to the 'modern theory', rightly rejects the view that arbitrageurs (and hedgers) deal directly with speculators in the forward market. Recall that speculators in the 'modern theory' supply forward funds to enable arbitrage to take place. The Cambists argue that the banks act as brokers in forward markets and are *always* willing to provide forward exchange *at the interest parity rate*. An example should make this clear.

Suppose a non-bank customer (hedger) requests his bank to deliver dollars in three months' time in exchange for Deutschmarks. The bank now has an open speculative forward position on its own books. In order to avoid an open position and a possible loss, if the spot DM–$ rate in three months' time differs from the current forward rate, the bank can use the eurocurrency market. The bank undertakes the following transactions: (i) borrows in the euro-deutschmark market; (ii) sells the deutschmark spot for dollars; (iii) invests the dollars in the eurodollar market. Thus when the forward market contract matures in three months' time, the bank is able to supply the dollars to the customer and use the deutschmarks received to pay off the euro-deutschmark loan. The bank has eliminated its exchange risk. At the outset of the transaction the bank knows the euro-deutschmark borrowing rate, the spot rate and the rate of interest on eurodollar bank deposits. If the bank 'charges' or quotes a forward rate to the customer equal to the interest parity rate (plus a brokerage fee) then the bank supplies the forward currency without any exchange exposure. Thus the banking mechanism ensures that eurocurrency rates always satisfy the interest parity condition.

Why are there no *net* capital flows in the spot market from covered arbitrage transactions by non-banks? Suppose a *non-bank* covered arbitrageur purchased deutschmarks in the spot market (to invest in German securities) and sold forward deutschmarks to the bank. The bank, in order to avoid an open position in the forward market, would sell deutschmarks (and purchase dollars) in the spot market and invest in the eurodollar market. *Net spot* transactions are therefore zero and covered arbitrage activity by non-banks does not affect capital flows, domestic interest rates nor the spot exchange rate.

What Causes Net Capital Flows?

First, and most obvious, non-bank *speculation* in the spot market influences net capital flows because there are no counterpart transactions by the banks. Second, speculation in the forward market (i.e. when $f \neq s^e$) by non-banks results in net spot capital flows because of the automatic response of banks in the spot market. To see this, suppose the bank's customers undertake speculative purchases of dollars from the banks in the forward market and supply deutschmarks as the counterpart transaction. These *non-bank* forward sales of deutschmarks lead the banks to borrow euro-deutschmarks, sell these *spot* for dollars and invest the proceeds in eurodollar bank deposits. There is therefore a net purchase of *spot* dollars.

In the Cambists' view, a rise in domestic interest rates induces a net capital in-flow (with possible repercussions on the spot exchange rate) because of (i) speculative spot transactions by non-banks (and banks); and (ii) the effect of interest rates on the forward rate and hence on speculative flows in the *forward* market, which in turn induce an automatic response by banks in the spot market.

Conclusions

The major point of difference between the Cambists and the modern theory concerns the impact of non-bank covered interest arbitrage on *net* capital flows in the spot market. The Cambists argue that non-bank covered arbitrage involves no *net* spot transactions and the analysis appears convincing for homogeneous eurocurrency assets. Both the 'modern theory' and the Cambist approach imply that net spot transactions result from speculative activity in either the spot or the forward market. Hence changes in domestic interest rates are likely to influence spot capital flows and the spot rate. We examine 'spot speculation' and the covered interest differential further in Chapter 5. Finally as far as eurocurrency markets are concerned, the banks keep the covered differential at zero and hence the rationale for the existence of the forward market must be based upon differential transactions (brokerage) costs in using the spot and forward markets (Niehans, 1984). Banks operating in the forward market reduce the transactions costs for 'customers' in avoiding currency risk: providing an example of financial intermediation (similar to that provided by banks in channelling domestic funds from lenders to borrowers).

Summary and Conclusions

The empirical results on the size of the arbitrage and speculative responses to changes in their respective yields vary considerably both over time and for different currencies. We are inclined to discount estimates of the arbitrage and spot speculative responses obtained from the *capital flows* equations. It is our view that the (quarterly) data period used in most studies is unlikely to measure adequately what are likely to be very fast responses. We therefore err towards the view that the forward rate equation yields more plausible estimates of the response of arbitrageurs and speculators (in the forward market). It seems to be the case that the banks operate so as to keep the covered interest differential at zero as argued by the Cambist school: hence *non*-banks do not have an incentive to engage in covered interest arbitrage. This would certainly explain why the arbitrage response coefficient a in the forward rate equation is very large: banks merely quote expected forward rates *equal* to the interest parity forward rate. If it is the case that the *covered* differential is always zero then hedgers incur equal 'costs' either by obtaining foreign currency through spot purchases or by forward purchases. Only differences in transactions (brokerage) costs or a differential interest cost on borrowing and lending funds can provide an incentive to use one or other of these two markets. Thus the forward market may exist only because it provides lower 'brokerage costs' than operations via the spot market (Niehans, 1984).

When estimating the forward rate equation the multicollinearity between the interest parity rate f^* and the expected spot rate s^e_{t+1} does not allow a precise estimate of the responsiveness of speculative flows in the forward market. On the basis of the evidence discussed above, our knowledge of the strength of *speculative flows* in both the spot and forward market is very limited. We shall investigate this aspect further albeit from a slightly different standpoint, when we discuss the efficient markets hypothesis (EMH) (see Chapter 5). Results from the EMH approach suggest that the speculative response in both the spot and forward market is large and tends to keep the *uncovered* speculative return close to zero, and the expected spot rate equal to the forward rate.

Notes

1. If u_t is a white noise error term, then: (i) the expected value of u_t is zero; $\mathrm{E}u_t = 0$; (ii) u_t is not serially correlated; $\mathrm{E}(u_t u_{t-j}) = 0, j \neq 0$; (iii) u_t has a constant variance, σ^2

(homoscedastic), that is, $E(u_t^2) = \sigma^2$.

2. *Stock* equilibrium for the asset stock, A, implies $A = f(r,W)$ where W = wealth, r = net yield, $f_r, f_w > 0$. Differentiating, we have $dA = f_r(r,W)dr + f_w(r,W)dW$. The first term is the *stock* effect of a change in r on the change in A. The second term indicates that at a new higher level of r a greater fraction (f_w) of any *increase* in wealth is used to purchase additional units of A. There is a continuing flow (wealth) effect on A of a *step* change in r, as long as total wealth is increasing (i.e. $dW > 0$).

4 INTERNATIONAL MONETARY MODELS

As their title suggests, international monetary models (IMM) deal primarily with the relationship between monetary variables (such as money supply and interest rates) and the spot exchange rate. With the increasing importance of capital flows in the 1970s, stimulated in part by Organisation of Petroleum Exporting Countries (OPEC) balances after the 1973 oil crisis, the emphasis switched from viewing the exchange rate as the 'price' which equilibrated the net *flows* of currency generated by trade in goods, to an 'asset view' of exchange rate determination. The equilibrium spot rate is then viewed as that rate at which asset holders do not wish to alter their portfolio of domestic and foreign assets. 'International monetary models' simplify the complex problem of portfolio choice. In the current account monetary models (CAM) only one asset, 'money', is included in the analysis. In the capital account monetary models (KAM) it is often assumed that domestic and foreign bonds are perfect substitutes. These 'simplified models' of asset behaviour provide an introduction to the analysis pursued in Chapters 11 and 12, where agents hold diversified portfolios with many assets which also interact with expenditure decisions. However the two broad types of international monetary models presented here are of interest in their own right since they provide useful and tractable methods of analysing movements in the spot rate. Indeed the CAM and KAM models provide the basic ideas behind equations and models used in practical exchange rate forecasting which are discussed in the final section of the book.

The CAM model uses the purchasing power parity (PPP) relationship (see Chapter 2) to represent equilibrium in traded goods (i.e. exports and imports) from which the term 'current account' arises. The model also assumes a conventional demand for money function in arriving at equilibrium in the money market. In the first half of this chapter we analyse the CAM model under fixed and flexible exchange regimes and then briefly discuss some tests of the PPP relationship and the CAM model itself. KAM models generally assume perfect capital mobility and hence the spot exchange rate has to satisfy the uncovered arbitrage condition. This essentially is the origin of the term 'capital account' and the assumption of equilibrium in the money market provides the 'monetary' element. In the second half of this chapter we begin with an account of the Dornbusch (1976) 'overshooting' KAM model of the determination of the spot rate. The conditions which determine 'over-shooting' or 'undershooting' are then presented. Next we discuss Frankel's KAM model which is an elaboration on the Dornbusch approach and provides useful insights into 'overshooting' and the relationship between changes in domestic interest rate and the spot rate that are of crucial importance for policy. We end the chapter with a brief overview of empirical results in KAM models and a short summary.

Current Account Monetary Models, CAM

There is such a diversity of models of exchange rate determination, each one sometimes only marginally different from its competitors, that it is somewhat hazardous to apply all-embracing labels to the models. However, it is probably fair to say that economists at the University of Chicago (USA) were early proponents of the IMM and it is often referred to as the 'Chicago View'. It is also known as current account monetarism, CAM, since under flexible exchange rates the purchasing power parity (PPP) condition is invoked and hence the exchange rate is seen as the 'price' that clears the current account.

Under *fixed exchange rates* the IMM predicts that the overall payments position (on current and capital account) is determined by the rate of growth of the domestic component of the money supply, that is, domestic credit. The International Monetary Fund (IMF) in the late 1960s, when considering the provision of loans to countries in payments difficulties, appears to have applied the IMM as it frequently requested such governments to reduce the rate of growth of domestic credit. In the IMM the exchange rate is viewed as the *relative* price of two currencies: this is the PPP condition, $s = p - p^*$. The *absolute* level of prices is primarily determined by each country's money supply, hence the exchange rate is determined by relative money supplies in the domestic and foreign countries. Countries with relatively high (low) monetary growth are expected to have depreciating (appreciating) currencies. The IMM appeared to fit the stylised facts of exchange rate behaviour in the early 1970s. The UK and Italy with relatively rapid monetary growth experienced depreciating currencies while Germany and Switzerland had appreciating currencies and low monetary growth.

The basic elements in the IMM are the goods arbitrage view of the PPP condition (see Chapter 2), a stable demand for money function, and the assumption of equilibrium in the money market. There is no explicit model of the capital account. We consider two variants of the IMM: a 'basic' model and a hyper-inflation model. The latter was successfully applied to explain exchange rate movements in the German hyper-inflation of the 1920s and in some Latin American countries in the 1970s.

IMM under 'Fixed' Exchange Rates

Under fixed exchange rates, PPP is used to determine the domestic price level: domestic prices are arbitraged to equal exogenous 'world prices' measured in domestic currency (SP^*). A one per cent change in either P^* or S (a step devaluation or revaluation) leads to an equal change in the domestic price level. If S is fixed, domestic inflation is 'imported' being determined by world inflation and is independent of the domestic money supply.

A step devaluation, from a position of payments equilibrium, leads to an equal change in domestic prices and no change in *relative* prices $(\tau \cong P^*S/P)$. There is no expenditure switching and the net trade balance remains unchanged. In the *long-run*, devaluation is ineffective in altering the balance of trade and the level of domestic output (if we ignore any 'indirect' effects such as 'wealth effects' on domestic demand).

What role does that money supply play? The domestic component of the money supply may be altered by transactions between the authorities and the non-bank private sector (NBPS). A budget deficit or open market purchases of government bonds by the authorities from the NBPS increase the money supply. Money received by the NBPS may lead to a multiple expansion of bank deposits as the cheque drawn on the central bank provides additional 'reserves' (high powered money) for the banks. Thus, the money supply may change because of transactions within the domestic sector and we refer to this as the 'domestic credit' (DC) part of the money supply.

The money supply also changes when there are net transactions with the overseas sector. For example, a UK exporter may receive payment directly in sterling: the 'foreign' importer (say US resident) sells dollars and purchases sterling from the central bank. Alternatively, the UK exporter may receive dollars and convert them into sterling himself at the central bank. (If he held the dollars in a US bank, this would constitute a capital out-flow to match the trade in-flow: there would be no net transactions with the overseas sector and no change in the domestic (UK) money supply.) In either case, the foreign exchange reserves (dollars) of the UK central bank rise and the UK money supply increases by an equal amount. Net transactions on the balance of payments (i.e. the current and capital account combined), cause changes in the domestic money supply that may be (crudely) measured by the change in foreign exchange reserves, R, measured in domestic currency. Thus, with a conventional demand for money function the money market may be represented as

$$M^s = DC + R \qquad (4.1)$$

$$M^d = M^d(Y, P, r) \qquad (4.2)$$

$$M^s = DC + R = M^d(Y, P, r) \qquad (4.3)$$

where demand for money M^d depends upon real output, Y and the price level P, and the rate of interest on domestic bonds, r.

A rise in the domestic price level caused by devaluation increases the desired demand for money. Excess demand for money balances leads to less spending on foreign goods, and foreign assets: a *temporary* payments surplus develops and the foreign component of the money supply, R, rises. Thus after a devaluation a 'real balance' effect on foreign purchases leads to a rise in the foreign component of the domestic money supply to match the increased money demand, caused by the higher domestic price level. After the money market reaches equilibrium there are no further net purchases of foreign goods and assets and the (flow) payments position returns to equilibrium (zero).

The money supply is endogenous under fixed exchange rates. Does this mean that the authorities cannot control the total money supply, M^s? The answer is yes, under our fixed exchange rate regime. Any increase in the money supply brought about via changes in 'domestic credit', which the authorities can influence, 'spills-over' into the balance of payments and is 'exported' via changes in the 'foreign' component of the money supply, R. The money market is equilibrated, not by changes in the arguments of the demand for money function (Y, P, r) but by equal and opposite changes in DC and R. The money supply does not affect the domestic price level (which is determined solely by PPP) but determines the balance of payments surplus or deficit (ΔR).

Under fixed exchange rates, our IMM, with Y and r exogenous, predicts: (a) the domestic price level is determined solely by 'goods arbitrage' and the PPP condition: inflation is 'imported'. Devaluation is ineffective in producing expenditure switching but produces a *temporary* payments surplus due to a real balance effect on foreign purchases; (b) the *growth* in the domestic element of the money supply determines the balance of payments surplus or deficit.

In the IMM it is not the absence of expenditure switching that is crucial in nullifying the long-run effects of devaluation but equilibrium in asset (money) stocks. The balance of payments is a flow, there cannot be asset stock equilibrium until flows are zero. A temporary payments surplus after a devaluation increases the money supply (via changes in R) and this real balance effect tends to reduce the surplus. Is it not possible for the authorities to offset the increase in the foreign component of the money supply and hence ensure a permanent surplus? Sales of government debt to the domestic NPBS, equal to the change in R (i.e. $\Delta DC = -\Delta R$) would prevent the total money supply increasing: this is a policy of *sterilisation*. Sterilisation of a payments surplus requires a *continuous* rise in the ratio of bonds to money (or to income) held by domestic residents which may only be sustainable if the interest rate on bonds *continuously* rises. (Here we ignore the wealth effect of the payments surplus on the demand for bonds.) Higher domestic interest rates may induce a further capital in-flow which requires more sterilisation. The time scale over which sterilisation is feasible depends in part on the size of any induced rise in domestic interest rates (i.e. interest elasticity of the demand for money) and the interest elasticity of capital flows. If there is perfect capital mobility, sterilisation is impossible since all sales of domestic assets by the authorities are purchased by overseas residents and the money supply held by domestic residents remains unchanged. As usually presented, the IMM assumes sterilisation is not feasible because of perfect capital mobility.

Domestic output is exogenous in the basic IMM, an assumption that is consistent with either the neoclassical view of the labour market and the supply of output, or, a 'Keynesian' model at full employment. Exogeneity of the interest rate is clearly a rather extreme assumption and we comment on this below.

IMM (or CAM) under Flexible Exchange Rates

Prices are determined by goods arbitrage and we are dealing with a flex-price model. Equilibrium occurs in the traded goods 'market' when there are no further profitable incentives for trade flows on the current account, that is, when PPP holds. Foreign prices are exogenous to the domestic economy (our small country assumption) leaving two endogenous variables P and S to be explained and these move proportionately to preserve PPP.

A freely floating exchange rate ensures that the change in foreign exchange reserves is zero ($\Delta R = 0$) and the money supply is under the control of the authorities ($M^s = DC$, Equation 4.1). With the 'usual' stable demand for money function given by Equation (4.5) below and the additional assumption that r and Y are fixed (Y, at the full employment level, perhaps), changes in the money supply lead to proportionate changes in the domestic price level. PPP ensures that the exchange rate moves in proportion to P and therefore to M. If foreign prices are determined by the exogenous foreign money supply, changes in the exchange rate reflect the *relative* growth in the domestic and foreign money supplies.

Using a log-linear demand for money function (with $m = \ln M$, etc.) the IMM (CAM) may be expressed:

$$s = k + p - p^* \qquad \text{weak PPP condition} \qquad (4.4)$$

$$m = p + \phi y - \lambda r \qquad \text{domestic monetary equilibrium} \qquad (4.5)$$

$$m^* = p^* + \phi^* y^* - \lambda^* r^* \quad \text{foreign monetary equilibrium.} \qquad (4.6)$$

Substituting for p and p^* from (4.5) and (4.6) in (4.4) we obtain:

$$s = k + (m - m^*) - \phi y + \phi^* y^* + \lambda r - \lambda r^* \qquad (4.7)$$

which for $\phi = \phi^*$ and $\lambda = \lambda^*$ reduces to:

$$s = k + (m - m^*) - \phi(y - y^*) + \lambda(r - r^*) \qquad (4.8)$$

and we also have

$$p = m - \phi y + \lambda r. \qquad (4.9)$$

In this model, the (domestic) price level and the exchange rate are determined simultaneously. An increase in the money supply creates an excess supply of money balances. Domestic prices rise if the excess supply of money spills over into an excess demand for domestic goods. This is the usual closed economy transmission mechanism for the money supply. Higher domestic prices then lead to purchases of foreign goods and the exchange rate falls to equilibrate the current account. This conventional transmission mechanism is consistent with the mathematical results but rather violates our interpretation of PPP as due to arbitrage with respect to 'goods' prices. An alternative transmission mechanism that preserves the arbitrage interpretation of PPP is possible. The excess supply of money cannot be relieved by changes in real income and domestic interest rates, which are exogenous. Excess money spills over into purchases of foreign goods and (non-money) assets, particularly the latter. Excess demand for foreign currency causes a fall in the domestic exchange rate, foreign prices in domestic currency (SP^*) rise and domestic prices are arbitraged upwards to yield equality of prices, in a common currency.

The response of the exchange rate to changes in output and the interest rate in the IMM (CAM) are of some interest and are in contrast to what might very loosely be called the orthodox view. In the IMM, any variable that leads to a decrease in the demand for money, allows the price level which clears the money market to be higher and hence (via PPP) the exchange rate to depreciate. Thus lower domestic output and a *higher* domestic interest rate lead to depreciation in the exchange rate.

A rise in the domestic interest rate in the IMM leads to a fall in the demand for money, and with the money supply unchanged, the excess supply of money causes a capital out-flow (or higher imports) and a depreciation in the exchange rate. However causal empiricism suggests that a rise in the domestic interest rate is quickly followed by an appreciation of the exchange rate. This is frequently the basis of government policies to 'support' the exchange rate. Armchair theorising suggests that a rise in domestic interest rates should lead to a substitution away from foreign assets into domestic assets, a capital in-flow and an appreciation in the exchange rate. Clearly, the current account monetary model must involve some rather restrictive implicit assumptions about the behaviour of the capital account.

Haache and Townend (1981) assert that in the IMM, r can increase (for a given r^*) if and only if the expected rate of depreciation of the domestic currency ($s^e - s$) increases so as to prevent a positive uncovered return ($r^* - r + s^e - s$), in favour of the domestic currency. The IMM therefore implicitly incorporates the open arbitrage condition for capital flows. A change in r is therefore not an exogenous event in this model as r responds only to changes in expectations about the exchange rate. There is, therefore, no incentive to switch into domestic bonds when the domestic interest rate rises. The IMM implicitly treats expectations about the exchange rate as exogenous to the model; a rather unattractive feature.

The testable predictions of the basic IMM are that the exchange rate responds proportionately to changes in relative money supplies, and that $\partial s/\partial y$, $\partial s/\partial r^* < 0$ and $\partial s/\partial y^*$, $\partial s/\partial r > 0$. Even though the RHS variables r, y and m are endogenous in the real world we can still test the pseudo reduced form equation (Equation 4.8) and the signs of the partial derivatives (as long as we use an appropriate instrumental variable (IV) estimating technique).

Overshooting

The above IMM model is static, overshooting does not occur and equilibrium is reached immediately. Almost all dynamic models are capable, in principle, of producing overshooting. Adjustment lags provide a rationale for dynamic responses to be appended to our static equilibrium model.

Suppose, for example, that the demand for money responds only slowly to changes in prices. Neglecting other factors, in equilibrium, $m = m^d = \gamma_0 p + \gamma_1 p_{t-1}$ with $\gamma_0, \gamma_1 > 0$ and $\gamma_0 + \gamma_1 = 1$ to preserve homogeneity. Suppose there are no lags in the arbitrage equation, so that $\Delta s = \Delta p$. In the *long run*, $\Delta m = \Delta p = \Delta s$. However, in the short run, a one per cent increase in the money supply leads to a $1/\gamma_0 > 1$ percentage change in the current price level to equilibrate the money market and a $1/\gamma_0$ percentage change in the current exchange rate ($\Delta s = \Delta p > 1$): hence, the *current* exchange rate overshoots its long run equilibrium value. Lags in the PPP relationship can also produce 'overshooting' of the exchange rate. Whether or not overshooting occurs in practice will depend upon the size of the lag responses (coefficients) in the whole model. For example if $\gamma_0 > 1$, overshooting will not occur in our simple example.

IMM–CAM in Hyper-inflations

During hyper-inflations, the demand for real money balances is thought to depend primarily on the expected rate of inflation. Changes in real incomes are small relative to movements in inflation. Higher rates of expected inflation encourage substitution out of money into goods. In the German hyper-inflation of 1920–3, workers bought goods as soon as wages were paid, for fear that goods would be too expensive in the near future. The demand for money function is:

$$m^d = p - \beta \pi^e + \phi y \qquad (4.10)$$

where π^e is the expected rate of inflation. With a similar equation for the foreign country, assuming $\beta = \beta^*$, $\phi = \phi^*$ and using the PPP condition we obtain:

$$s = k + (m - m^*) + \beta(\pi^e - \pi^{*e}) - \phi(y - y^*). \qquad (4.11)$$

This equation is equivalent to Equation (4.8) derived in our basic IMM, provided we accept the Fisher hypothesis that real rates of interest are constant: $r - \pi^e = \gamma$ and $r^* - \pi^{*e} = \gamma^*$ (where γ, γ^* are constants). r and r^* can then be replaced in Equation (4.8) by π^e and π^{*e} (and the γ's are absorbed into the constant term). Equation (4.11) is the hyper-inflation version of the IMM–CAM. Countries with high (increasing) expected rates of inflation have 'low' (depreciating) exchange rates. Again, we have the unit elasticity of S with respect to relative money supplies.

Policy Implications of IMM–CAM

Under fixed exchange rates domestic inflation in the small open economy is largely determined by world inflation. If sterilisation is not possible because of a high degree of capital mobility then devaluation only has a temporary effect on the balance of payments working via a real balance effect on overseas purchases (rather than via expenditure switching). Under fixed exchange rates the authorities cannot control the *total* money supply: excessive growth in domestic credit is the cause of a payments deficit.

There is a straightforward message for policy that arises from the CAM model with floating exchange rates: high domestic monetary growth leads to a depreciating exchange rate and high domestic inflation. Control of the money supply is the required policy instrument to reduce inflation and stabilise the currency.

Empirical Evidence on PPP and Current Account Monetarism

Direct tests of the PPP relationship for different frequency of data (monthly, quarterly, annual) and for different countries and time periods (particularly the 1920s and 1970s) are voluminous. The 1920s provide a period of very large nominal shocks; for example Germany experienced hyper-inflation, while in the UK prices fell. If PPP is valid, data with such high variability should provide precise estimates of the PPP relationship.

The PPP hypothesis is usually tested in an equation of the form

$$s = \alpha_0 + \alpha_1(p - p^*) + u_t \tag{4.12}$$

where there may also be lagged values of the relative price level included in the equation to pick up any adjustment lags. The 'strong version' of PPP implies $\alpha_0 = 0$ and $\alpha_1 = 1$ and the weak version imposes only $\alpha_1 = 1$. In both versions we expect the error u_t which picks up all other influences on s_t to be independent of any other economic variables and to be serially uncorrelated with zero mean. The PPP equation is an equilibrium condition and causation may therefore be in both directions, that is, from p to s or vice versa. Hence, 'simultaneous estimators' such as instrumental variables rather than OLS should be used. The price indexes used should be for homogeneous goods, traded freely between the two countries. There should be no changes in quotas or tariffs on the goods in the price indexes. (A constant level of tariff would be reflected in the constant α_0.)

Krugman (1978) provides a most comprehensive survey of tests of the PPP hypothesis. As expected, the hypothesis fits the 1920s best, when, by and large, $\alpha_0 = 0$ and $\alpha_1 = 1$. However, for the 1970s, particularly for rates against the dollar, the hypothesis tends to break down.

Frequently, $\alpha_0 \neq 0$ and $\alpha_1 \neq 1$ and the errors u_t are subject to high positive autocorrelation, that is, any deviation from PPP (as measured by u_t) tends to persist in the future. Deviations from PPP are therefore substantial in the short run. Indeed, in the 1970s the monthly deviations from PPP, that is $u_t = s - p - p^*$ nearly follow a random walk (i.e. $u_t = \varrho u_{t-1} + \varepsilon_t$, with $\varrho \approx 1$). The deterioration in the results for the 1970s as compared with the 1920s is hardly surprising, given the probable increase in capital mobility and the importance of capital account flows in determining the exchange rate.

Results consistent with the success of PPP in the 1920s and its breakdown in the 1970s are obtained when current account monetarist equations (like 4.8) are estimated. These equations test the joint hypotheses of PPP, money market clearing and correct demand for money function.

For the 1920s for Germany, Frenkel (1976), Frankel (1980) demonstrates that the hyper-inflation CAM performs well.

Bilson (1978) and Haache and Townend (1981) provide tests for the basic IMM–CAM. For the 1960s and 1970s Bilson (1979) cites a number of studies of various bilateral rates which support the general tenets of the monetary approach, namely a unit response of the exchange rate to relative money supplies and high domestic interest rates leading to a lower exchange rate. Haache and Townend (1981) on monthly data for the sterling-dollar rate obtain:

$$s = -10.2 + 0.57m + 0.34m^* - 0.24y + 0.63y^* + 0.19r - 0.007r^* + u_t$$
$$\quad\ (12.7)\quad (6.5)\quad\ (1.5)\quad\ \ (1.6)\quad\ (5.0)\quad\ (8.0)\quad\ \ (1.4)$$

$$u_t = 0.62u_{t-1} = e_t$$
$$\quad (5.0)$$

February 1972 – October 1977; $\bar{R}^2 = 0.98$; $SEE = 1.7$ per cent; $dw = 1.8$.

Although the domestic money supply and interest rate terms are of the 'right' sign and statistically significant, the former is not unity. The coefficient on m^* (the US money supply) has the 'wrong' sign and the equation exhibits first-order correlation in the residuals. The equation, cannot therefore, be said to support the IMM–CAM of exchange rate determination. Overall the voluminous evidence on the basic IMM–CAM tends to reject the model for the 1970s for countries with moderate inflation although the hyper-inflation version works well for Germany in the 1920s and for some high inflation (e.g. Latin American countries) in the 1970s.

Capital Account Monetarist Models, KAM

In most of the industrialised nations there was a large build-up of domestic assets held by foreigners and foreign assets held by domestic residents throughout the 1970s (e.g. OPEC balances). Lower transactions costs of switching between assets as a result of improved technology (e.g. computers), and the gradual removal of exchange controls, led to increased capital mobility. Gradually it became increasingly accepted that capital account flows, potential and actual, were far more important than current account flows in determining movements in the exchange rate especially in the short run. The exchange rate was considered to be a 'jump' variable that could move instantaneously to 'clear' (i.e. bring about equilibrium in) the capital account. The inability of the international monetary current account model, CAM, to explain volatile short-term exchange rate movements acted as a catalyst to the development and widespread acceptance of capital account monetarist models, KAM.

Large movements in the *real* exchange rate (or 'competitiveness') were not expected to occur under floating exchange rates. Proponents of floating rates had argued that the nominal exchange rate would move to preserve purchasing power parity, PPP, and hence the real exchange rate would remain broadly constant. However with the advent of floating rates in the 1970s a number of countries, most notably the UK, experienced wide movements in the real exchange rate. In the UK, for example, price competitiveness deteriorated by over 40 per cent between 1979 and 1981 while over the succeeding three years the real exchange rate fell by roughly the same amount. Such 'overshooting' in the real exchange rate causes volatile movements in real net trade and hence in domestic output and employment. Indeed the UK experienced a very severe recession over the 1979–82 period. The real output and employment consequences of changes in the real exchange rate are an important policy issue for which the KAM models provide some useful insights.

Another important policy issue on which the KAM models throw some light concerns the response of the spot rate to changes in the domestic interest rate. When discussing the determinants of capital flows we noted that a higher domestic interest rate leads to a speculative capital in-flow and hence under a floating exchange rate regime one would expect an *appreciation* in the spot rate. However, in the current account monetary model a higher domestic interest rate leads to a *depreciation* in the spot rate. For policy purposes it is important to know the response of the spot exchange rate to changes in interest rates brought about by domestic monetary policy actions (such as open market operations). A particular

KAM model due to Frankel (1979) suggests that this conundrum may be resolved by distinguishing between those changes in the interest rate that compensate for inflation and those that are due to 'tight' monetary policy. Tight monetary policy in the Frankel model occurs when the interest rate rises relative to the rate of inflation, that is when there is a rise in the *real* interest rate. The Frankel model is sometimes referred to as the 'real interest rate' model of the exchange rate.

KAM models also provide a framework for analysing the impact of a resource discovery in a small open economy. The obvious example here being the consequences for the UK of the discovery and extraction of oil in the North Sea. Under certain plausible conditions, models of the KAM variety can be used to analyse why an oil (or natural gas) discovery might lead to an appreciation in the real exchange rate and a domestic recession as occurred in the Netherlands and in the UK in the late 1970s and early 1980s, respectively.

One of the main distinguishing features shared by a number of KAM models is the assumption that well informed speculators in the spot market do not allow the uncovered (speculative) return, $r^* - r + s^e - s$, to be non-zero. A non-zero uncovered return implies that speculators *expect* to make a profit by switching between domestic and foreign assets. In a number of KAM models it is assumed that potential or actual speculative capital flows are so large that the uncovered differential immediately returns to zero. The latter condition is referred to as *uncovered* interest parity.

Perfect capital mobility (and risk neutral[1] speculators) ensure that uncovered interest parity is maintained. (Somewhat confusingly this condition is also sometimes referred to as the uncovered interest arbitrage condition. Clearly the use of the word 'arbitrage' here does not signify that the transaction is devoid of risk.) Another general assumption of this type of model is that goods prices (and real output) are 'sticky': prices are not perfectly flexible in the short run and PPP holds only in the long run. Although the goods market does not 'clear' in the short run it is usual to assume in KAM models that the foreign exchange and the money market 'clear' in every period. Rational expectations by foreign exchange dealers are usually a feature of KAM models although we shall not deal with this aspect formally.

Dornbusch Overshooting Model

The Dornbusch (1976) model has the general characteristics of KAM models referred to above. The model exhibits exchange rate overshooting and a tight monetary policy may lead to a recession in the short run.

In response to changes in the domestic interest rate, the spot exchange rate acts as a 'jump' variable and instantaneously adjusts to keep the uncovered (speculative) return at zero. However, because prices are sticky this leads to a short-run change in the *real* exchange rate and hence in the net real trade balance and domestic output. In the long run there are no effects on real variables, output returns to its 'natural' (initial equilibrium) rate and PPP is restored. (Note that the reason real output is unchanged is because the Phillips curve is vertical in the long run.)

Possible causes of an initial 'jump' (and overshoot) in the exchange rate might be a change in the money supply, government expenditure, foreign interest rates, a resource discovery or a change in world interest rates. Thus in the Dornbusch model domestic output is not insulated in the short run either from domestic policy or from changes in 'world' variables. In contrast early proponents of floating exchange rates had stressed the 'insulating' properties of floating rates and had argued that such a policy would provide considerable independence of the domestic economy from 'world shocks'.

Assumptions behind the Dornbusch Model

The capital account is modelled by assuming that uncovered interest parity holds:

$$\mu = r - r^* \tag{4.13}$$

where $\mu = s^e - s$, the expected rate of depreciation of the domestic currency. Exchange rate expectations are assumed to be regressive.

$$\mu = \theta(\bar{s} - s) \qquad 0 < \theta < 1 \tag{4.14}$$

where $\bar{s}$ is the long-run equilibrium exchange rate. If the actual exchange rate s is below $\bar{s}$, then speculators expect s to rise towards $\bar{s}$ (at the rate θ per period); that is, they expect a depreciation in the exchange rate. The model incorporates a conventional demand for money function, and equilibrium in the money market is given by

$$m = -\lambda r + \phi y + p. \tag{4.15}$$

At this stage let us merely note that the Phillips curve in the goods market does not allow a *long-run* effect of money on real output or on the domestic interest rate. Also PPP holds in the long run. In the long run, a one per cent increase in the money supply leads to a one per cent increase in the price level (i.e. homogeneity) and because PPP holds there is also a one per cent depreciation in the nominal exchange rate. These are precisely the implications of the CAM model but in the Dornbusch model they hold only in the long run.

In the Dornbusch model, unlike the CAM model, the domestic interest rate is allowed to adjust in the short run to clear the money market. For convenience assume for the moment that y and p are 'sticky' in the short run. An increase in the money supply then requires a fall in the bond rate r to 'clear' the money market $(dr = -(1/\lambda)dm)$. The fall in r causes a potential capital out-flow which is arrested as the spot exchange rate *immediately depreciates* below its long-run equilibrium, to induce an *expectation* of a *future* appreciation. The capital account is then in equilibrium: the lower domestic interest rate is matched by an expected appreciation $(d\mu = dr)$ and an actual depreciation. Hence uncovered interest parity holds continuously.

In the Dornbusch model changes in the interest rate reflect changing monetary tightness and a fall (rise) in the interest rate is accompanied by a depreciation (appreciation) in the exchange rate in the short run, $\partial s/\partial r < 0$. This is the converse of the CAM result.

To preserve the uncovered arbitrage condition after a fall in the domestic interest rate, the actual spot rate must instantaneously depreciate *below its long-run equilibrium* value; hence the exchange rate *overshoots* its long-run value. Overshooting in the Dornbusch model is due to the restrictive channels through which monetary policy is forced to operate. If output and prices are 'sticky' in the short run, the interest rate must accommodate all the disequilibrium in the money market after a change in the money supply. In the longer run, output and prices equilibrate the money market, the interest rate returns to its initial value and expected exchange rate changes are zero.

Mathematically the overshooting result after an increase in the money supply is easily derived (in our simplified account). In the *long run*, y and r are unchanged and money market equilibrium implies homogeneity, $dp = dm$, while long run PPP gives, $d\bar{s} = dp = dm$. The change in the actual exchange rate in the short run is given from Equation (4.14):

$$ds = d\bar{s} - d\mu/\theta = dm - d\mu/\theta. \tag{4.16}$$

But to preserve uncovered interest parity $d\mu = dr$ and in the *short run* with y and p fixed, money market equilibrium gives $dr = -dm/\lambda$. Thus substituting $d\mu = -dm/\lambda$ in Equation (4.16) yields

$$ds = dm + dm/\theta\lambda = [1 + (1/\theta\lambda)]dm. \tag{4.17}$$

Since $1/\theta\lambda > 0$ the initial change in the spot rate $(1 + 1/\theta\lambda)dm$ is greater than the long-run effect $(d\bar{s} = dm)$.

Although we have not made explicit reference to the rational expectations hypothesis it turns out that if agents form expectations according to Equation (4.14), this is consistent with (Muth) RE. In the above exposition of the Dornbusch model there are no random error terms and therefore the assumption of RE is equivalent to assuming perfect foresight on the part of spot speculators. We do not formally present the full RE account of the Dornbusch model.

Undershooting?

The assumptions of the Dornbusch model do not appear unreasonable for a small open economy with a high degree of capital mobility. Although the model explains the qualitative movements in the real exchange rate (and output) for a number of industrialised open economies in the late 1970s period nevertheless it is worth investigating the sensitivity of the overshooting result to changes in the basic assumptions of the model.

In the UK in the period 1979–82 the broad money supply (£M3) was growing well in excess of the target range set by the authorities and it could be argued that monetary policy was lax. Nevertheless the real exchange rate appreciated over this period. This would appear to contradict the prediction of the Dornbusch model that a real appreciation is associated with a tight monetary policy. There are two ways we might interpret these facts within the framework of the Dornbusch model. First, some would argue that £M3 was a misleading indicator of the tightness of monetary policy over this period. The authorities removed the constraints it had imposed on the banks' ability to expand deposits (i.e. Supplementary Special Deposits Scheme or 'the corset'; see Bank of England, 1982) which artificially boosted bank lending and the money supply. If in fact monetary policy was tight over this period then movements in the exchange rate are consistent with the Dornbusch model. The level of interest rates might be a better indicator of the tightness of monetary policy under these abnormal conditions and since over this period UK interest rates were high, this could have triggered 'overshooting'.

The second explanation of these events could be termed the 'credibility hypothesis' (Currie, 1984). If the private sector thought that the government's commitment to its stated monetary targets was strong then it would expect that any current overshoot would be met by a tightening in the future. The latter would imply higher interest rates *in the future* and via the uncovered interest parity condition an actual appreciation of the domestic currency. (The latter pushes the actual spot rate above its long-run equilibrium rate so that a depreciation is *expected* and uncovered interest parity is maintained.) However if speculators in the spot market are 'rational' and obey the postulates of the REH they will foresee this future appreciation and consequent capital gain from holding the domestic currency. Knowing that all other RE speculators will not wait until the day before the appreciation to purchase the domestic currency, all speculators purchase the domestic currency *today*, in order to reap the benefit of the future expected capital gain. However this causes the exchange rate to appreciate at the time the overshoot in the money supply is noted. Hence a lax monetary policy will be accompanied by an appreciation in the current spot rate if it is thought that the authorities will stick to their medium-term monetary targets. The above account provides a useful example of how the assumption of RE brings forward in time events that are anticipated to take place in the future. The distinction between anticipated (or announced) policy changes and unanticipated changes is crucial in RE models and the path of the economy will be different under the two types of policy (or under other 'shocks' to the economy depending on whether they are anticipated or unanticipated). Unanticipated events are often referred to as 'news' and we discuss this source of exchange rate volatility in Chapter 5.

Let us continue with this anticipated/unanticipated distinction in the Dornbusch model by considering an *anticipated* reduction in the money supply. RE agents would be aware that a reduction in the money supply leads to an equiproportionate fall in the price level. If prices are perfectly flexible then a fall in the price level reduces the demand for money in proportion to the fall in supply and the money market remains in equilibrium *without any change in the interest rate*. The latter implies that there will be no change in the real exchange rate even in the short run. The nominal exchange rate immediately adjusts to preserve PPP and there is no overshooting. It is sometimes argued by New Classical economists, who believe in continuous market clearing in *all* markets and that expectations are 'rational', that only unanticipated changes in the money supply produce overshooting in the Dornbusch model. However it is clear that the assumption of sticky goods prices is crucial in producing the overshooting result.

Let us now assume less than perfect capital mobility. If speculators are risk averse we noted in Chapter 2 that speculative activity will not push the uncovered speculative return to zero. Under these conditions the exchange rate will move to clear the current and capital account combined, that is:

$$B = a(p^* + s - p) + b(r - r^* + s - s^e) = 0. \qquad (4.18)$$

The current account is influenced by competitiveness and speculative capital flows by the uncovered arbitrage condition (but b is not infinite since we do not have perfect capital mobility).

Perhaps the simplest way to illustrate how the overshooting result is crucially dependent on the assumption of a high degree of capital mobility is to investigate the polar case, namely zero capital mobility (i.e. $b = 0$). With zero capital mobility the change in the interest rate consequent on a change in the money supply will have no effect on capital flows and hence no effect on the current spot rate. From Equation (4.18) we see that, in order for the balance of payments to remain in equilibrium, any change in the price level must be accompanied by an equal change in the spot rate: hence PPP must be maintained even in the short run and therefore there is no overshooting of the real exchange rate.

We can make the analysis more realistic by allowing a non-zero but low degree of capital mobility. To clear the capital account after a monetary contraction and rise in interest rates requires an *expected* depreciation and hence an *actual* appreciation as in the 'original' Dornbusch model. However the appreciation tends to lead to a current account deficit. The exchange rate must therefore appreciate by less than in the perfect capital mobility case in order to maintain overall payments equilibrium. It can be demonstrated (Frenkel and Rodriguez, 1982) that undershooting is more likely the lower the degree of capital mobility and the larger is the elasticity of net trade with respect to competitiveness (i.e. the larger is a in Equation 4.18).

Both undershooting and overshooting in the exchange rate are possible in a Dornbusch type model depending on the degree of price flexibility and capital mobility. However we now return to the basic Dornbusch model to investigate the implications of alternative 'shocks' impinging on the economy.

Other Shocks in the Dornbusch Model

In the Dornbusch model the domestic interest rate in the uncovered interest parity condition provides the link between other domestic variables and the foreign exchange market. For example an increase in government expenditure will raise the demand for transactions balances and hence the interest rate (for a given money supply). This is the familiar IS-LM result. The rise in domestic interest rates may then lead to exchange rate overshooting.

A resource discovery such as North Sea Oil *may* produce a recession in a Dornbusch type model. The analysis pursued here is different to that in Chapter 12. In the latter the real resource and relative price implications of North Sea Oil are examined. Here we concentrate on demand factors in a RE model.

North Sea Oil provides income (an annuity) for UK residents which tends to increase the transactions demand for money (i.e. LM curve moves to the left) and has a direct impact on expenditure (i.e. IS curve shifts to the right). Both of these effects tend to push up interest rates and hence lead to a sharp appreciation in the exchange rate to maintain uncovered interest parity. It may be shown (Eastwood and Venables, 1980; Neary and Wijnbergen, 1984) that if the income from North Sea Oil is immediately paid out then the direct expenditure effects outweigh any reduction in output caused by a short-run loss of competitiveness and a recession is avoided. The authorities, who receive the major proportion of North Sea Oil wealth in the form of tax receipts, may either spend it or redistribute it in the form of tax cuts to the private sector or retire outstanding government debt. In the first two cases there is a direct demand effect but in the latter case, which appears to be that taken by the UK government, there is not. Under such circumstances the fall in net trade caused by the appreciation in the exchange rate will lead to a recession in the short run. How long the recession lasts depends of course on the parameters of the model and the lag between the receipt of North Sea Oil taxes by the government and any disbursement in the form of tax cuts or increased expenditure.

Summary of the Dornbusch Model

The Dornbusch model is able to account for the short-run volatility in the nominal exchange rate and for large swings in the real exchange rate. The latter may lead to large swings in real net trade and output and highlights the possible repercussions of a tight monetary policy in a small open economy. The demand effects of a resource discovery such as North Sea Oil in the UK can also be analysed in the Dornbusch model. The exchange rate does not overshoot when we relax some of the assumptions of the Dornbusch approach. In particular the assumption of sticky goods prices and a high degree of capital mobility is required to produce overshooting.

Frankel Real Interest Differential Model

Our reasons for examining the KAM model of Frankel (1979b) are: (i) it allows us to derive a single equation to explain movements in the spot rate which can be tested and used for forecasting (we take up the latter issue in Chapter 13); (ii) the model is more general than the Dornbusch and CAM models and we are able to undertake a simple test to discriminate between these rival models; (iii) the Frankel model provides an explanation of the different response of the spot rate to changes in the domestic interest rate in the Dornbusch and CAM models.

Taking up the last point we noted that in the CAM model an increase in the domestic interest rate leads to a depreciation in the exchange rate ($\partial s/\partial r$ is *positive*). In the hyper-inflation version of the CAM model changes in the nominal interest rate depend upon changes in the expected rate of inflation $r = \gamma + \pi^e$ (where π^e is the expected rate of inflation and γ is the constant real interest rate). This is the Fisher relationship: nominal interest rates are 'arbitraged' upwards to maintain a constant real return in the face of higher expected inflation. In the hyper-inflation CAM model a higher nominal interest rate does *not* reflect a tight monetary policy but a higher expected rate of inflation. A higher expected rate of inflation leads to a higher nominal interest rate and a fall in the demand for money (at any given price level) and a depreciation in the exchange rate as excess money 'spills over' into purchases of foreign goods and bonds. The expected inflation rate and the level of the exchange rate are *positively* related ($\partial s/\partial \pi^e > 0$).

In the Dornbusch model prices are 'sticky' and there is no hyper-inflation effect on interest rates and the demand for money. (Because of the sticky price assumption this model is sometimes loosely referred to as 'Keynesian'.) Here a rise in interest rates signals a tight monetary policy. A capital in-flow ensues, the spot exchange rate instantly appreciates (relative to its long-run equilibrium rate) in order to induce an expectation of a depreciation in the future and thus stem the capital in-flow. The nominal interest rate and exchange rate are negatively related. We have broad competing theories which give a different relationship between r and s on the one hand and π^e and s on the other.

Frankel (1979) provides a general model for which the above two approaches are special cases; he refers to this as the 'real interest differential model'. It provides a Dornbusch relationship with respect to the nominal interest rate ($\partial s/\partial r < 0$) and a hyper-inflation-CAM solution with respect to the expected rate of inflation ($\partial s/\partial \pi^e > 0$). Also, the exchange rate may overshoot its equilibrium value.

The Frankel Model in Detail

Frankel's model assumes uncovered arbitrage but modifies the Dornbusch expectations equation for the exchange rate by adding a term reflecting relative expected secular inflation: $\pi^e - \pi^{*e}$. The expectations equation is:

$$s^e - s = \theta(\bar{s} - s) + (\pi^e - \pi^{*e}) \qquad (4.19)$$

and uncovered interest parity yields

$$s^e - s = r - r^* \qquad (4.20)$$

The expected rate of depreciation depends in part on the deviation of the exchange rate from its equilibrium value, which as we know gives Dornbusch type results. In addition if $s = \bar{s}$, the expected rate of depreciation is given by the expected inflation differential between the domestic and foreign currency: as we shall see this term generates hyper-inflation-CAM results. In order that expectations are not systematically in error we require the actual change in the exchange rate to equal its expected change and hence equal the expected inflation differential. In long run equilibrium $\Delta \bar{s} = \pi^e - \pi^{*e}$ and the weak form of PPP holds. In the short run the actual exchange rate can deviate from PPP because of the Dornbusch term, $\theta(\bar{s} - s)$, and sticky prices.

Frankel asserts that the expectations equation is a plausible expectations generating mechanism *per se* but it may also be shown to be consistent with *rational* expectations. We do not deal with the latter aspect here.

Combining Equations (4.19) and (4.20) and re-arranging we have:

$$\bar{s} - s = (1/\theta) \left[(r - \pi^e) - (r^* - \pi^{*e}) \right] \tag{4.21}$$

The movement in the spot rate around its equilibrium value is determined by the relative *real* interest differential. Further, when $s = \bar{s}$, then $\bar{r} - \bar{r}^* = \pi^e - \pi^{*e}$, hence the term in square brackets may be re-written $[(r - r^*) - (\bar{r} - \bar{r}^*)]$. It is only when a tight monetary policy raises the nominal interest differential above its long-run level, given by relative expected inflation, that the 'current' exchange rate appreciates above its long-run equilibrium level ($\bar{s} - s > 0$).

We now assume that PPP holds in the long-run and with the usual demand for money function we obtain an expression for the long-run exchange rate (as in the CAM).

$$\bar{s} = \bar{p} - \bar{p}^*$$
$$= \bar{m} - \bar{m}^* - \theta(\bar{y} - \bar{y}^*) + \lambda(\bar{r} - \bar{r}^*)$$
$$= (m - m^*) - \theta(y - y^*) + \lambda(\pi^e - \pi^{*e}) \tag{4.22}$$

where we have used $\bar{r} - \bar{r}^* = \pi^e - \pi^{*e}$ (an international Fisher effect), which is the hyper-inflation-CAM.

The crucial elements in the Frankel model are the expectations equation (Equation 4.19) and the distinction between the short-run and long-run determinants of the exchange rate. The long run is pure CAM with PPP (Equation 4.22). In the short run, s can differ from $\bar{s}$ because of the expectations formation equation embedded in Equation (4.15).

Substituting for $\bar{s}$ from Equation (4.22) in Equation (4.21) we obtain

Frankel's ('reduced form') exchange rate regression equation:

$$s = \bar{m} - \bar{m}^* - \theta(\bar{y} - \bar{y}^*) - (1/\theta)(r - r^*) + [(1/\theta) + \lambda](\pi^e - \pi^{*e}) \tag{4.23}$$

$$s = \bar{m} - \bar{m}^* - \theta(\bar{y} - \bar{y}^*) + \alpha(r - r^*) + \beta(\pi^e - \pi^{*e}) \tag{4.24}$$

where $\alpha = -1/\theta$ and $\beta = (1/\theta) + \lambda$.

Table 4.1 characterises our three competing models in terms of the parameters α and β. In addition we expect $\theta > 0$ and to have a value close to the income elasticity of the demand for money estimated in other studies. From our estimate of α we can obtain an estimate of θ, the speed of adjustment of expectations, and from β we can then obtain an estimate of λ, the interest elasticity of the demand for money. Finally in all the models we expect the coefficient on long-run relative money supplies to be unity.

Table 4.1

Model		Parameters
Frankel		$\alpha < 0 \quad \beta > 0 \quad |\beta| > |\alpha|$
'Chicago'	CAM	$\alpha > 0 \quad \beta = 0$
	CAM-hyper-inflation	$\alpha = 0 \quad \beta > 0$
'Keynesian'	Dornbusch	$\alpha < 0 \quad \beta = 0$

Testing the Frankel Model

Frankel assumes that the long-run values of m and y equal their current actual values. The relative expected inflation rate is proxied by long-term bond interest differentials under the assumption that long-term *real* interest differentials are constant. (A proxy using past rates of inflation was not successful.) The equation estimated on the DM/\$ rate using monthly data between July 1974 and February 1978 (using an auto-regressive instrumental variable, package AIV) is

$$s = 1.4 + 0.97(m - m^*) - 0.52(y - y^*) - 5.4(r - r^*) +$$
$$\quad (0.12) \quad (0.21) \quad\quad\quad (0.22) \quad\quad\quad (2.1)$$

$$29.3(\pi - \pi^*) + 0.64\, u_{-1} \tag{4.25}$$
$$(3.3)$$

AIV; data period July 1974–February 1978, monthly; standard errors in parentheses.

All the coefficients of the Frankel real interest rate model are of the correct sign and statistically significant, thus rejecting the 'Chicago' and

'Keynesian–Dornbusch' type models. The implied estimate for θ is 0.2, so that 80 per cent of the deviation in $(\bar{s} - s)$ persists after one quarter, and 44 per cent after one year. The implied income elasticity of the demand for money of 0.5 and the semi-elasticity with respect to the interest rate of 6.0 are reasonably plausible.

The estimated equation is 'corrected for' autocorrelation, whereas the theory suggests random errors. More importantly however the 'corrected' equation may itself contain autocorrelated errors (the plot of actual and fitted values shows significant systematic positive and negative errors) but no test statistics are given. If the 'corrected equation' has auto-correlated errors the test-statistics (standard errors) will be incorrect. Further, there are no formal tests of *outside sample* predictions. Frankel's assumption that the actual monthly money supply may be equated with the long-run money supply, given that the latter is probably highly volatile, seems rather cavalier. Nevertheless, the 'theory' and empirical results appear to be superior to those of the two competitors cited.

Haache and Townend (1981) test the Frankel synthesis for the sterl-ing effective rate and obtain very poor results. After correcting for substantial autocorrelation, the inflation expectations variable is barely significant, the nominal interest differential has the 'wrong' sign and the relative money term is statistically insignificant. However by using the effective rate they have to use 'proxy' world variables and it is pro-bably better to test the theory on bilateral rates.

Hooper and Morton (1980) argue that the serial correlation in the Frankel model may be due to: (a) variable risk premium in the uncovered arbitrage equation; (b) omission of real variables to pick up any changes in the determinants of the steady state *real* exchange rate. Two *ad hoc* crude proxy variables are proposed and added to the Frankel equation (Equation 4.24). To measure changes in the steady state real exchange rate they use the cumulative *unanticipated* current account surplus (i.e. the cumulative residuals from a regression of the current account on other variables) and for the risk premium the cumulative sum of foreign exchange reserves. On quarterly data for several currencies against the US dollar (1974 (1)–1978 (4)) they find only the 'steady state' variables to be significant (when using instrumental variables) but the residuals are no longer serially correlated.

In a general CAM model, Haache and Townend (1981) find that changes in oil prices have strong effects on the sterling-dollar rate. This variable may be picking up changes in the real exchange rate. Clearly the possibility of changes in the real exchange rate and the existence of a risk premium need further study. We report on the latter when discussing the EMH in Chapter 5.

Summary and Conclusions

There can be no doubt that KAM models have increased our understanding of exchange rate movements particularly in the short run. They provide a useful framework for investigating the interaction between the foreign exchange market and other sectors of the economy. The incorporation of RE in such models allows the distinction between anticipated and unanticipated policy changes and their impact on the exchange rate to be analysed. Movements in the exchange rate today may be in response to anticipated changes in policy variables. When the latter actually occur there may be little movement in the exchange rate since RE speculators will have already acted on the information. Clearly the credibility attached to future policy changes will influence the degree to which the exchange rate will 'jump' and it must be admitted that this is an area where our understanding is weak. Unanticipated changes in policy (and other variables) will have very different repercussions on the exchange rate compared with anticipated changes as we saw with the basic Dornbusch overshooting model. Clearly the volatility of short run changes in the nominal and real exchange rate are explained in broad qualitative terms by the KAM approach.

Turning to the quantitative performance of KAM models it must be remembered that in testing the various models we are simultaneously testing a number of hypotheses. There are several equations in the system which are then solved to give a (pseudo) reduced form equation for the exchange rate, which is then estimated. The single equation exchange rate equation may break down because of a weakness in any of its constituent parts. We have noted that the PPP condition seems to hold approximately for the 1970s. It is fairly well known that the demand for money functions of the type used to derive the exchange rate equation have suffered substantial structural breaks in the 1970s for a number of industrial countries. The models studied pay little attention to the possible determinants of the real exchange rate or the risk premium on open arbitrage transactions. Expectations are at the heart of exchange rate determination and the way in which agents react to unanticipated events in the foreign exchange market are bound to have an influence on the spot exchange rate. These elements receive a relatively simple treatment in the models discussed (primarily to keep the analytics of the models tractible rather than a belief that such mechanisms are the last word concerning expectations formation). In Chapter 5 we bring the issue of expectations to the fore.

Overall what can we say about the empirical performance of the single equation exchange rate models discussed? By and large they provide a description of exchange rate movements that broadly fit the facts in the 1970s. In particular relative money supply growth and interest rate movements appear to influence exchange rate movements but the relationship is far from precise. We have said little about the performance of our exchange rate equations in predicting outside the sample period of estimation and this is taken up in Chapter 13 on exchange rate forecasting.

Note

1. Risk neutral speculators consider only the expected return when making their portfolio decisions. They disregard higher moments of the probability distribution of outcomes such as the variance which may provide a measure of riskiness.

5　ASSET MARKETS, THE EFFICIENT MARKETS HYPOTHESIS AND 'NEWS'

Introduction

In the 1960s the predominant view of the working of the foreign exchange market was that under floating rates, the exchange rate would be determined so as to equalise the *flow* demand for foreign exchange by importers and the supply by exporters. In contrast to this 'flow theory', the *asset market approach* stresses that the equilibrium exchange rate is that rate at which the market as a whole is prepared to hold the total outstanding *stocks* of assets of different countries. The foreign exchange market is to be viewed like any other highly organised asset market, such as the market in stocks and bonds. We have already implicitly discussed variants of the asset market approach when analysing the current account monetarist models, CAM, and the capital account monetarist models, KAM. In the former the exchange rate is viewed as the relative price of domestic and foreign money and in the latter perfect substitutability between domestic and foreign bonds is usually assumed. (Of course these models also embody assumptions about the behaviour of other markets, for example the goods market.)

In this chapter we wish to examine the behaviour of the foreign exchange market in a manner similar to that used by economists to analyse the behaviour of other asset markets such as the stock market. Mussa (1979a) notes that since in these 'spot auction' markets, assets are continuously traded and the assets in question are durable then: 'the price of an asset is tightly linked to the market's expectation of the future price of that asset. Whenever information is received that alters the market's view of the likely future price of an asset, the current price of that asset immediately reflects that alteration.'

Implicit in the above statement in the view that the foreign exchange market is an *efficient market* in that prices fully and instantaneously reflect all available information. If the current spot rate does not immediately 'jump' to reflect people's changed expectations about the future course of the exchange rate then abnormally large profits could be earned. The efficient markets hypothesis, EMH, also emphasises that the behaviour of rational, sensible agents might nevertheless result in highly volatile movements in exchange rates. It therefore provides an explanation as to why floating exchange rates in practice are far more volatile than their early supporters had suggested (prior to the decision to float in the early 1970s).

A further characteristic of an 'efficient market' is that changes in asset prices will be heavily influenced by unexpected events or 'news'. This enables one to account for a number of stylised facts of exchange rate behaviour. First, 'news' leads to a revision of the direct impact of current 'fundamental' variables (e.g. relative money supplies) on exchange rates. If today's 'news' affects one's *expectation* of tomorrow's exchange rate this too will have further repercussions on the *current* spot (or forward) rate. 'News' may therefore cause overshooting in the exchange rate. Second, if the forward rate at time $t-1$ is the market's best guess of next period's spot rate, it may nevertheless be a poor predictor if 'news' items lead to a revision of the forces acting on the spot rate between $t-1$ and t. Third, if 'news' has a powerful effect on spot and forward rates it essentially increases the risk associated with an open forward position. Banks who act as brokers in the market have to cushion themselves against losses on open forward positions. They can do so by charging an implicit risk premium in the transactions costs they charge to their customers when obtaining forward exchange. Hence the 'news' hypothesis goes some way to explaining the widening of the banks' bid-ask spreads in the forward market in the 1970s and the difficulties in obtaining forward contacts of long maturity.

The EMH suggests that agents use all available information when deciding on the equilibrium price of foreign exchange. It follows that *anticipated* events will be immediately reflected in the spot rate. The EMH plus the idea of new information or 'news' therefore provides a framework for analysing the impact of anticipated and unanticipated events on the foreign exchange market.

Spot and forward exchange rates are rather volatile, particularly over short time periods such as a month or less. Up to now our theories of exchange rate determination (e.g. KAM and CAM) have in the main attempted to explain these volatile movements with variables that exhibit less variability than the exchange rate series themselves. The news approach to exchange rate determination does not discard our earlier theories but seeks to augment them. Longer term cyclical movements in the exchange rate may be caused by such 'fundamentals' as relative money supplies, but 'news' causes the *observed* exchange rate to differ from its underlying level. To give a simple example: unexpectedly 'good' trade figures when announced at time t are likely to lead to an appreciation in the spot exchange rate. However, if 'good' trade figures (for time

t) had been expected at $t - 1$ by participants in the foreign exchange market then it is likely that the exchange rate would *not* alter when these 'good' figures are *actually* announced. Dealers in foreign exchange markets would have already acted upon their expectation that 'good' figures were likely and this fact would have been immediately reflected in the spot rate, at time $t - 1$. Otherwise a known opportunity for making speculative profits would have been foregone.

It should be fairly obvious from the above discussion that the 'news' interpretation may be grafted on to the EMH, since the latter is concerned with agents seeking to eliminate knowable profitable opportunities. For example, the EMH and the news hypothesis, when taken together, predict that the *actual* one period ahead spot rate is equal to the forward rate *plus* the impact of any unexpected events that occur between time, $t - 1$ and t. Tests of the EMH therefore need to be modified in the light of the 'news' hypothesis.

The 'news' hypothesis enables one to distinguish between expected and unexpected changes in the domestic interest rate. The reader may recall that the CAM and the Dornbusch (KAM) models gave conflicting results concerning the impact of the domestic interest rate on the spot exchange rate, which Frankel attempted to reconcile (see Chapter 4). It turns out that if increases in the domestic interest rate due to future inflation are taken to be expected events, whilst increases due to tight monetary policy are considered to be unanticipated events (at least in part) then the conundrum referred to can be satisfactorily resolved.

One of the most repeated criticisms of the floating rate regime is that exchange rate movements are 'excessive' and 'unjustified'. The implication usually drawn is that the authorities should therefore intervene heavily and frequently in the market or that countries should return to some kind of adjustable peg system (for example, the European Monetary System (EMS) — see Chapter 7). Defenders of the floating rate system have used the EMH and 'news' approach to repudiate the view that actual exchange rate changes are too volatile. They argue that because it is an 'efficient market' we ought to expect volatile movements even though private agents act rationally. If foreign exchange dealers use all available information in a rational manner what possible reasons could there be for goverment intervention in the market? Indeed supporters of the EMH in the foreign exchange market have suggested that government intervention in the market leads to *increased* volatility since private agents have to guess what the authorities might do next and this introduces additional uncertainty and 'news'. So acceptance of the EMH carries the implication that the authorities should not intervene in the foreign exchange market.

The EMH suggests that foreign exchange dealers react quickly to remove any profitable opportunities that arise in the market. Ignoring risk attached to uncovered (or open) transactions this implies that the return to uncovered speculation in the spot market (i.e. $r^* - r + s^e - s$) and in the forward market (i.e. $f - s^e$) will be continually pushed to zero by 'efficient' speculators acting in the two markets. In covered arbitrage transactions there is no exchange risk and the EMH would imply that arbitrage will keep the covered interest differential at zero (i.e. $r^* - r + f - s$). Further, since agents in an efficient market use all available information the above 'returns' to arbitrage and speculation should be independent of (orthogonal to) any information available at the time expectations are formed. Tests of the above propositions provide a test of whether the foreign exchange market is 'efficient'. In the previous chapter we came to the conclusion that empirical evidence from capital flows and the forward rate equation suggested that arbitrage transactions were highly elastic but that spot and forward *speculative* activity did not push the uncovered return to zero. The EMH provides additional evidence on the speed and strength of speculative activity in spot and forward markets.

It is perhaps useful at this point to summarise the important issues concerning the behaviour of the spot and forward markets that may be analysed using the EMH and 'news' approach. First we may examine the view that covered and uncovered (speculative) returns are zero and hence that capital flows are highly elastic. The reader will recall that the uncovered interest parity condition is crucial in producing 'overshooting' in KAM models and it is clearly of some importance to establish whether this relationship holds in practice. Second, it is important to determine whether exchange rates are 'excessively' volatile. If the EMH/news approach can account for the volatility of changes in the forward and spot rates then this severely weakens the case for government intervention in the foreign exchange market. Third, is the forward rate a useful predictor of the future spot rate or does the importance of 'news' imply that an open position in the forward market is a highly risky option for companies, banks and individuals to take? If 'news' is important then the best one can do is obtain a good model of the 'fundamental' economic variables that determine broad swings in exchange rates and ignore the high frequency 'news' elements that cause day-to-day and month-to-month variations. Fourth, do participants in the foreign exchange market react differently to anticipated and unanticipated events? In particular we shall discover that the distinction between anticipated and unanticipated changes in interest rates can resolve the conundrum referred to in the previous chapter, namely, the response of the spot rate to changes in the domestic interest rate. Fifth, does the addition of 'news' variables improve the statistical performance of (reduced form) exchange rate equations? Finally, do results using the EMH give any indication of the importance of transactions costs and risk (premia) in foreign exchange transactions?

Outline of the Chapter

The rest of the chapter is divided into three main sections: the first deals with some key postulates of the rational expectations hypothesis, the second covers the EMH and the third incorporates 'news' into the analysis of the foreign exchange market.

Tests of the EMH involve the use of the uncovered interest parity condition and the return to forward speculation. Both variables contain the unobservable expected spot rate. Since the rational expectations hypothesis, REH, is used to obtain a data series for the expected spot rate we briefly summarise the unbiasedness and orthogonality properties of RE predictions in the next section. Tests of the news hypothesis require measures of unanticipated events. It turns out that the REH is also of use here since the RE *forecast error* provides one measure of an unanticipated change in a variable.

We then discuss tests of the EMH in the spot and forward markets. First we discuss the behaviour of the covered interest differential and whether observed deviations from *covered* interest parity may be explained by transactions costs. Next we discuss speculation in the forward market and the relationship between the expected spot rate and the one period ahead forward rate. In particular we discuss whether the forward rate is an unbiased predictor of the expected spot rate and assess the evidence in favour of a risk premium. We then examine tests of the *uncovered* interest parity relationship and hence the degree of capital mobility in the spot market due to speculative activity. To anticipate some of our key results we find that the EMH suggest a high degree of capital mobility and that risk and transactions costs appear to play only a minor role in influencing behaviour in the foreign exchange market (at least in non-crisis periods).

In the next major section of this chapter we augment our tests of the EMH by explicitly considering the impact of 'news' on the spot and forward markets. We begin with a discussion of how the REH may be used to generate a data series for 'news' and how the latter may be incorporated in our tests of the EMH. Next we analyse how 'news' may result in volatile movements in spot and forward rates and how the distinction between anticipated and unanticipated events may be used to explain the relationship between movements in the spot rate and domestic interest rates. We then present some illustrative empirical tests of the 'news' hypothesis before finally presenting a brief summary and conclusions.

Rational Expectations Hypothesis, REH

As we noted in Chapter 2, in the exchange rate literature some form of the rational expectations hypothesis, REH, is usually used to model expectations formation. The REH assumes that individuals form consistent expectations; consistent, that is, with the *predictions* obtained from the economic model which explains the phenomenon in question. For example, if the appropriate model was CAM then an individual's expectations about the future spot rate would be determined by relative money supply growth (as well as other variables). However, even if the CAM were the 'true' model the expected future spot rate generated according to rational expectations (RE) would not equal the actual (ex-post) future spot rate in all periods because of random elements in the economic system. The individual's expectations would be correct on *average* over a number of periods: that is, they would be unbiased.

There are two obvious methods of generating rational expectations for a set of data relating to the past. In such a case the investigator has in front of him the actual values of variables relating to the present, past and future for each time period in his data set. Thus as a first method, one can use the *actual* future values of the variable since these differ from the true subjective expectations only by a random error. Second, one can regress actual future values of the variable on current and past values of variables that 'theory' suggests influence the variable in question. Having estimated the coefficients in this equation one can use it to predict ahead and provide a data series for the expected value of the variable. The difference between the actual future value and the predicted future value (that is the 'residual' in the regression equation) provides an estimate of the unexpected component or 'news' element.

In RE the individual's subjective probability distribution concerning future events is the same as the actual probability distribution, conditional on the information available to him. In principle the REH considers all moments of the probability distribution, but in most RE models only the mean or expected value of the distribution is considered and higher order moments such as the variance are ignored (the latter make .

the analysis much more difficult).

In forming RE the individual is concerned with three elements: the horizon over which expectations are being formed, the time expectations are formed and the 'information set' available to him. For example, expectations of a variable S formed at time $t - 1$, about time period t, conditional on information I available at time $t - 2$ may be written $E_{t-1}(S_t|I_{t-2})$. In RE it is not the time at which expectations are formed that is important but the *dating of the information set* available to individuals. However, we shall assume these two dates are the same and unless otherwise stated we shall for the most part assume a one period forecast horizon. Thus, for example, we shall write $E_{t-1}(S_t|I_{t-1})$ simply as S^e and $E_t(S_{t+1}|I_t)$ as S^e_{t+1}. Where any ambiguity might arise we shall explicitly use the expectations operator E_{t-j} with the implicit assumption that I is also dated $t - j$.

Two Basic Postulates of RE Forecasts

A number of propositions about the relationship between outcomes and forecasts (expectations) follow from the above view. We do not prove these propositions here but merely assert them (and except when explicitly stated otherwise, we refer to one period ahead expectations only).

1.   *Unbiased Forecasts.* Over time, with rational expectations we expect an *individual* to forecast correctly. Hence for a variable S, with an actual value S_{t+1}, the REH implies

$$S_{t+1} = S^e_{t+1} + u_{t+1}. \tag{5.1}$$

The expectation error in each period u_{t+1} will generally be non-zero but it will be zero on average over a number of predictions as over-predictions and under-predictions cancel out, i.e. $E_t u_{t+1} = E(S_{t+1} - S^e_{t+1}) = 0$. When dealing with *aggregate* expectations, the forecast error u_{t+1}, averaged over *all* individuals for a number of predictions, will also be zero. Under RE, expectations can be wrong but they cannot be systematically wrong. Since prediction errors, u_{t+1}, are random and unpredictable, once the forecast error is observed ex-post, it does not affect future expectations since it contains no new information (this contrasts with 'adaptive expectations' where past forecast errors influence current expectations). Errors in expectations are the result of unanticipated shocks, caused for example by unanticipated changes in government policy or in exogenous variables such as world interest rates.

The RE forecast error should also be serially uncorrelated (i.e. uncorrelated with its own future and past values) as well as having a zero mean.

If these two properties of u_{t+1} both hold (and if u_{t+1} has a constant variance) then u_{t+1} is said to be a 'white noise' error.

2.   *Information and the Orthogonality Property.* When RE prevails speculators use all the relevant information available at time t, (I_t), to form a view about S_{t+1}^e. If X_t is a subset of the information set actually used by agents, then the forecast error, u_{t+1}, must be independent of (orthogonal to) any information in X_t. The forecast error u_{t+1} is due to unpredictable shocks and will be unrelated to any relevant information available at the time expectations are formed.

The orthogonality property is sometimes referred to as the 'efficiency' property since it implies that agents use all relevant information in an 'efficient' manner thus avoiding knowable forecast errors.[1] In view of the use of the term efficiency in widely different contexts in economics and econometrics we do not use this term in this context and always refer instead to the orthogonality property. We reserve the term 'efficient' in the sense used in the efficient markets hypothesis EMH.

Having formally presented these two basic postulates of RE we are now ready to discuss test of the EMH in the spot and forward markets.

The Efficient Markets Hypothesis, EMH

The EMH pre-dates the REH but both theories consist of closely related concepts. A capital or asset market is said to be an 'efficient market' when prices (e.g. bond prices, exchange rates) fully and instantaneously reflect all available relevant information so that opportunities for super-normal profits are eliminated.[2] Since all available information is used by agents in an 'efficient market', they must form their expectations according to the REH Otherwise, opportunities for making supernormal profits would arise by exploiting the systematic forecasting errors made by some participants in the market. An *efficient market* has low trans-actions costs, low costs of collection and processing of information, flexible prices, and no impediments to voluntary exchange (but assets need not be perfect substitutes as in the case of a 'perfect market', see Chapter 2).

The efficient markets *hypothesis* EMH assumes an 'efficient market' where agents use REH, together with a particular view (model) of how prices are determined (e.g. the market clears instantaneously). The EMH is therefore a *joint* assumption about market behaviour and the forma-tion of expectations.

The EMH introduces the notion that prices reflect all the available relevant information. If this is the case, why do agents bother to collect information on variables other than prices since the former, by definition, contain no additional information? This conundrum has been investigated in the literature (Grossman and Stiglitz, 1980) but need not concern us here.[3] For our purposes we may take the EMH as being equivalent to the joint assumption of a 'perfect market' (or perfect capital mobility) and RE. The EMH is useful because it allows the application of RE' without having to deal with a full structural model of the phenomenon under study. Of course the EMH, although it yields tractable tests, need not necessarily be a true description of particular markets, for example, the foreign exchange market. There is an additional difficulty if the EMH is found to be invalid. We do not know whether it is our model of the behaviour of the market that is incorrect or our assumption of rational expectations: the EMH is a joint hypothesis. We now apply the EMH in turn to the covered interest return and the uncovered return in the forward and spot markets.

Covered Interest Parity

The EMH suggests that except for the existence of transactions costs and 'sovereign risk' (e.g. risk of imposition of exchange controls, Aliber, 1973) the uncovered interest return should be continually pushed to zero so that no abnormal profits are made. There are two broad approaches to testing this proposition. First one can plot the actual deviations from interest parity (i.e. $r^* - r + f - s$) to see if they differ 'significantly' from zero. The second method involves regression analysis.

For example, Frenkel and Levich (1975, 1977) use the first method. For 'non-homogeneous' assets, for example UK-US Treasury bills, they find that 85 per cent of the deviations from interest parity in the 1960s and early 1970s in 'tranquil' (i.e. non-crisis) periods can be accounted for by their estimates of the relevant transactions costs. For 'homogeneous' eurocurrency assets *all* deviations from covered interest parity lie within the bands set by transactions costs. However, some have questioned the calculation of transactions costs as used by Frenkel and Levich. Alternative measures of transactions costs (e.g. McCormick, 1974) give results for non-eurocurrency assets that are less favourable to the EMH.

If covered interest parity holds, then in the regression of the forward premium/discount, $f - s$, on the interest differential, $r - r^*$, that is:

$$(f - s) = a + b(r - r^*) \tag{5.2}$$

we expect $b = 0$ and a to give an estimate of transactions costs for covered arbitrage.

The evidence would appear to reject the EMH for non-homogeneous assets and to reject marginally the hypothesis for a number of euro-currency rates (e.g. Marston, 1976; Cosandier and Lang, 1981) since b is found to be significantly different from unity in a substantial pro-portion of cases. (Regression estimates of the transactions cost term a are broadly consistent with Frenkel and Levich's calculations.)

There are no exchange risk factors in covered arbitrage transactions so that the apparent failure of the EMH can only be defended by argu-ing that the data periods used cover periods where sovereign risk was present or that the variables are measured incorrectly or that inappropriate estimation techniques are used. The rejection of the EMH for euro-currency arbitrage is hard to reconcile with the Cambist or bankers' view of operations in the forward market that we discussed in Chapter 3. On balance, therefore, we err towards the view that the EMH holds to a very close approximation for covered transactions.

The EMH and the Forward Market

Stylised Facts. A graph of the 30-day forward rate F and the actual spot rate led by 30 days S_{t+1} for the \$/DM (using weekly data) is shown in Figure 5.1. It is obvious that the broad trends in the \$/DM *actual future* spot rate are picked up by the current forward rate. This is the case for most currencies since the root mean square of the prediction error, $S_{t+1} - F$, is of the order of 2–2.5 per cent against the dollar for the curren-cies shown in Table 5.1. This is particularly true for those currencies that experience a trend in the exchange rate (e.g. Japan and the UK). The 4-week variability in the spot rate in column 2 of Table 5.1 is about 2-2½ per cent per cent for most currencies. The forward market has not predicted *changes* in the spot rate at all accurately; forecast changes in the spot rate $(F - S)$ are of the same order of magnitude as actual changes $(S_{t+1} - S)$ (column 3 of Table 5.1). For example, only 2 per cent of the changes in the \$/DM rate are predicted by the forward rate (column 3, Table 5.1). In some cases this percentage is negative indicating that the forward rate is a worse predictor than the contemporaneous spot rate. The large size of these prediction errors does not necessarily imply a failure of market efficiency since all alternative predictors of S_{t+1} given information at time t, may give larger forecast errors than using F_t does.

It is clear from Figure 5.1 that a regression of S_{t+1} on F will produce (positively) serially correlated residuals since F provides a run of under-

Table 5.1: Prediction Errors of 4-week Forward Rates

Currency against $	(1) Per cent, RMS prediction error $= \sqrt{\dfrac{\Sigma(s_{t+1} - f)^2}{n}}$	(2) Per cent, RMS change in spot rate $= \sqrt{\dfrac{\Sigma(s_{t+1} - s)^2}{n}}$	(3) Per cent of changes in spot rate predicted by forward rate
1. Deutschmark	2.10	2.12	2.2
2. French franc	2.21	2.09	− 11.4
3. Pound sterling	2.18	2.23	6.0
4. Italian lira	2.76	2.53	− 18.8
5. Swiss franc	2.51	2.61	7.4
6. Dutch guilder	2.10	2.0	− 10.0
7. Japanese yen	1.84	1.84	0

Source: Frankel (1980), *Southern Economic Journal*, April.

Data period: weekly data 5 July 1974–4 April 1978 (193 data points).

and over-predictions of S_{t+1}. If the \$/DM future spot rate S_{t+1} is lagged one period, the solid line would shift to the right and would nearly coincide with F. Hence the current forward rate appears to be more highly correlated with the *current* spot rate than with the *future* spot rate. This suggests that influences on S also impinge upon F: this is the basis of the 'news' interpretation of exchange rate which we discuss later in this chapter.

Basic Model. Below we are able to show that if the forward market conforms to the EMH and speculators are risk neutral (i.e. pay no regard to risk) then the forward rate is an unbiased predictor of the expected future spot rate, s^e_{t+1}. We shall see that the assumption of RE, allows us to replace the unobservable s^e_{t+1} by its 'expected value', namely the *actual* future spot rate, s_{t+1}.

The modern theory of the forward rate (see Chapter 3) predicts $f = s^e_{t+1}$ if the elasticity of the speculative schedule for forward foreign exchange c_f, is infinite. $c_f \rightarrow \infty$ if the disutility from risk is zero, that is, if agents disregard any 'risk', in making their portfolio decisions. Thus risk neutrality in the 'modern theory' produces the same result as the EMH, namely $f = s^e_{t+1}$.

A speculator, as we have seen, is able to make an *expected* profit if the current forward rate, f, differs from his view of the *expected* future spot rate. If the forward market is efficient and eliminates knowable

Figure 5.1: Forward Rate (30 days) and Spot Rate (led 4 weeks): Dollar-Deutschmark

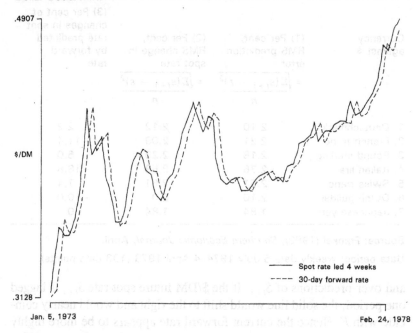

Source: Frankel (1980)

opportunities for profit, 'speculators' should invest in forward contracts until profitable opportunities are exhausted, that is, until

$$f_t = s^e_{t+1} + v'_t \tag{5.3}$$

where v'_t is the risk premium at time, t. Risk neutrality implies $v'_t = 0$. The risk premium v'_t is the expected profit margin of the speculator and may also capture any transactions costs (e.g. manpower costs) associated with the forward contract. Speculators will match arbitrage demand and supply for a particular currency and may carry only a small 'open position'.

We cannot test the 'efficient markets' assumption of Equation (5.3) unless we have a data series for the expected future spot rate. We do not have direct evidence on expectations since *surveys* of foreign exchange dealers' expectations are not normally available. We therefore require a relationship between s^e_{t+1} and observable variables. Although in principle one could hypothesise any expectations formation process for s^e_{t+1} (for example, the 'no-change' view, $s^e_{t+1} = s_t$) it is usual to assume RE:

Figure 5.2: The Forward Premium and Actual Percentage Changes in the
Spot Rate for the US Dollar versus the Deutschemark, Monthly, 1973–1977

% p.a.

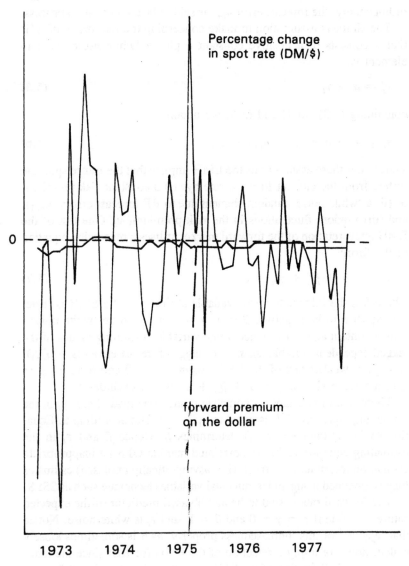

Source: Mussa (1979)

$$s_{t+1} = s_{t+1}^e + u_{t+1} \tag{5.4}$$

with $E_t(u_{t+1}|I_t) = 0$ and u_{t+1} serially uncorrelated (u_{t+1} is a 'white noise' error). RE also implies that u_{t+1} is independent of (or orthogonal to) all information available at t. Given the conditions of zero mean and orthogonality, the forecast error u_{t+1} is said to be an innovation process.

The simplest assumption to make concerning the risk premium v_t' is that it consists of a positive constant α plus a 'white noise' random element v_t:

$$v_t' = \alpha + v_t \tag{5.5}$$

combining (5.3), (5.4) and (5.5) we obtain

$$s_{t+1} = -\alpha + f_t + (u_{t+1} - v_t). \tag{5.6}$$

Thus under these assumptions the EMH implies that the future spot rate differs from the current forward rate by: (i) a constant risk premium, α; (ii) a 'white noise' random element due to RE forecast errors (u_{t+1}); and (iii) random fluctuations in the risk premium, v_t. One test of the EMH interpretation of the forward market utilises a regression equation of the form:

$$s_{t+1} = \alpha + \beta f_t + \gamma I_t + \varepsilon_t \tag{5.7}$$

where I_t is the information set available at time t. If the EMH is 'true' we expect α to be negative, $\beta = 1$, $\gamma = 0$ and ε_t to be 'white noise'. I_t may contain any relevant economic variables including values of the lagged dependent variable (s_t, s_{t-1}) or lagged forecast errors ($s_t - f_{t-1}$). A slightly weaker test of the EMH *assumes* $\gamma = 0$ and tests for $\beta = 1$ in the regression $s_{t+1} = \alpha + \beta f_t + \varepsilon_t$, which excludes I_t.

There is an important econometric point to be made here. ε_t in the estimating equation (5.7) is equal to $u_{t+1} - v_t$. But according to Equation (5.3), v_t' (and hence v_t) determines f_t. Hence f_t and ε_t in the estimating equation (5.7) are correlated making OLS an inappropriate estimation technique. 'Correct' (i.e. asymptotically unbiased) estimates may be obtained using an instrumental variables technique such as 2SLS.

The forward rate is said to be an unbiased predictor of the expected future spot rate if $\alpha = \gamma = 0$ and $\beta = 1$, and ε_t is white noise. Notice that rejection of this 'unbiasedness property' as it is sometimes loosely called, does *not* imply a rejection of the EMH (or RE) since the latter allows $\alpha \neq 0$. Rejection of the EMH (i.e. rejection of either RE or the notion of an 'efficient' market) occurs if $\gamma \neq 0$ and $\beta \neq 1$ or if ε_t is not white noise.

Alternative formulations of the unbiasedness property are sometimes used. For example unbiasedness also implies that the forward premium/discount $(f - s)$ is an unbiased predictor of the *change* in the spot rate. We obtain this relationship by subtracting s_t from both sides of $s_{t+1} = f_t + u_t$ giving:

$$(s_{t+1} - s_t) = (f_t - s_t) + u_t \tag{5.8}$$

A *test* of unbiasedness is then a test of $\alpha = \gamma_1 = 0$, $\beta = 1$ and that ε_t is white noise, in the regression:

$$\Delta s_{t+1} = \alpha + \beta(f - s) + \gamma_1 I_t + \varepsilon_t. \tag{5.9}$$

Tests of the EMH in the Forward Market

There are a great many published tests of the EMH and we can only give a flavour of the results here. Frankel (1980) provides a useful set of tests of increasing severity for the EMH using weekly data on six major currencies against the dollar and the 4-week forward rate.

The currencies are those of Table 5.1 (excluding the yen). Frankel uses logarithms of the forward and spot rates, f and s_{t+1} (to avoid the Siegal paradox, see below).

A weak test of the EMH is provided by an IV regression of $(s_{t+1} - f)$ on a constant, α. In general although the point estimate of α is non-zero (about ½ per cent) its standard error is large and statistically we may accept that $\alpha = 0$. This provides evidence against a risk premium.

A slightly stronger test is to run the regression:

$$s_{t+1} = \hat{\alpha} + \hat{\beta} f_t + u_t \tag{5.10}$$

where for a zero risk premium we expect $\hat{\alpha} = 0$, and for the EMH we also expect $\hat{\beta} = 1$ and u_t to be serially uncorrelated (Table 5.2).

Except for Italy (i.e. the lira-dollar rate) the EMH is accepted for the floating period July 1974–August 1978 on an OLS regression although the test is much less favourable to the EMH when the data period March 1973–July 1974, just after floating rates were introduced, is added to the data set. We may interpret the latter as a period of learning by forward market operators about their new environment. Representative OLS results for the most favourable period, July 1974–April 1978, are given in Table 5.2. However IV results to overcome the errors in variables bias give much less favourable results for the hypothesis that $\alpha = 0$, $\beta = 1$. In addition most of the regressions suffered from autocorrelated errors: a direct refutation of the REH which we now deal with in more detail.

So far we have implicitly used only 'property I', the 'unbiased

Table 5.2: EMH and Forward Rate (Frankel, 1980)

Currency against $	$\hat{\alpha}$ (standard error)	$\hat{\beta}$ (standard error)	F-test $\hat{\alpha} = 0, \hat{\beta} = 1$
Deutschmark	0.016 (0.045)	1.015 (0.050)	2.02
French franc	−0.098 (0.072)	0.933 (0.046)	2.99
Pound sterling	0.028 (0.016)	0.957 (1.96)	1.96
Italian lira	−0.383* (0.186)	0.942 (0.028)	3.46

Source: Frankel (1980).

Data period: 5 July 1974–4 April 1978, weekly data.
* indicates statistically different from $\alpha = 0$ or $\beta = 1$ at 5 per cent significant level.
$F < F^c$ indicates acceptance of joint hypothesis, $\hat{\alpha} = 0$, $\hat{\beta} = 1$ where F^c is the critical value.

forecast' assumption of RE. Property II of RE, the 'orthogonality assumption', requires the forecast errors $s_{t+1} - f_t = u_t$ to be independent of any other variables including previous prediction errors $(s_t - f_{t-1})$. We can perform the following regressions:

$$s_{t+1} - f_t = \hat{c}_0 + \hat{c}_1 (s_t - f_{t-1}) + w_t \qquad (5.11)$$

$$s_{t+1} = \hat{c}_0 + \hat{c}_1 (s_t - f_{t-1}) + \hat{\beta} f_t + w_t \qquad (5.12)$$

If the EMH is correct we expect $\hat{c}_1 = 0$ and $\hat{\beta} = 1$ and for a zero risk premium $\hat{c}_0 = 0$.

Prima facie Frankel's (1980) results using Equations (5.11) and (5.12) reject the EMH (except for the DM-dollar rate 1974–8) but it is impossible to discern whether the RE or the 'efficient markets' assumption is to blame. As always there are qualifications to add before rejecting EMH even on Frenkel's data. We have not modelled any variation in the risk premium or in transactions costs. Instrumental variables are chosen *a priori* by the researcher and different instruments yield different results. We cannot be certain that the IV results cited so far are the most favourable to the hypothesis. (On the other hand the information set included in our tests consists only of one period lagged forecast errors, other variables if included might reject the EMH more decisively.) Different proxy variables for the expected future spot rate might produce different results. Finally there is a technical measurement problem known as the Siegal paradox. If $s_{t+1}^e = f_t$ in units of domestic per unit of foreign currency, this relationship does not hold when spot and forward rates are measured in units of foreign per unit of domestic currency.

Use of the logarithm of spot and forward rates mitigates this problem. Frankel (1980) suggests that the poor results for the EMH might be due to agents recognising the *possibility* of discontinuously large errors if the authorities were to withdraw from the market. In such cases the residuals are not normally distributed and our test statistics are incorrect.

Further Tests. Additional tests of the EMH have followed three broad approaches: (i) use of alternative proxies for s_{t+1}^e; (ii) more sophisticated estimation techniques; and (iii) inclusion of a wider range of variables in the information set I_t. We discuss these aspects briefly.

Jacobs (1982) uses an explicit model to determine s_{t+1}^e. An autoregressive model

$$s_{t+1} = b_0 s_t + b_1 s_{t-1} + b_2 s_{t-2} + \ldots + e_t \qquad (5.13)$$

is estimated, yielding values for $\hat{b}_i$, which can then be used to generate predictions that act as a proxy variable for s_{t+1}^e, that is $\hat{s}_{t+1}^e = \hat{b}_0 s_t + \hat{b}_1 s_{t-1} + \ldots$ The variable $\hat{s}_{t+1}^e$ is then used in the regression $f = a_0 + a_1 \hat{s}_{t+1}^e + u_t$ to obtain estimates $\hat{a}_0$ and $\hat{a}_1$. (This is an instrumental variables approach to RE, McCallum, 1976.) Jacobs finds that $a_0 \neq 0$, $a_1 \neq 1$ for seven major currencies against the dollar using monthly data for the period 1973–80. In fact $a_1 > 1$ and is larger for quarterly than for monthly data indicating that the risk premium probably increases with the length of the time horizon, as one might expect.

Frankel (1982) provides weak tests of the unbiasedness of the forward rate using both instrumental variables IV to overcome the errors in variables problem, and OLS regressions of the form:

$$s_{t+1} = \alpha + \beta f_t + \beta_1 f_{t-1} + \varepsilon_t. \qquad (5.14)$$

Monthly data for the \$/£, \$/French franc and \$/DM over the period June 1973–July 1979 are used. Frankel obtains mixed results. For the \$/DM rate, $\alpha = \beta_1 = 0$, and $\beta = 1$ jointly, and ε_t are white noise. But for the \$/£ and \$/franc rates $\alpha \neq 0$, although the joint hypothesis $\alpha = 0$, $\beta = 1$ is accepted at 5 per cent level for sterling (but not for the franc). Frankel provides a test of the degree of bias in the OLS coefficients and finds that OLS does not give significantly different results to IV (this is the Hausman 1978 test) *when applied to each equation singly.*

Frankel (1982) also reports a regression of the *change* in the spot rate Δs_{t+1} on the forward premium/discount, $(f - s)$ and other variables known at time t (e.g. Δs_t). He is not able to reject the null hypothesis that $\alpha = \beta_1 = 0$, $\beta = 1$ and ε_t is white noise in Equation (5.9). However the 'power' of this test is rather low since one can also accept the joint hypothesis $\alpha = \beta_1 = \beta = 0$ (i.e. reject $\beta = 1$). We should not find the latter result surprising since we noted that the forward premium/discount explains little of the change in the spot rate (see column 3, Table 5.1).

MacDonald (1983) tests the unbiasedness property by allowing for any contemporaneous correlation between errors *across equations* of the form $s_{t+1} = \alpha + \beta f_t + \varepsilon_t$. If unanticipated events which are reflected in ε_t impinge upon more than one currency (which seems likely) the ε_t for each currency will be correlated. Using Zellner's (1962) seemingly unrelated regression procedure (SURE) better estimates of the standard errors of α and β are obtained. MacDonald finds that for quarterly data over the period 1972 (1)–1979 (4) for six major currencies against the dollar only sterling and the Canadian dollar pass the joint hypothesis that $\alpha = 0$, $\beta = 1$. Rejection of the null-hypothesis appears to be mainly due to $\alpha \neq 0$ rather than $\beta \neq 1$, and is more severe when Zellner's estimation method is used, compared with the more favourable results in the OLS regressions. However MacDonald does not use instrumental variables estimation so errors in variables bias remain a problem.

Baillie *et al.* (1983) are concerned that in testing for unbiasedness in Equation (5.7), $s_{t+1}^e = \alpha + \beta f_t + \gamma I_t + \varepsilon_t$, the information set I_t may be unduly restrictive. They suggest using a set of several lagged values of f and s as the information set. Implicitly they include higher order lagged values of the forecast error since terms like f_{t-j} and s_{t-j+1} may always be re-written as the past forecast error $(f_{t-j} - s_{t-j+1})$ (plus an additional term s_{t-j+1}). Since s_{t+1} and f_t are jointly determined, a more general model includes an additional regression in which f_{t+1} is regressed on its own lagged values $f_t, f_{t-1}, \ldots$ and lagged values of the spot rate $s_t, s_{t-1}, \ldots$ The two regressions may be written

$$s_{t+1} = \alpha(L)\, s_t + \beta(L)\, f_t + \varepsilon_{1t} \tag{5.15}$$

$$f_{t+1} = \gamma(L)\, s_t + \lambda(L)\, f_t + \varepsilon_{2t} \tag{5.16}$$

where $\alpha(L) = \alpha_0 L + \alpha_1 L^2 + \ldots$; L is the lag operator $L^n X = X_{-n}$; and ε_{it} are white noise errors. (The two equation system above is known as a (bivariate) vector autoregression.) Baillie *et al.* (1983) show that the unbiasedness property (that is $\alpha = 0$, $\beta = 1$ in our simple model) implies a complex non-linear restriction between the lag operator coefficients $\alpha(L)$, $\beta(L)$, $\gamma(L)$ and $\lambda(L)$. A test of the unbiasedness property is provided by a test of this non-linear restriction. Using weekly data on 30-day forward rates against the US dollar, for sterling, DM, lira, French franc, Canadian dollar and Swiss franc for the 1970s, they find that the non-linear restriction does not hold for all currencies considered.[4] The 30-day forward rate is not, in general, an unbiased predictor of the future spot rate. This need not lead to rejection of the EMH (and RE) since the EMH does not imply the unbiasedness property unless there is a zero risk premium.

Baillie and McMahon (1982) have extended the above results in a trivariate autoregression where the uncovered interest differential (r^* $- r$) is included as an additional variable. The latter is included since covered and uncovered arbitrage in the spot market and hence ($r - r^*$) might influence f and s_{t+1}^e, since all are jointly determined variables. Results using weekly observations on the 90-day forward rates for the £/$, DM/$ and Italian lira/$ from 1 June 1973–8 April 1980 (362 observations) reject the unbiasedness hypothesis.

Summary: EMH and the Forward Rate. The balance of evidence appears to reject the unbiasedness property of the forward rate for the major currencies. In the main this appears to be due to a statistically significant constant term in the equation $s_{t+1} = \alpha + \beta f + \varepsilon_t$, rather than β being wildly different from unity. This suggests that speculators may charge a risk premium in some forward market transactions. Alternatively $\alpha \neq 0$ may contain an element of transactions costs (i.e. paper work). Apart from the naive assumption that the risk premium is constant over time, no attempt has been made to model the risk premium in the forward market literature (but see the beginning of this section on the efficient market hypothesis, and the reference to Hooper and Morton, 1980).

The existence of a risk premium is not inconsistent with the EMH (and RE). In the above empirical work the orthogonality property of RE (EMH) generally holds but the existence of serially correlated errors, ε_t, appears to reject the EMH for a number of currencies (against the dollar) in the 1970s.[5] However the starting date for such tests is crucial. Immediately after the introduction of floating exchange rates for most major currencies in 1972, foreign exchange operators may have been learning about the new system and RE (and therefore the EMH) may not have applied. Tests starting with post-1974 data are marginally more favourable to the EMH. If one views the evidence as being against the EMH then either expectations are not rational or our instantaneous market clearing model of the forward market does not hold. The former would appear to be the most likely cause of failure of the EMH. Survey evidence on exchange rate expectations by operators in the foreign exchange market would be useful in providing ancillary evidence on the RE hypothesis (as, for example, with price expectations and interest rate expectations data, Mullineaux, 1978 and Friedman, 1979).

If there is a risk premium in forward market speculative transactions, domestic and foreign currencies are not perfect substitutes. Hence private agents are concerned about the composition of their assets held in different currencies, and by altering supplies of currency in the forward market, the authorities can influence the forward rate. (On the other hand if domestic and foreign assets are perfect substitutes then the authorities cannot influence the forward rate.) With imperfect substitutability, by operating in the forward market, the authorities can influence spot transactions by banks (see bank arbitrage, Chapter 3) and hence the spot exchange rate. Whether on balance such intervention is desirable is a much wider question and requires a cost-benefit calculation and the application of welfare economics. We have merely established that government intervention to alter the forward rate is probably feasible for a large number of currencies. We reserve further discussion of the forward market and the EMH until we have analysed the role of 'news' in the foreign exchange market.

EMH and the Uncovered Speculative Return

We noted in Chapter 2 that: if we have perfect capital mobility (foreign and domestic assets are perfect substitutes, instantaneous market clearing, zero transactions costs) and a zero risk premium then the uncovered speculative return is zero

$$s_t^e - s_{t-1} = d_{t-1} \tag{5.17}$$

where $d_{t-1} = r_{t-1} - r^*_{t-1}$, the uncovered interest differential. (Somewhat confusingly Equation (2.6) is also referred to as the open *arbitrage* condition.) Also we noted that Equation (5.17) holds if the spot market is 'efficient' and hence eliminates knowable opportunities for supernormal profit (providing there is a zero risk premium). However, the EMH also assumes that all available information is used in forming expectations, hence the unbiasedness property of RE holds, $s_t = s_t^e + u_t$. We may therefore substitute the actual spot rate in place of the unobservable spot rate in Equation (5.17) yielding:

$$s_t = s_{t-1} + d_{t-1} + u_t. \tag{5.18}$$

Equation (5.18) has the testable implication that the current spot rate depends upon the previous period's spot rate and the uncovered interest differential, with a unit coefficient on each variable. The orthogonality property of the RE forecast error u_t implies that no other variables known at time $t - 1$ or earlier should influence s_t (other than s_{t-1} and

d_{t-1}). Tests of Equation (5.18) have followed similar lines to those used to test the EMH in the forward market.

Early empirical work tested Equation (5.18) by regressing ($s_t - s_{t-1} - d_{t-1}$) on a wide variety of economic variables available at time $t - 1$ or earlier. Frankel (1979a) found that for the DM/\$ rate on quarterly data over the 1970s that all additional variables tried were insignificant. Haache and Townend (1981) using monthly data on the sterling effective rate (July 1972–February 1980) found that the interest rate coefficients, when included as independent variables, have unit coefficients, but lagged values of the change in the exchange rate and Domestic Credit Expansion are also significant. Hence the RE forecast error u_t is not independent of all information at time $t - 1$ or earlier and the joint hypothesis of zero risk premium and the EMH fails; similar results are obtained for the £/\$ rate. Cumby and Obstfeld (1981) using weekly data (July 1974–June 1978) on six major currencies against the dollar found that lagged values of the dependent variable ($s_t - s_{t-1} - d_{t-1}$) of up to 16 weeks are statistically significant for all six currencies. The RE forecast error is therefore serially correlated contrary to part of the maintained hypothesis.

Our interim conclusions concerning the validity of the EMH (plus the assumption of a zero or constant risk premium) for speculative spot transactions are similar to those for the forward market. Not all aspects of the maintained hypothesis hold and we surmise that there may be a (variable) risk premium in uncovered spot market transactions. The latter implies that intervention by the authorities in the spot market *may* succeed in altering the spot rate or domestic interest rates since foreign and domestic assets may be imperfect substitutes. Evidence from Equation (5.18) nevertheless supports the view that the elasticity of substitution between foreign and domestic assets may be high — considerably higher, in fact, than estimates obtained from regression equations using actual capital flows as the dependent variable, as reported in Chapter 3. As the speculative return responds to potential as well as actual flows, the estimates from the open arbitrage equation (Equation 5.18) may better characterise asset substitutability across the foreign exchanges.

A recent development in the exchange rate literature has been to consider the role of 'news' in causing 'jumpiness' in exchange rate movements. These ideas have a bearing on tests of the EMH in the spot and forward markets and we discuss these aspects in the next section.

Exchange Rates and News

Introduction

A prominent feature of the movement in bilateral exchanges is their extreme volatility. Weekly changes are extremely volatile with monthly and quarterly changes less so. Most of the hypotheses examined so far have attempted to explain such movements by economic variables, such as the money supply, output or prices, that show less volatility than exchange rate changes. This, in part, accounts for the poor performance of such variables in 'tracking' the short-run or high-frequency data on exchange rates. On the other hand, causal empiricism tells us that 'news', for example, new money supply figures or new data on the current account position, can lead foreign exchange dealers to buy and sell currencies and affect the spot and forward rates. Newspaper headlines, such as 'Sterling falls because of unexpectedly high money supply figures' are not uncommon. The implication here is that if the published money supply figures had been *as expected* the exchange rate would have remained unchanged. On the other hand expected events that are later confirmed may already be incorporated in the current exchange rate — an implication of an efficient market. For example, another headline might be 'Exchange rate improves as Chancellor announces lower monetary targets for the future'. The emphasis here is that expected future events may influence the exchange rate today.

We shall use the term 'news' as a shorthand solely for unexpected events. Our task in this section is to examine whether the above common-sense notions concerning the behaviour of the foreign exchange market may be formally incorporated in the exchange rate models discussed previously. The volatility of exchange rates may then be explained by news and changing expectations of future events.

Why are Exchange Rate Movements Volatile?

Two stylised facts about exchange rate volatility have a bearing on the analysis that follows. First, although the forward rate is (approximately) an unbiased predictor of the future spot rate, the *predicted change* in the exchange rate, given by the forward discount, namely $(F - S)$, on a month-to-month basis is poor. The variance of the actual change in the spot exchange rate can often exceed that for the forward discount by a factor of 20 (Frenkel, 1982) — see Figure 5.2. This suggests that the bulk of exchange rate changes is due to 'new information' which by definition could not have been anticipated and reflected in the forward rate which prevailed in the previous period.

Second, contemporaneous spot and forward rates move very closely together and have nearly equal values (i.e. $F_t \doteqdot S_t$ — see Figure 5.1). For example for the \$/£, \$/DM and \$/yen exchange rates the correlation between the *contemporaneous* spot rate and one month forward rate exceeds 0.99 and correlations between the corresponding *percentage changes* in spot and forward rates exceed 0.96 for these three currencies. The following simple model (Frenkel and Mussa, 1980) involving uncovered interest parity can help explain these facts:

$$r_t - r_t^* = E_t s_{t+1} - s_t \qquad (5.19)$$

substituting for $r_t - r_t^*$ from Equation (5.19) in the current account monetary model, e.g. like Equation (4.8):

$$s_t = k + (m - m^*) - \alpha(y - y^*) + \beta(E_t s_{t+1} - s_t) \qquad (5.20)$$

$$s_t = [1/(1 + \beta)] Z_t + [\beta/(1 + \beta)] E_t s_{t+1} \qquad (5.21)$$

where $Z_t = k + (m - m^*) - \alpha(y - y^*)$. The current spot rate depends upon current 'fundamental' variables Z_t and expectations (formed today) about the future exchange rate. By repeated forward substitution for $E_t s_{t+1}$, that is assuming rational expectations, we obtain:

$$s_t = [1/(1 + \beta)] \sum_{j=0}^{\infty} [\beta/(1 + \beta)]^j E_t Z_{t+j} \qquad (5.22)$$

Thus the influence of Z on the current spot rate declines as the time horizon extends (i.e. $[\beta/(1 + \beta)]^j \to 0$ as $j \to \infty$).

In general, Equation (5.22) may be obtained without invoking the current account monetarist model. From Equation (5.19) we see that the current spot rate depends upon the current and all future values of the interest differential and therefore on all future values of variables that determine this differential. The latter need not be monetary variables.

An implication of Equation (5.21) is that the current spot rate and the expected spot rate for one period ahead should be closely related: the higher is β the closer to unity is the coefficient $\beta/(1 + \beta)$ on $E_t s_{t+1}$ and the closer this correspondence should be. If 'news' does not affect the variables in Z because they are relatively 'sticky', but does affect $E_t s_{t+1}$ then 'news' will also affect the current spot rate in a similar direction and possibly by a similar amount (if β is large).

If the forward rate at time t, f_t, is formed in an efficient market it should reflect the 'news' received *in the current period*. Hence, given the model embedded in the expectations equation (Equations 5.21 or 5.22), we would expect changes in the contemporaneous (one month) forward rate, f_t and the current spot rate s_t to be highly correlated.

Changes in the current spot rate should be correlated with the expected future spot rate in all future periods but with declining weights $[\beta/(1 + \beta)]^j$. However, if 'news' is thought to involve a temporary rather than a permanent change it will not affect expectations far into the future. Hence we expect a much weaker correlation between the current spot rate and forward rates (which we take as unbiased predictors of, $E_t s_{t+1}$) of longer maturity. In general this is confirmed by the evidence. Changes in, say, *annual* forward rates are less correlated with changes in the contemporaneous spot rate than are one month forward rates.

Three further conclusions from Equation (5.22) are worth noting. If CAM is used to determine $(r - r^*)$ then β is the interest elasticity of the demand for money. If $\beta = 0$, the current spot-rate depends only upon Z_t (relative money supplies and income) and not on expectations about future exchange rate movements. Even though Equation (5.22) embodies the efficient markets hypothesis (i.e. instantaneous market clearing, plus RE) the exchange rate does not follow a random walk and will be serially correlated if the variables in Z are serially correlated. Finally, overshooting may occur if current changes in Z (e.g. change in the money supply) are viewed as permanent and affect expectations about the future exchange rate: efficient markets reflect all available information, immediately.

Direct Tests of the News Hypothesis in the Spot and Forward Market

Our first problem is to measure news or unexpected events. There are three main approaches, one using actual data on expectations, another public forecasts and the third, RE and regression analysis.

Expectations data exist for prices, inflation and output for a number of industrial countries. Data on interest rate expectations are also available for the US (see Holden *et al.*, 1985). Usually, but not always, expectations information is qualitative, that is respondents answer 'up', 'down' or 'the same'. In this case there are methods for transforming the data into a quantitative figure for expectations (Carlson and Parkin, 1975; Pesaran, 1984). Whether we think that economic variables like those mentioned influence the exchange rate depends on our model of exchange rate determination. However, if we do have expectations series on relevant variables, *EX*, the unexpected or 'news' variables are simply actual minus expected, $(X - EX)$. Public forecasts can be used in a similar manner to form news variables.

If neither expectations nor forecast data are available, we can construct pseudo expectations and 'news' variables using regression analysis.

Our (reduced form) model of the exchange rate may suggest that:

$$s = \beta X + w_t \tag{5.23}$$

where X is the set of fundamental variables that influence s and w_t is a 'white noise' error. For example, for the CAM model, X would include relative money supplies, output and interest rates. With information available at $t - 1$, and noting that under RE, $E_{t-1}w_t = 0$, we have from Equation (5.1) $s^e = E_{t-1}s = \beta(E_{t-1}X) = \beta X^e$. Subtracting $s^e = \beta X^e$ from Equation (5.23) we obtain:

$$s - s^e = \beta(X - X^e) + w_t \tag{5.24}$$

$$s = s^e + \beta(X - X^e) + w_t = s^e + \text{'news'} + w_t. \tag{5.25}$$

Thus, the rational expectations forecast error $(s - s^e)$ is composed of a genuinely random component w_t and unexpected changes ('news') in the fundamental variables, X, that determine s. The 'news' variable is a type of forecast error which is *not known* at $t - 1$ and therefore helps to determine the forecast error in the spot rate, $s - s^e$. If expectations are rational, $(X - X^e)$ will be orthogonal (uncorrelated) with any other variables (at $t - 1$ or earlier), hence so will the RE forecast error for the spot rate $(s - s^e)$. The relationship between s and X should come from some relevant economic theory. In practice there may be several contending hypotheses about the determinants of s, each giving different series for the 'news' variable. Tests of the hypothesis that 'news' influences the spot or forward rate is always tested jointly with a hypothesis concerning the formation of expectations of news variables (EX). This is one reason why different researchers obtain different results when testing the 'news' hypothesis.

The news approach expressed in Equations (5.6) and (5.10) may be usefully applied to explain why tests of the EMH in the spot and forward markets discussed so far may be deficient.

We may now assume that we either have or can generate a series of the relevant 'news' variables $(X - X^e)$. From Equation (5.25)

$$s = s^e + \beta(X - X^e) + w_t. \tag{5.26}$$

If we assume EMH and a constant risk premium α and α' in the spot and forward markets respectively, then

$$s^e = s_{t-1} + d_{t-1} + \alpha \tag{5.27}$$

and

$$s^e = f_{t-1} + \alpha' \tag{5.28}$$

Substituting in Equation (5.26) we obtain testable equations:

$$s = \alpha + s_{t-1} + d_{t-1} + \beta(X - X^e) + w_t \quad \text{EMH-spot market} \quad (5.27)$$

$$s = \alpha' + f_{t-1} + \beta'(X' - X'^e) + w_t \quad \text{EMH-forward market} \quad (5.28)$$

and α and α' may also measure non-zero transactions costs.

(A) Illustrative Results: Spot Market. Dornbusch (1980) tests the EMH (constant risk premium) model of the spot market using several 'news' variables. First it is worth noting that, for the effective dollar rate, anticipated depreciation as measured by $r - r^*$ ($= s^e_{t+1} - s$) constitutes only a small proportion of the actual change in the spot rate: the latter is dominated by *un*anticipated depreciation, $u_t = s_{t+1} - s + r^* - r$ (see Figure 5.3).

Dornbusch models unanticipated interest rate differentials ($d_t - E_{t-1}d_t$) as residuals from a regression of d_t on past values of d. 'Current account' news (CAN) and 'cyclical' news (CYN), are measured as deviations of realised values from OECD *forecast* values. Dornbusch imposes and does not test the unit restrictions on s_{t-1} and d_{t-1} since he uses ($s_t - s_{t-1} - d_{t-1}$) as the dependent variable. Using biannual data (1973–9) for the $/yen and $/DM, the results are mixed. For the yen the 'news' variables perform reasonably well but for Germany only interest rate 'news' is significant. Representative results are:

$/Yen

$$s_t - s_{t-1} - d_{t-1} = -3.8 + 1.35 \, \text{CAN} - 2.6 \, \text{CYN} + 1.27 \, \text{CYN*} + 0.75 \, u_{t-1}$$
$$\phantom{s_t - s_{t-1} - d_{t-1} = } (0.4) \quad (4.2) \quad\quad (4.0) \quad\quad\quad (1.13)$$

OLS, $R^2 = 0.73$; $DW = 2.1$

$/DM

$$s_t - s_{t-1} - d_{t-1} = 2.29 + 1.38 \, \text{CAN} - 0.53 \, \text{CYN} + 26.1 \, (d_t - E_{t-1}d_t) - 0.40 u_{t-1}$$
$$\phantom{s_t - s_{t-1} - d_{t-1} = } (1.2) \quad (1.9) \quad\quad (0.8) \quad\quad\quad (3.5)$$

OLS, $R^2 = 0.62$, $DW = 2.2$, 1973 (2nd half)–1979 (2nd half)

An unanticipated surplus on the Japanese current account CAN leads to a yen appreciation (dollar depreciation). 'News' of a cyclical expansion in Japan CYN leads to a yen depreciation while 'news' of expansion in OECD countries, CYN*, leads to a yen appreciation. News concerning interest rate differentials is not found to be statistically significant.

Figure 5.3: Anticipated and Unanticipated Depreciation of the Dollar, February 1973–January 1980[a]

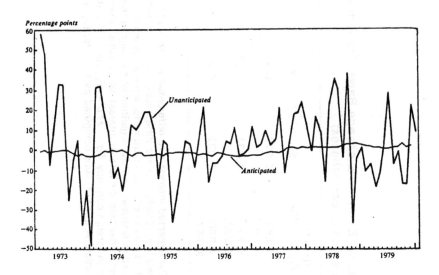

Sources: Dornbusch (1980).
a. The data are monthly, expressed at annual percentage rates. The unanticipated depreciation of the dollar is the difference between actual depreciation and anticipated depreciation. The exchange rate is the nominal effective rate. Anticipated depreciation is measured by short-term interest differentials between the United States and a trade-weighted average of the interest rates of five foreign countries. The weights equal those used in calculating the exchange rate.

(B) Illustrative Results: Forward Market. Frankel (1982) tests the EMH-constant risk premium hypothesis for the forward market, $s_t = \alpha' + \beta' f_{t-1} + \gamma' r_t + $ 'news' $+ w_t$. Representative results are shown in Table 5.3 for one month forward rates and three currencies: $/£, $/French franc, $/DM using an IV estimation technique.[6]

The *actual* interest differential is not significant in any of the three equations and, as hypothesised, interest rate 'news' is significant for the pound and the franc. The unexpected interest rate series consists of the residuals from a regression of d on its own lagged values and lagged values of the forward rate. The positive coefficient on interest rate 'news' Frankel interprets as unexpected changes in inflationary expectations which one would associate with a rise in the spot rate (depreciation). Clearly a negative coefficient is also plausible if unexpected changes in interest rates are seen as a reflection of tight monetary policy *à la* Dornbusch (1976). The news equation appears to be free of first order

Table 5.3: One-month Interest Rate Differentials and Forecast Errors of Exchange Rates; Instrumental Variables Monthly Data; June 1973–July 1979 (standard errors in parentheses)

Dependent variable $\ln S_t$	Constant	$\ln F_{t-1}$	$(r - r^*)_t$	$[(r-r^*)_t - E_{t-1}(r-r^*)_t]$	SE	R^2	DW
Dollar/pound	0.018 (0.017)	0.969 (0.022)	−0.156 (0.100)	0.562 (0.191)	0.023	0.97	1.81
Dollar/franc	−0.136 (0.112)	0.915 (0.076)	−0.312 (0.209)	0.547 (0.282)	0.031	0.75	2.19
Dollar/Deutschmark	0.002 (0.044)	0.996 (0.015)	−0.173 (0.286)	0.599 (0.457)	0.032	0.93	2.07

Source: Frenkel, 1982.

Note: Interest rates are the one-month (annualised) Euromarket rates. The expected interest rate differential $E_{t-1}(r - r^*)_t$ was computed from a regression of the interest differential on a constant, two lagged values of the differential, and the logarithm of the lagged forward exchange rate. Two stage least squares estimation method was used. The instruments were a constant, two lagged values of the interest differential, Durbin's rank variable of the unexpected differential, and the logarithm of the lagged forward exchange rate. $(r - r^*)_t$ denotes the actual interest rate differential where r denotes the rate of interest on securities denominated in US dollars and r^* denotes the rate of interest on securities denominated in foreign currency. $[(r - r^*)_t - E_{t-1}(r - r^*)_t]$ denotes the unexpected interest rate differential. SE is the standard error of the equation. A quasi-R^2 was computed as $1 - \text{Var}(u_t)/\text{var}(\ln S_t)$.

autocorrelation, unlike earlier regressions of s on f excluding 'news' variables (see Chapter 4) (although the only diagnostic statistic presented is the Durbin-Watson statistic for first order autocorrelation). Thus Frankel is able to accept the EMH and the absence of a risk premium since $\hat{\alpha}' = 0$, $\hat{\beta}' = 1$.

MacDonald (1983) provides a rather stronger test of the EMH-'news' view of the forward market. 'News' is represented by the unexpected components of both the *domestic* and *foreign* money supplies. The underlying model of the spot exchange rate being tested is therefore the CAM. An 'unexpected' money supply series is obtained from the residuals of a regression of money on several lagged values of the current account surplus, the budget deficit (or alternatively, government expenditure), the rate of inflation, real output and interest rates. For several countries the signs of these variables in the money supply regressions did not conform with *a priori* views (e.g. one might expect the budget deficit to have a positive coefficient). MacDonald's basic 'news regression' is of the form:

$$s_t - f_{t-1} = \alpha + \gamma_0(L) \ (m - E_{t-1}m_t) + \\ \gamma_2(L) \ (m^* - E_{t-1}m_t^*) + w_t \qquad (5.29)$$

where $\gamma_i(L)$ indicate that lagged 'news' about m may influence $s_t - f_{t-1}$. We expect the coefficient on the domestic monetary 'surprise' to be positive and that on the foreign monetary 'surprise' to be negative. Also if the forward market is efficient then lagged values of 'money surprises' should be insigificant, since these are already incorporated in f_{t-1}. Using quarterly data 1972 (1)–1979 (4) and Zellner's (1962) seemingly unrelated regression procedure (to take account of contemporaneous correlations of errors *across* equations), his results are rather unfavourable to both the EMH and the 'news' hypothesis for most of the six major currencies studied. Frequently no *current* period 'news' variables are significant and some are of the wrong sign. Lagged values of some of the 'news' variables are sometimes significant indicating that the EMH may not hold. Although the study is very thorough as far as it goes, nevertheless results should be interpreted with caution since IV estimation techniques are not used and the regression equation used to generate the expected money supply series is rather unsatisfactory, frequently having 'wrong signs'.

News and Single Equation Models of the Exchange Rate

The current account and capital account models discussed in Chapter 4 yield (reduced form) equations for the spot rate. Tests of these models that we have discussed exclude news variables. Our above analysis indicates that these equations may perform better if news variables are included. For example take the CAM model. The expected spot rate may be formed by looking at current and past values of the money supply, but Equation (5.25) indicates that an equation with the *actual* spot rate as the dependent variable requires additional 'news' variables. However if agents use RE then even if news variables are omitted the error in the exchange rate equation will still be 'white noise' and the parameters unbiased because of the orthogonality property of RE forecast errors, $X - X^e$.[7] But the test statistics used for hypothesis testing (e.g. *t*-statistics) will be misleading.

Tests of single equation models of the exchange rate that incorporate news variables are in their infancy. They appear to improve the within-sample fit of the equations but do not wholly overcome some of the problems outlined in previous chapters (see for example, Wickens and Smith, 1984; Davidson, 1982; and MacDonald, 1983).

Dornbusch Approach to the 'News' Hypothesis

Domestic Interest Rates and the Spot Rate. Dornbusch (1978) shows that a change in the exchange rate may be attributed to a component that is expected, having been anticipated in the interest differential (at time $t - 1$), and an unanticipated component reflecting fresh information or 'news'. This formulation enables one to test the 'news' hypothesis and also to explain why the exchange rate responds differently to anticipated and unanticipated changes in interest rates. The latter provides another way of resolving the paradox concerning the spot rate response to the interest rate, noted when discussing Frankel's (1979) real interest differential hypothesis (Chapter 4).

Earlier in this chapter we found that the EMH applied to the spot market, together with the assumption of a zero risk premium gives

$$E_{t-1}s_t = s_{t-1} + d_{t-1} \tag{5.30}$$

$$s_t = s_{t-1} + d_{t-1} + u_t \tag{5.31}$$

where u_t is the RE forecast error $(s_t - E_{t-1}s_t)$ and is independent of all information available at $t - 1$ or earlier and has zero mean.

Equation (5.31) predicts that a high positive interest differential, d_{t-1}, is associated with an increase in the spot rate $(s_t - s_{t-1} > 0)$, that is, a depreciation. As noted earlier (see Chapter 3), that is contrary to the portfolio view that a high differential leads to a capital in-flow and an appreciation in the exchange rate. The paradox may be resolved as follows. Consider individuals at time $t - 1$, with a *two* period decision ($t - 1$, to $t + 1$). Uncovered arbitrage gives:

$$E_{t-1}s_{t+1} - s_{t-1} = E_{t-1}d_t + d_{t-1}. \tag{5.32}$$

For a *one* period decision *at time t*, we have:

$$E_t s_{t+1} - s_t = d_t. \tag{5.33}$$

Subtracting (5.33) from (5.32) we obtain:

$$s_t = s_{t-1} + d_{t-1} + [(E_t s_{t+1} - E_{t-1}s_{t+1}) - (d_t - E_{t-1}d_t)] \tag{5.34}$$

But Equation (5.31) still holds, hence comparing (5.31) and (5.34):

$$u_t = [(E_t s_{t+1} - E_{t-1}s_{t+1}) - (d_t - E_{t-1}d_t)].$$

We may interpret Equation (5.34) as follows: d_{t-1} reflects the rate of depreciation between $t - 1$ and t that was expected at $t - 1$, ($s_t^e - s_{t-1} = d_{t-1}$). u_t, which equals the terms in square brackets, represents 'news' or unexpected events which form the basis of the RE forecast error. The unexpected component of the interest differential ($d_t - E_{t-1}d_t$), represents a *revision* of expectations about appreciation next period. The final term represents revisions to expectations formed at t and $t - 1$ about the exchange rate that is expected to prevail in period, $t + 1$. Equation (5.34) is an implication, solely, of the uncovered interest parity condition and it is independent of any specific model of exchange rate determination (such as the CAM).

According to Equation (5.34), an *un*anticipated increase in the interest differential ($d_t - E_{t-1}d_t$) leads to an appreciation in the exchange rate, while a known high interest differential d_{t-1} is associated with a depreciating exchange rate. (However if an unanticipated increase in the differential at time t leads to a re-appraisal concerning the expected rate then $E_t s_{t+1} - E_{t-1}s_{t+1}$ will change. In practice this may well occur and then the simple negative relation between $d_t - E_{t-1}d_t$ and s_t may not hold.) Disregarding the above caveat, if interest differentials at time $t - 1$ reflect underlying inflationary expectations then we would expect a rise in interest rates to lead to a depreciation as in the CAM-hyper-inflation model. An unanticipated reduction in the money supply, which causes an unanticipated increase in r will, according to Equation (5.34) yield an appreciation in the exchange rate, as in the Dornbusch KAM (1976) model. Thus both the CAM-hyper-inflation model and the

Dornbusch model may be accommodated in Equation (5.34).

According to the EMH and news approach the distinction between anticipated (expected) events and unanticipated events is crucial to an understanding of movements in the spot exchange rate, particularly in the short run. It may well be that the success of the CAM and KAM models in the early 1970s is due to the fact that complex difference terms in the 'independent variables' such as the money supply (e.g. Δm_{t-j}) and interest rates may act as a proxy for unanticipated events. For example if expectations about interest rates are formed according to the 'no change' view $E_{t-1}r_t = r_{t-1}$, then the unexpected change in interest rates, $r_t - E_{t-1}r_t$, is given by $r_t - r_{t-1} = \Delta r_t$. In more general terms one might expect $E_{t-1}r_t = \gamma(L)r_{t-1}$ where $\gamma(L)$ is the lag operator. In this case current and lagged values of r_t which often appear in empirical versions of these exchange rate models may act as a proxy for unexpected changes.

Summary and Conclusions

The following are the main conclusions to emerge from our analysis of the EMH/news approach to behaviour in the spot and forward market. These conclusions represent our own view of the conflicting evidence on these matters: others may believe the balance of the evidence points to different conclusions.

(1)   For homogeneous assets such as eurodollar deposits any deviations from *uncovered* interest parity may be attributed to transactions costs (in non-crisis or 'tranquil' periods). Covered arbitrage between such assets conforms to the EMH. This result should not be surprising given our (Cambist) analysis of the role of banks in the forward market discussed in the previous chapter.

(2)   For non-homogeneous assets (e.g. UK and US Treasury Bills) the evidence for an infinitely elastic arbitrage schedule remains an open question. There may therefore be scope for the authorities to influence covered arbitrage flows and hence the spot rate by intervention in the forward market.

(3)   The forward rate does not appear to be an unbiased predictor of the future spot rate and *un*covered interest parity does not appear to hold in speculative *spot* market transactions. However the results support the view that the elasticity of substitution between domestic and foreign assets may be high and certainly higher than estimates

obtained in the previous chapter from equations for spot capital flows and for the forward rate equation of the 'modern theory'.

(4)   The results in (3) do not necessarily reject the EMH. We could have chosen an incorrect 'equilibrium' model of the exchange rate, measured expectations incorrectly or failed to take adequate account of a (possibly time varying) risk premium. The existence of serial correlation in some of the equations used to test the EMH is indicative of a time varying risk premium. However, the fact that variables known at the time the forecasts of future exchange rates are made influence the forecast error, seems to reject the EMH. The apparent failure of the EMH may be due to a number of factors. It may be that regime changes (including changes in the rules governing the authorities' intervention in the market) may require a period of learning and the RE-EMH does not allow for this.[8] It is always possible that in the short run the exchange rate may deviate from its true underlying determinants because of irrational speculative 'bubbles'. One may continue to hold a currency even if 'fundamentals' dictate otherwise because if others act on whim, rumour or fashion (in the very short run) this may lead to a rise in its value. In short, some agents may not know the 'true' model yet their collective actions may influence the rate in the short run. Clearly 'outsiders', maybe even company treasurers, would be taking a large risk if they took an open speculative position on the basis of such rumours.

(5)   Incorporating 'news' into the EMH does not alter the conclusions concerning market efficiency noted above. 'News' does help to explain the short-run (e.g. monthly) volatility of the spot and forward rate. The response of the spot rate to anticipated and unanticipated changes in economic variables is likely to be very different. Whether unanticipated changes are expected to persist or not also leads to different movements in the spot rate.

For example an anticipated increase in interest rates is unlikely to influence the current spot rate when the increase actually occurs since in an efficient market it will already have been incorporated in the spot rate. Also an unanticipated increase in the domestic interest rate which is expected to persist may lead to a revision in expectations concerning the future value of the exchange rate and hence the current spot rate may alter (overshoot) substantially.

In short, the notion that the exchange rate is determined in a well organised 'spot auction' market has considerably enhanced our understanding of the behaviour of the spot exchange rate and its relationship to the forward rate. The failure of formal tests of the EMH may well be due to the fact that agents take time to learn about regime changes caused for example by changes in external events or in the way the authorities' policy rules (behaviour) changes. The analysis of how agents learn about changes in their environment is likely to provide a rewarding area for future research into the efficient markets approach.

Notes

1. We shall not be directly concerned with the *consistency* property of RE. But for completeness this property of REH simply states that it is impossible to know in advance how one will change one's expectations. For example if speculators knew in January that in three months' time they would alter their expectation of the spot rate for July, then they should use that information today to alter their view of the spot rate for six months hence, formed in January. To ignore such information would (by definition) be irrational.

2. Efficiency can be more precisely defined with respect to the information set I_t. The market is said to be 'weakly efficient' if a trader cannot make abnormal returns using only the past history of the 'price' about which expectations are being formed. For 'semi-strong form efficiency' the information set is broader and includes *all* publicly available information. 'Strong form efficiency' holds when abnormal profits cannot be made when *all* public and private information is known by the trader. In the text we simplify matters by referring only to 'efficiency' where the latter covers 'weak-form' and 'semi-strong form' efficiency only.

3. The conundrum is resolved by noting that data are only collected at discrete intervals, while the EMH assumes that the process of arbitrage has already occurred *within* the period.

4. The regressions are actually computed using the first differences of the variables to obtain 'stationarity'. It is not clear therefore that the results reject the unbiasedness property in terms of the *levels* of the forward and expected spot rates. However, if as here, a regression in differences of the variables has white noise errors a regression in levels of the variables *may* exhibit *residual* serial correlation. If the latter is indicative of error autocorrelation then the unbiasedness property will not hold in the levels of the variables. Differences versus levels equations is a highly contentious area of econometrics at present and no clear cut inferences can be made in moving from difference regressions to regressions in levels (see Hendry and Mizon, 1978; and the reply by Williams, 1978). The unbiasedness property also predicts that the *change* in the spot rate depends upon the forward/discount, $f_t - s_t$, that is

$$s_{t+1} - s = (f - s) + u_t. \tag{i}$$

A regression in only *differences* of the variables s and f is not a special case (nested version) of (i) and hence is not a test of the unbiasedness property in the form (i).

5. Serially correlated errors may arise if the maturity date of the forward contract exceeds the frequency of observations. For example, if we use the one month forward rate and weekly data the error term follows a third order moving average process. In the text we ignore this technical issue by having the data period the same as the maturity period on the forward contract. Minford and Peel (1983) also make the important technical point that if agents have incomplete current information at the time the forward rate is set, then the error term will also follow a moving average error process the order of which is

determined by the length of the information lag. The latter provides a further plausible reason why autocorrelation might occur in tests of the EMH in the forward market. Thus the presence of serial correlation may not be indicative of the failure of the EMH.

6. The equation is estimated using instrumental variables but as Durbin's rank variable (Durbin, 1954) is used as an instrument the coefficients will be biased.

7. If news variables are erroneously omitted from the spot rate equation then in the language of econometrics the parameter estimates will be consistent but not 'efficient' (where the latter means 'minimum variance').

8. B. Friedman (1979) has argued that agents can never determine an unbiased estimate of the true parameter even when there are no regime changes. It follows from his analysis that we should not expect the orthogonality property of RE to hold.

Part 1: Further Reading

An introduction to the terminology used by professionals in the foreign exchange market may be found in the books by Heywood (1981) and Kenyon (1981), with a slightly more academic approach in McKinnon (1979) and Llewellyn (1980). The latter two books also deal extensively with the forward market for foreign exchange and provide more detail than herein on the eurocurrency markets. Those readers specifically interested in eurocurrency markets should also consult Johnston (1983). Beenstock (1978) provides a useful survey of empirical results on the determinants of the forward rate and capital flows.

Purchasing power parity (PPP) is discussed in a number of articles in the *Journal of International Economics* (1978); in particular see Krugman (1978). Frenkel (1981) and Haikko (1984) provide recent surveys.

Accounts of the CAM and KAM models are to be found mainly in journal articles. On the former see the articles in the special issue of the *Scandinavian Journal of Economics* (1976), and Bilson (1978). The seminal article on KAM is Dornbusch (1976) which is also discussed with other open economy models in Dornbusch (1980). Extensions of the basic Dornbusch model are to be found in a special issue of *Oxford Economic Papers* (1981); and in particular see Haache and Townend (1981).

The literature on the empirical evidence of the EMH and the role of 'news' in explaining the volatility of exchange rates is voluminous; useful starting points include: Mussa (1979); Frenkel and Mussa (1980); Frenkel (1981b). For evidence on whether the forward rate is an unbiased predictor of future spot rates see: Bilson (1981); Frankel (1980); Hansen and Hodrick (1980). For a clear introduction to the rational expectations hypothesis see Attfield *et al.* (1985).

PART 2

ALTERNATIVE EXCHANGE RATE REGIMES

There has been no shortage of ideas and suggestions about how the international monetary system should be run. Practice has varied considerably, from the gold standard before the First World War to floating exchange rates after it and then back to the gold standard in 1925. The Second World War saw the formation of the Bretton Woods system of fixed-but-adjustable exchange rates backed by the International Monetary Fund (IMF) to aid international liquidity. In the 1960s the fixed exchange rate system came under increasing pressure and collapsed altogether at the beginning of the 1970s. The ensuing system of flexible exchange rates between the main trading countries has operated in a number of different ways since then with different levels of intervention by the authorities.

Not only has there been variation in the system as time has passed but there is very considerable variation in the way exchange rates are determined across the world at any one time. At present some exchange rates are floating — sterling and the dollar for example. Others are floating but with rather more official intervention, such as the Greek drachma. All the EC countries with the exception of the UK and Greece are members of a joint float through the Exchange Rate Mechanism of the European Monetary System (EMS), in which their currencies only move by a limited amount against each other but float more freely together against the other major currencies. Many of the smaller countries either peg their currencies to a major currency such as the US dollar, or peg it to a weighted basket of currencies, where the weights are related to the importance of the countries in their foreign trade. Thus, for example, the Norwegian, Swedish and Finnish currencies tend to move fairly closely together because of their strong trading links.

This part of the book is divided into three chapters. In the first, Chapter 6, we seek to explain the evolution of the exchange rate system since the Second World War and examine some of the major alternative regimes and their properties. In particular we look at fixed rate regimes, concentrating primarily on the system set up by the Bretton Woods agreement in 1944 which lasted until the early 1970s. Then in Chapter 7, we consider the European Monetary System (EMS), beginning with its origins in what was known as the 'snake', so called because of the way the currencies fluctuated within a narrow band in a system which was first fixed and then floated against third countries. We also look forward to the ways in which the EMS can develop in aiding the integration of the EC countries.

In the reminder of Part 2, Chapter 8 covers other major exchange rate regimes which have been tried or are currently used and are documented in Table 8.1. Among these are dual exchange rate systems such as that currently practised by Belgium, the investment currency market which existed in the UK, the 'crawling peg' system and other similar slowly-moving exchange rate regimes such as that which has been employed by New Zealand.

Most of these systems are used either to enable the imposition of selective controls on certain categories of transactions while permitting convertibility of the currency in the general run of transactions or to ease the speed of adjustment. There is considerable argument over whether a sudden step devaluation by a relatively large amount which the market does not anticipate is a more satisfactory method of depreciating the currency than a clearly announced series of small steps over a longer period of time. While the latter may enable asset holders to cover themselves against much of the adverse effect of the change on their wealth it may also remove much of the short-run gain to economic activity thought to stem from a devaluation.

In the final section we consider examples of trade where currency is not used directly, first in the bilateral agreements with the Eastern bloc countries, and second in the rapid rise in 'counter trade' which has taken place in the wake of the balance of payments difficulties encountered by developing countries following the second oil crisis.

Each of the systems has various merits and drawbacks and it is unlikely that any one system could be described as optimal for all time periods or indeed for all countries at the same time. 'Fixed' exchange rates, for example, permit greater certainty in planning transactions and hence are likely to lead to increased trade. However, when the rates are fixed but adjustable the uncertainty returns, especially since under those circumstances the realignments of parties are likely to be substantial. Fixed rates also entail that countries must correct external imbalances by altering the overall stance of their economic policy, thus leading to conflicts between external and internal objectives. Flexible rates on the other hand allow continuous adjustment which may avoid massive destabilising capital flows in an open market. They also permit national authorities to influence domestic inflation rates in a way not possible under the fixed rate system. However, one problem with all such systems is that they are circular. For some countries to move up others must move down, for some to run deficits others must run surpluses. In unconstrained systems attempts by several countries to move simultaneously in the same direction will not only be self-defeating but may result in more deflation or indeed inflation than is necessary to achieve the self-same result.

6 THE EVOLUTION OF THE EXCHANGE RATE SYSTEM SINCE THE SECOND WORLD WAR

The Bretton Woods System

The exchange rate system which dominated the 1950s and 1960s was evolved during the war and came into force despite the plethora of war-time controls which persisted as the major industrialised countries sought to restructure themselves onto a balanced peace time footing and to repair and replace assets that had been damaged or destroyed. It is a tribute to the thought which went into these arrangements that they came into force and endured so long. The system was set up at an international conference at Bretton Woods, New Hampshire in the United States during July 1944 after two years of development, principally between Keynes and others in the United Kingdom and Harry Dexter White from the US Treasury.

The main purpose of the Bretton Woods proposals was to establish a system of trade and payments which would enable rapid recovery and economic growth after the war. The proponents appreciated that the participants would come out of the war with very unbalanced economies and were concerned that in trying to get matters right and achieve the necessary structural change they would not resort to the protection and competitive devaluations which characterised the 1930s when countries tried to recover from the slump.

The major feature of the Bretton Woods proposals was the setting up of the International Monetary Fund (IMF). This institution was intended to be the vehicle of international monetary co-operation through which the members could sort out their difficulties. The system was intended to enable orderly international payments, which were free of restrictions, at stable exchange rates. It was appreciated that to achieve such a system countries would have to be able to run deficits in the short run while they adjusted their domestic policies to achieve what was described as balanced development in the long run. To do this it was necessary to set up a Fund, to which all the members subscribed, from which loans could be made to countries which were in 'temporary' deficit under terms which would ensure that the deficits were relatively quickly eliminated.

The exchange rate system envisaged involved each member state establishing a par value for its currency in terms of gold or, equivalently, in terms of the US dollar. The price of gold was fixed in terms of US dollars at $35 per ounce. They would then maintain the actual rate of exchange within 1 per cent of this par value. As long as the dollar maintained free convertibility with gold it automatically adhered to this position. Other countries would have to maintain their rates by buying or selling dollars or gold. Exchange rates could only be varied outside the limits with the IMF's approval, which could only be given if a country was in 'fundamental disequilibrium'. Thus the system was intended to be one of fixed exchange rates and reflected a pre-existing commitment to the 'gold standard' by the United States (see the next section).

Countries were given quotas in the Fund which approximated to their relative economic size. These quotas determined both subscriptions and the size of borrowings that could be made. Member countries could draw on their quotas in a series of equal sized tranches. The first quarter could be drawn without restriction but thereafter the conditions imposed increased in severity to force the country to eliminate the cause of the borrowing. Thus under this sort of system of fixed exchange rates the member countries had to use domestic policies to eliminate balance of payments difficulties which could not be met by use of their own foreign exchange reserves or by the first tranches of borrowing from the IMF. Such moves would involve some combination of monetary and fiscal policy, raising interest rates to encourage an inflow of funds or cutting back the demand for imports relative to exports, say by deflation.

One of the problems of this system is that the major onus is on the deficit countries to adjust whereas of course, taking the world as a whole, surpluses exactly equal deficits. This problem was most acute immediately after the war when there was a major shortage of dollars. Countries hit hard by the war needed to import food and manufactured goods because their own productive capacity had been cut back and also needed to import capital goods to set up further production in the future. The United States had the least affected manufacturing industry and an agricultural surplus so Europe rapidly ran up a deficit. This shortage of dollars was offset in 1947 by the offer of Marshall Aid which led to the formation of the Organisation for European Economic Cooperation (OEEC), which was the precursor of the Organisation for Economic Co-operation and Development (OECD) which exists today. The conditions of Marshall Aid deliberately tried to rectify the problems causing the dollar shortage, encouraging non-dollar trade and exports to the dollar area.

This in itself proved insufficient and in 1949 the United Kingdom decided to devalue by some 30 per cent. This was the first major change of parities under the Bretton Woods system and it revealed some of the problems in it. The actual size of the devaluation 'required' is difficult to estimate as it depends upon a complex set of international responses. It is widely argued that the UK devaluation was too great first because it encouraged most other European countries to devalue as well, hence the United Kingdom gained no competitive edge over them. Secondly because of the size of the devaluation the changes in output required to adjust the balance of trade to the new relative prices were greater than could be undertaken quickly. As a consequence some of the adjustment took the form of relative prices increases which eroded some of the original gain. The whole subject of the relation between devaluation and price inflation is developed in Part 3 of the book. Suffice it to say at this point that while devaluation lowers the price of exports to foreign purchasers it simultaneously raises the costs of imports in the home market. Although the full price rise may not be passed on, both through substitution by domestically produced products and through reductions in importers' margins, a proportion of the effect will filter through to domestic costs and hence domestic price inflation. These price increases will themselves contribute to a boost to the price–wage spiral affecting all prices throughout the economy, including export prices. It is thus an empirical matter whether and how quickly the initial price advantage is eroded.

The whole analysis was upset by the advent of the Korean War in 1950 which led to a massive boom in raw material prices — measured in dollars — which did much to annul the effects of the devaluation within a short period of time. However, from 1950 onwards the United States moved from being a surplus country to being one with a deficit and this totally altered the complexion of the Bretton Woods system and enhanced its chances of success. These deficits enabled the European countries to build up their foreign exchange reserves with dollars for trading. 1950 also saw the formation of the European Payments Union under which the European countries were able to pool their reserves of scarce dollars and provide a measure of guaranteed credit from those in surplus to those in deficit. The co-operation was a precursor of the more extensive arrangement involved with the European Monetary System, which is discussed in the next chapter. Aided by these changes the Bretton Woods system developed well and the European countries grew rapidly in the 1950s, seeing the formation of the European Community (EC) and European Free Trade Association (EFTA). During the same period restrictions on currency transactions were removed and by the end of the decade the Bretton Woods system was very much as intended by its designers.

There had been some deviations — the Canadians elected to float their currency for much of the period (1950–62) and France devalued in 1957 and 1958 but the system worked well as long as the US deficits could be tolerated and the European surpluses accepted. Although the Marshall Plan terminated in 1952, partly as Europe appeared to be able to stand on its own feet, US net transfers to Europe continued at a high level. The dollar in effect operated as the universal reserve currency rather than gold.

By 1959 the position began to change as US overseas liabilities began to reach equality with her gold reserves. On the other side of the coin West German surpluses also began to cause concern by 1960. In the short run, deflation of the American economy and revaluation of the mark in 1961 served to resolve the difficulties. However, further restrictions on the dollar out-flow became necessary in the 1960s with the Interest Equalisation Tax being imposed in 1963 to discourage private US portfolio investment abroad.

As the 1960s progressed it also became clear that the United Kingdom was having problems coping with the system (see Table 6.1). In the years of fastest growth (1951, 1955, 1960), the UK had moved into substantial deficit; a pattern repeated again in 1964. However, in the ensuing years it became increasingly difficult to prevent deficits despite quite restrictive domestic measures, and in 1967 the pound was devalued for a second time. Even in nominal terms the UK foreign exchange reserves failed to grow from their peak of $3¼ billion in 1950 after the 1949 devaluation and, with an increase in trade from £3½ billion to more than $6 billion over the period 1950–67, these reserves covered an increasingly small proportion of transactions. In one sense this was symptomatic of a general problem of the low rate of increase in international reserves which still restricts the international payments system in the 1980s. It meant that countries could not accommodate some of the fluctuations in financial flows readily in the short run and were either pushed into interest rate changes which were unwelcome for domestic policy or to changing the exchange rate's peg. Quite naturally, during the 1960s there were extensive discussions over how the system could be reformed to get round some of its drawbacks but none was implemented before the devaluation of sterling.

What is particular interesting about the way in which the Bretton Woods system was operated is that although countries were permitted to change exchange rates (with approval) they went to great lengths to

Table 6.1: United Kingdom Current Balance and Official Reserves 1946–75

	£ million Current balance	$ million UK official reserves* (at end of period)
1946	− 230	2,696
1947	− 381	2,079
1948	+ 26	1,856
1949	− 1	1,688
1950	+ 307	3,300
1951	− 369	2,335
1952	+ 163	1,846
1953	+ 145	2,518
1954	+ 117	2,762
1955	− 155	2,120
1956	+ 208	2,133
1957	+ 233	2,273
1958	+ 360	3,069
1959	+ 172	2,736
1960	− 228	3,231
1961	+ 47	3,318
1962	+ 155	2,806
1963	+ 125	2,658
1964	− 328	2,315
1965	− 30	3,004
1966	+ 130	3,100
1967	− 269	2,694
1968	− 244	2,421
1969	+ 505	2,528
1970	+ 823	2,827
1971	+ 1,124	6,582
1972	+ 247	5,646
1973	− 981	6,476
1974	− 3,273	6,789
1975	− 1,521	5,429

Source: *Economic Trends*.
* Apart from transactions, the level of official reserves has been affected since 1970 by changes in the valuation of gold, Special Drawing Rights and convertible currencies. In addition, from July 1972, the official reserves were re-defined to include the reserve position in the IMF.

avoid doing so. The UK used substantial holdings of reserves and arranged various credits with other central banks in an effort to support the pound during 1964–7. By the end of the crisis the UK had borrowed $8 billion to try to keep sterling within the permitted bounds and yet had nevertheless had to devalue. In fact it did not take long to repay most of this debt after the UK balance of payments moved into surplus in 1969.

A major problem with the Bretton Woods system was the asymmetry of adjustment for surplus and deficit countries. While deficit countries were forced towards devaluation no corresponding pressures to revalue were felt by surplus countries, which could maintain their exchange rates and accumulate reserves. Such pressures might only be felt if the increased capital in-flows led to unwelcome pressure on the domestic money supply.

Gold and Gold Standards

In the Bretton Woods system the dollar was pegged to gold and all other currencies were pegged to the dollar. Hence the international price of gold was in effect fixed. However, gold has more uses than purely as an international reserve asset for central banks. Consequently throughout the period there was a thriving gold market, particularly in London. With the variations in supply and demand for gold which developed during the late 1950s it became necessary for central banks to collude to keep the market price of gold close to its official $35/oz convertible value — otherwise it would have paid any central bank which did not wish to participate to speculate in the market. Shortly after the devaluation of sterling in 1967 it became apparent that this system could not be maintained indefinitely in view of the very high rate at which the US particularly was having to sell gold from its reserves to keep the market price down. The eventual result was that in March 1968 the central bank market for gold was divorced from the private market and a two-tier system operated (until November 1973).

The problem was that convertibility of the dollar with gold no longer appeared credible. Dollar holders therefore sought to convert their assets into gold before the price rose, thereby forcing just that rise. To a major extent this problem was exacerbated by the large surpluses of dollars flowing out of the United States as a result of expenditure related to the Vietnam war. Once the two-tier market was formed there was little incentive to transact at the $35/oz price and the world system had effectively moved to a dollar standard.

Before the two-tier market the Bretton Woods system operated in many ways very much like a gold standard since the dollar remained convertible into gold at a fixed price. In the gold standard systems of the period up to the First World War and between 1925 and 1931 each currency was pegged to gold and gold could be freely traded between countries. However, it also had the feature that in effect each currency was backed by gold. Although not 100 per cent of the bank notes issued may have been backed by gold, the proportionate cover was sufficient not to call the system into question. If a country suffered an outflow of gold it would need to deflate to return to balance and similarly a surplus currency country would need to do the reverse. Since gold would in effect form part of the money supply some of this change would be automatic.

While the gold standard appeared to work quite well in the years before the First World War this was partly because of the dominant role of sterling in the system. The UK ran surpluses in most years on current account and varied her overseas investment largely to match fluctuations in those surpluses (Argy, 1981). Argy suggests five other contributory factors: a relatively stable period free from wars, highly co-ordinated economic cycles among the main countries, careful monetary policies, a readily functioning adjustment mechanism and an adequate supply of gold.

These features point to the difficulties that can emerge from any fixed rate system whether gold based or not. It has difficulty coping with large fluctuations in economic fortunes — as in other markets price as well as quantity adjustment is necessary. Large deficits and surpluses will appear if countries do not follow the same growth paths. It is not possible to run a monetary policy with different domestic aims if this does not result in an acceptable international balance. If the process of adjustment is very difficult, as the UK found in the 1960s, the system has to give way; and lastly, as in the case of the dollar after the war, serious problems occur if the reserve asset is in short supply. Since supply of new reserve assets under a currency standard is in effect determined by the current account surplus of the country whose currency forms the reserve asset, in this case the dollar, that country needs to follow a macroeconomic policy which is acceptable to all the participant countries in the system if the arrangement is to continue. The collapse of the gold standard in the inter-war years was also related to these factors, the Depression proved too big a shock, adjustment seemed to be more difficult to achieve and economic cycles were not so well co-ordinated.

Additionally, in moving to a fixed rate system it is important to fix the rates well at the outset. It is widely thought, for example, that when the UK rejoined the gold standard in 1925 it did so at too high a parity. Again after the Second World War parities could not be maintained and were extensively adjusted in 1949. The post-war problem with gold and with reserve assets in general was simply that their magnitude and distribution was not sufficient to enable the international system to expand and for various countries to adjust their surpluses and deficits at steady rates. By 1967 it was clear that convertibility of the dollar into gold would have to cease as increasing monetary and non-monetary demand for gold drove the gold reserves down and threatened to drive the price up. While the two-tier system alleviated the problem in the short run it was clear that the only solution of a more permanent nature was to expand international reserves by creating further reserve assets. The further assets, called 'Special Drawing Rights', were eventually created after a great deal of discussion, in 1968. Although they did not come into operation until 1970.

SDRs are somewhat odd. They represent the right to obtain foreign exchange through the IMF and can perhaps be thought of as 'artificial gold'. The amount of SDRs available in total is determined by the Fund in relation to estimated international liquidity needs, and the amount allocated to an individual country is proportionate to its ability to borrow under the normal quotas from the Fund. This need for international liquidity by each individual country is directly related to the size of its international trade and its overall level of domestic economic activity. They are in effect a book entry for transactions between central banks to settle their international payments. A country can borrow SDRs from the IMF and use them to settle its debts. Drawings within the allocated limit for any country can be made at any time provided that the average drawing does not exceed 30 per cent of the allocation over a five year period. Recipient countries which are members of the IMF are obliged to accept SDRs in payment up to a holding of three times their own allocation under the scheme. The value of an SDR was initially set equal to $1 and hence to 1/35 oz gold. IMF members are not compelled to enter the SDR scheme. Only central banks and authorities of countries are allowed to hold SDRs.

As is clear from Table 6.2, SDRs have not been used extensively compared to total reserves in the world system but their drawings have been quite substantial in the context of total borrowings from the IMF. Table 6.2 also illustrates the way in which reserves have provided a decreasing cushion for fluctuations in trade balances and current account deficits in general. Up to 1969 the ratio of trade to reserves rose steadily. A second surge took place with the first oil crisis in 1974 and yet a third increase in the ratio has occurred since 1978. The size of trade is not so important in these calculations as is the sum of countries' surpluses and deficits. Reserves are used to finance net payments rather than trade as a whole.

Table 6.2: International Reserves and their Relation to World Trade (SDR bn)

Year	Total reserves[d] (1)	SDRs (2)	World trade (3)	Ratio of trade to reserves (%) (4)
1950	46[c]		56	122
1955	54		94	174
1960	60		128	213
1965	71		186	262
1966	73		204	279
1967	74		215	291
1968	78		239	306
1969	79		272	344
1970	93	3	312	335
1971	123	6	321	261
1972	147	9	382	260
1973	152	9	475	313
1974	180	9	684	380
1975	194	9	746	385
1976	223	9	851	382
1977	266	8	926	348
1978	283	8	996	352
1979	307	12	1243	404
1980	355	12	1563	440
1981	370	16	1692	457
1982	365	18		
1983	390[a]	19[b]		

Source: IMF, *Financial Statistics*. UN, *International Trade Yearbooks*.
a. September.
b. October.
c. 1949.
d. End year.

The Collapse of the Bretton Woods System

As we mentioned earlier, systems of fixed exchange rates seem to be accompanied by pleas for more flexibility while systems of flexible exchange rates are accompanied by pleas for more stability. However, the Bretton Woods system became increasingly difficult for countries to operate as divergences in their balances occurred and imbalance appeared to be increasingly difficult to eliminate. We have seen how the UK was obliged to devalue in 1967. In 1968 the disturbances coupled with an already weak foreign sector led to pressure for a French devaluation. The reverse pressure applied in Germany where continuing surpluses and strong growth led to massive in-flows of funds in anticipation of a revaluation. Eventually France did indeed devalue, by 11 per cent, in August 1969. The following month the mark was floated and a new parity some 9 per cent higher was fixed in October. In both cases considerable lengths had been gone to in order to avoid these exchange rate changes. The German economy was expanded and the French deflated. The Germans introduced a border tax and the French arranged large credits. Nevertheless the exchange rate changes were not avoided, merely postponed.

However, the Bretton Woods system was effectively killed by the weakness in the dollar in 1970–1. After a recession in 1969 with a surplus on the balance of payments, the US economy expanded during 1970 and 1971. As a result the US current account moved heavily into deficit, coupled with an out-flow of short-run capital as US interest rates fell relative to those in most of the other developed countries. One country's out-flow is another's in-flow, which was reflected in increasing upward pressure on some European currencies, principally the mark and the guilder. At the same time discussions of means of increased flexibility in exchange rates, fuelled partly by the brief float of the mark in 1969, made a change in the system more likely. The Canadian dollar had begun floating again in 1970. By mid-1971 the Bundesbank could not cope with the speculative in-flow any longer. The mark and the guilder were allowed to float and Austria and Switzerland revalued. This reaction to pressure on the mark was aided by the existence of money supply targets which restricted the expansionary route to accommodation of it.

Interestingly enough the upward float was very slow despite the massive flows of payments that had taken place. It thus appeared that relatively small movements in exchange rates might be all that was necessary to prevent the massive destabilising flows of short-term capital which had occurred, starting with the British crisis in 1967. However, the pressure on the dollar continued and the American government was forced in August 1971 to end convertibility with gold, to raise taxes, cut federal expenditures and impose a 10 per cent import surcharge.

Ending convertibility with gold broke the formal link in the fixed exchange rate system but in any case the disturbance to the international monetary system had been such that it was not clear where new stable rates should be fixed. A period of confusion followed. In December a re-alignment of currencies was agreed at the Smithsonian Institution in Washington with the dollar being devalued to $38 per ounce with respect to gold and the main other currencies being revalued by varying amounts with respect to the dollar: yen 16 per cent, Swiss franc 14 per cent, mark

13½ per cent, guilder and Belgian franc 11½ per cent, sterling and French franc 8½ per cent and the lira and Swedish krona by 7½ per cent. The overall change in the dollar was thus approximately 10 per cent with respect to the main currencies and 7½ per cent overall as many other currencies maintained their dollar parities.

A measure of greater flexibility was also introduced with countries being permitted to allow their currencies to fluctuate 2¼ per cent either side of their central parities compared with the earlier 1 per cent. However, the underlying changes in the approach to exchange rate determination were really rather fundamental. It had been shown that multiple independent floating of currencies was possible in an ordered manner. The burden of adjustment in the system could not be just one sided, the United States would have to play a similar role in the system to everyone else. 'Benign neglect' was an insufficient approach. This was in part an outcome of the rapid relative increase in the economic strength of the other major Western countries (including Japan). Lastly, it had been shown that major speculative movements in short-term capital could not be fought off without either major domestic distortions or a change in the rate of exchange.

The Creation of the System of Floating Exchange Rates

The Smithsonian agreement was an attempt at reform within the generalised framework of the Bretton Woods system but its existence was rather fragile. The EC countries attempted a closer alignment of their currencies, permitting only 1¼ per cent variations round their central or par values, sustained by more co-operation in the intervention of their central banks. This closer alignment, known as the 'snake' is discussed in more detail in Chapter 7.

The UK had participated briefly in the snake in mid-1972 in anticipation of its membership of the EC in 1973, however, within a few weeks the pound had to be floated separately. In early 1973 there was further pressure on the system resulting first in the floating of the Swiss franc and second in the devaluation of the dollar by a further 10 per cent. The yen was floated at the same time and shortly thereafter the EC currencies, excluding sterling, began a joint float. March 1973 thus represents the end of the fixed rate system and although there have been various moves to limit fluctuations the major currencies have all been floated since that date. Although the dollar was nominally fixed in terms of gold at $42.22 per ounce the free market price was double that and hence

Table 6.3

	SDR weights %	
	1 July 1974	1 July 1984
US dollar	33.0	42
Deutschmark	12.5	19
UK Sterling	9.0	13
French franc	7.5	13
Japanese yen	7.5	13
Italian lira	6.0	
Canadian dollar	6.0	
Dutch guilder	4.5	
Belgian franc	3.5	
Swedish krona	2.5	
Spanish peseta	1.5	
Norwegian krona	1.5	
Australian dollar	1.5	
Danish krona	1.5	
Austrian schilling	1.0	
South African rand	1.0	

transactions did not normally take place at the official rate.

Some further changes to put the floating exchange rate system on a fully organised basis was still required as, unlike the Bretton Woods system, it had evolved rather than been created according to a carefully planned set of steps. The first was the breaking of the link between the SDR and gold. In July 1974 the SDR was defined in terms of a basket of the 16 most important currencies in international transactions and thus thereafter it reflected the relative movement in all those currencies. The weights have been adjusted on a number of occasions since then and the current weights are also shown in Table 6.3. At the same time changes to end the fixed price of gold were set in train so that eventually countries could, when necessary, use their gold reserves at market prices, which effectively increased world liquidity.

The second main change was that the position of the IMF has become rather anachronistic without the fixed rate system and amendments to the articles of agreement were clearly required. These took some time to develop and although they were largely agreed in 1976 they did not come into force until 1978. They legitimised the forms of fixing exchange rates currently practised: pegging to SDRs or other currencies, cooperative arrangements, and 'other' arrangements. However, the option of returning to stable but adjustable par values was also included. The IMF's explicit role in the system in providing 'firm surveillance' was set out so that members behaved in a manner 'to assure orderly exchange arrangements and to promote a stable system of exchange rates'. Principles were put forward to members to try to ensure orderly economic growth and reasonable price stability. To these ends countries were enjoined not to intervene in a destablishing manner and were obliged to try to maintain a system which avoided erratic disruptions.

To some extent these remarks were rather more expressions of hope as the means of co-ordination and avoidance of fluctuations were not set out. However, it did express the fears that a floating regime could be unstable and that member countries could by their actions reduce or increase that instability.

The generality of the remarks about the exchange rate systems permitted were necessary in the light of the variety of systems actually implemented — as is set out in Table 8.1. In terms of number of currencies, the most widespread system adopted has been a rate pegged to a major currency, most frequently the US dollar. This choice often reflects the main currency of invoicing of foreign trade — take the case of the former French colonies, which are pegged to the French franc, for example. These rates will not of course be fixed with respect to other currencies which are not pegged to the same major currency. They will vary against them by the same amount that the major currency varies. This fixing to a major currency gives credibility to the minor currency. Similarly its external debt is normally denominated in foreign currencies in part to remove the risk of deliberate devaluation of the holding by the borrower.

Countries which have chosen to peg to the SDR or some other weighted basket of currencies will find their exchange rates fluctuating with respect to all other currencies except those which are pegged in exactly the same way. One of the reasons for pegging to a composite is to try to fix the exchange rate with respect to the country's trade pattern, as in the case of Sweden, Finland and Norway. This minimises the effect of variations in the other exchange rates on the country's balance of payments. However, the greater the difference between the import and export trade patterns the less these fluctuations can be eliminated. Such attempts at choosing the appropriate basket can only be approximate as the exact impact of the goods traded is altered by the currency of invoicing which may not be that of either the supplier of the purchaser. The ideal basket would probably be set in terms of the distribution of the currencies used in the country's international payments.

These fixed rate systems are in one sense even more fixed than the Bretton Woods system, which did permit fluctuations round central rates within 1 per cent bounds. The two groups of currencies shown in the middle section of Table 8.1 reflect a version rather nearer the previous system with limited fluctuations permitted round a single currency, the dollar, in the case of the first group, and round each other in the case of the European Monetary System, whose members form the second group. The remaining currencies move more flexibly but only those in the last column are floating in the traditional sense of the term. Even then this does not tell us how managed the float is, merely that it does not involve the following of some explicit rule. It does not prevent the following of an exchange rate policy by the countries involved. Indeed it is clear that some have done so, manipulating interest rates and intervening in the market to try to achieve particular objectives. In the next chapter we explore one of these parts of the current international system of exchange rates in more detail — the European Monetary System.

7 THE EUROPEAN MONETARY SYSTEM

Antecedents

The European Monetary System (EMS) and its precursors can be thought of as reflecting two requirements of its members. The first is simply relative stability of exchange rates and the second the operation of a monetary system appropriate to the transactions and co-operation required between the members of the European Community (EC). When the 'snake' came into being in April 1972 it was in the context of the Smithsonian agreement of fixed but more widely adjustable exchange rates. The snake quite deliberately cut down the range of fluctuations permitted between the member countries from the 2¼ per cent of the Smithsonian system to half that, virtually the same as the old Bretton Woods agreement. This arrangement of more limited fluctuation than the general system became known as the 'snake in the tunnel'.

When general floating began a year later there was no longer a tunnel in which to float. (For those who like these descriptive terms, the arrangement between Belgium and the Netherlands to keep the fluctuations between their currencies to the even narrower range of 1½ per cent was nicknamed the 'worm'.)

Before the snake, the EC countries had already undertaken a number of measures to ease adjustment between them. The first was for Short-term Monetary Support, set up in 1970. This enabled debtor countries to draw for a period of up to three months on credits from the creditor countries up to a quota limit. This in effect created a mini-IMF arrangement particularly if a country wished to draw more than its quota. However, perhaps the best known antecedent was the much older European Payments Union, started in 1950, to treat European surpluses and deficits on a multilateral basis and thereby ease the limitations of liquidity on trade.

In 1970 also, the Werner Committee, which was charged with investigating what steps could be taken towards monetary union in the EC, reported its findings to the EC commission. These findings were generally endorsed by the Council of Ministers in 1971. The initial steps involved setting up a system of medium-term financial assistance and limiting the range within which the EC currencies were permitted to vary against each other. While the former was introduced straight away the latter had to be postponed and was introduced in a more limited form as the snake in the following year.

The short- and medium-term credit arrangements reflect a wish by the EC members which had coloured earlier international negotiations with the United States, particularly by France, that the process of adjustment should be symmetric. It should apply just as much to creditor as well as debtor countries, unlike the Bretton Woods system where the onus was largely on the deficit country.

The snake arrangements did not work out too well as the UK (and the Irish Republic whose currency was, at that stage, maintained at par with sterling) left the system almost immediately; Italy left after less than a year; France left in 1974, rejoining after 18 months but then leaving again less than a year later. Of the EC countries and the four applicant members (UK, Irish Republic, Denmark and Norway) only Germany, Belgium–Luxembourg, the Netherlands, Denmark and Norway were still in the scheme when it was replaced by the EMS — Norway not having joined the EC.

On the other hand, for those countries which did retain membership it does appear that not only was the path of their exchange rate movements smoother but (de Grauwe and Peters, 1979) their path of price inflation also had a smaller variance than that of the EC countries as a whole. However, it is important not to confuse cause and effect in this considera-tion. The countries which withdrew did so because they found themselves unable to maintain their parities within such narrow margins. The ability to remain in the system reflects not just more limited fluctuations among the members, in economic activity and prices but reasonably coincident fluctuations, where the coincidence can be unplanned or the result of deliberate policy decisions. Furthermore, it also reflects the ability to ride out short-run pressures from capital flows.

Of the currencies which remained in the snake the Deutschmark was by far the most important. The other major currencies, pound, French franc and the lira were unable to move with it and the size of speculative flows between them were greater than could be offset by action by either party. The flows between the other snake countries and the mark would, however, each be considerably smaller in relation to the size of total mark transactions and hence fairly small in relation to the German ability to intervene in the market. Co-ordination is likely to be possible among several large countries only if all parties try to iron out differences in economic performance which lead to international imbalances, say, through co-ordinated control of monetary growth. The snake system did not involve any substantial measures of co-ordination of economic policies between the EC countries with surplus countries trying to reduce their surpluses by monetary or fiscal expansion and deficit countries seeking to reduce their imbalances by deflationary means.

In assessing the success of the system it must also be noted that the period following the inception of the snake was one of unusual international economic distortion as it included the first oil crisis in 1973–5 which contributed towards substantial deficits in several of the main industrialised countries, as shown in Table 7.1. It is, however, noticeable that despite being an oil producer the United States showed a deficit, while West Germany which is a major oil importer showed an increased surplus. In the case of the UK the crisis was exacerbated by the miners' strike, with its associated 3-day working week, and the lagged inflationary effect of the rapid expansion in the economy and the money supply in 1972–3. It is perhaps not surprising that under those conditions coordination was rather limited. However, the variability should not be exaggerated. As is clear from Figure 7.1 there was relatively little fluctuation between the pound and the Deutschmark between the middle of 1976 and the end of 1979. The greater fluctuations were between both currencies and the dollar.

Little closer integration appeared during the period although a common currency for accounting between the members in their EC dealings, the European Unit of Account (EUA), had been introduced. The EUA was composed, rather like the Special Drawing Right (SDR), of a weighted sum of the currencies of the member countries where the weights reflected the economic importance of the countries within the EC. When the European Monetary System was set up in 1979 this developed the common currency further with the establishment of European Currency Unit (ECU) on the same weighted basket basis.

The Structure of the EMS

The EMS is a substantial strengthening of the previous system. It was set up in March 1979 following the EC Council meeting in Bremen in 1978. The central feature is the ECU which like the SDR was measured as a sum of fixed weights of the member currencies which includes sterling (see Table 7.2). The ECU is the EC unit of account and currency for international settlement between the members. Participation in the ECU system is necessary for transactions with the EC institutions but that does not entail membership of the exchange rate mechanism of the EMS and UK and Greece have not (yet) joined.

Table 7.1: Balance of Trade (T) and Current Balance (C) 1972–6, Main Industrialised Countries ($bn)

	1972		1973		1974		1975		1976	
	T	C	T	C	T	C	T	C	T	C
United States	-6.4	-6.0	0.9	6.9	-5.3	4.5	9.0	18.4	-9.4	4.3
Japan	9.0	6.6	3.7	-0.1	1.4	-4.7	5.0	-0.7	-5.9	3.7
West Germany	8.3	0.8	15.2	4.3	22.2	9.8	17.6	4.0	16.6	3.8
France	1.3	0.3	0.7	0.7	-3.9	-6.0	1.4	-0.1	-4.7	-6.1
United Kingdom	-1.8	0.3	-5.8	-2.6	-12.2	-8.6	-7.2	-4.1	-6.4	-2.0
Italy	0.1	2.0	-4.0	-2.7	-8.5	-8.0	-1.2	-0.8	-4.2	-2.8
Denmark	-0.4	-0.1	-1.2	-0.5	-1.8	-0.9	-1.3	-0.5	-2.9	-1.9
Irish Republic	-0.3	-0.1	-0.4	-0.2	-1.0	-0.7	-0.3	-0.0	-0.5	-0.3
Netherlands	0.6	1.3	1.2	2.4	0.8	2.1	1.3	2.0	1.8	2.7
Norway	-1.0	-0.1	-1.5	-0.3	-2.3	-1.1	-2.8	-2.4	-3.6	-3.8
Belgium	1.3	1.4	1.3	1.3	-0.2	-0.2	-0.3	-0.1	-0.8	-0.1

Source: *OECD Balance of Payments, 1960–77.*

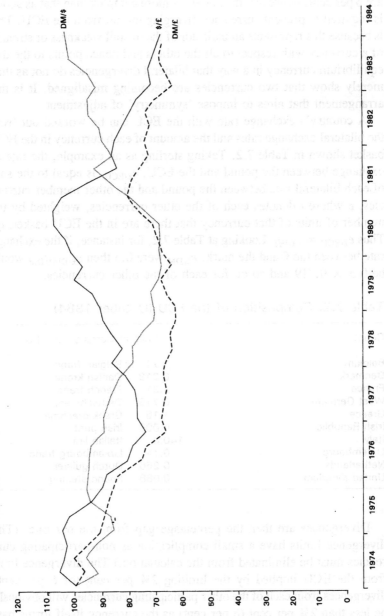

Figure 7.1: Exchange Rates (Index 1974 QI = 100)

DM/$

$/£

DM/£

Source: IMF database SIA.

Note: Downward movements in these series indicate a depreciation of the denominator currency relative to the numerator.

The EMS is a fixed but adjustable peg system of exchange rates. There are central or par values round which the individual rates are not to vary by more than 2¼ per cent for all countries except Italy where the bounds are 6 per cent. However, the system is more complex than that as action is required to prevent currencies diverging too far from the ECU. This is because this represents an indicator of the overall weakness or strength of a currency with respect to all the others and hence points to the disequilibrium currency in a way that bilateral divergencies do not as they merely show that two currencies are becoming misaligned. It is this arrangement that aims to impose 'symmetry' of adjustment.

A country's exchange rate with the ECU can be worked out from the bilateral exchange rates and the amount of each currency in the ECU basket shown in Table 7.2. Taking sterling as an example, the rate of exchange between the pound and the ECU, $e_{£/ECU}$, is equal to the sum of each bilateral rate between the pound and the other member currencies, e where i denotes each of the other currencies, weighted by the number of units of that currency that there are in the ECU basket, q_i. Thus $e_{£/ECU} = e_{£/i}q_i$. Looking at Table 7.2, for instance, if the exchange rate between the £ and the mark, $e_{£/DM}$ were 0.3 then $e_{£/DM}q_{DM}$ would be 0.3 × 0.719 and so on for each of the other currencies.

Table 7.2: Composition of the ECU (October 1984)

Country	Units of Currency in 1 ECU	
Belgium	3.71	Belgian franc
Denmark	0.219	Danish krona
France	1.31	French franc
West Germany	0.719	Deutschmark
Greece	1.15	Greek drachma
Irish Republic	0.009	Irish punt
Italy	140.0	Italian lira
Luxembourg	0.14	Luxembourg franc
Netherlands	0.256	Dutch guilder
United Kingdom	0.088	Pound sterling

Divergences are then the percentage gap from the par rate. (The divergence limits have a small complication as non-participating currencies must be eliminated from the calculation.) The divergence limit from the ECU implied by the limiting 2¼ per cent (or 6 per cent) divergences from each of the other participating currencies will obviously be less than 2¼ per cent (6 per cent) as the currency itself forms part of the ECU. Hence the ECU, in effect, moves to the extent of that

Table 7.3: EMS European Currency Unit Rates

	ECU central rates	Currency amounts against ECU 24 September	% change from central rate	% change adjusted for divergence	Divergence limit %
Belgian franc	44.8320	45.1097	+0.62	+0.90	±1.5425
Danish krona	8.12857	8.07815	−0.62	−0.34	±1.6421
Deutschmark	2.23840	2.22390	−0.65	−0.37	±1.1455
French franc	6.86402	6.78901	−1.09	−0.81	±1.3654
Dutch guilder	2.52208	2.50363	−0.73	−0.45	±1.5162
Irish punt	0.724578	0.717381	−0.99	−0.71	±1.6673
Italian lira	1520.60	1505.71	−0.98	−0.70	±4.0856

Source: *Financial Times*, 25 September 1985.

Changes are for ECU, therefore positive change denotes a weak currency.
Adjustment calculated by *Financial Times*.

currency's weight, in the same direction as the currency itself moves. This is illustrated in Table 7.3.

The central rates are shown in column 1 and the actual rate in column 2. Column 3 then shows the percentage devaluation of the actual rate from the central rate. However, when non-participating countries are excluded we can see from column 4 that the divergence is shifted upwards (sterling is substantially below its central rate). The divergence limits shown in column 5 are narrower when the currency's own weight in the ECU is taken into account.

When divergence of a currency from the ECU central rate reaches 75 per cent of its permitted range it crosses the 'divergence threshold', at which point that country is expected to take corrective action either alone or in concert with the other members.

The system of payments between member countries, including the UK, was made more flexible by the expansion of the role of the European Monetary Co-operation Fund (EMCF) by requiring them to deposit 20 per cent of their gold and dollar reserves in exchange for ECUs. These ECUs can then be used to settle accounts between the member countries. These reserves are revalued every three months and interest is payable (receivable) according to whether their net holdings of ECUs fall below (exceed) the initial deposits, i.e. according to whether a country is a debtor or creditor compared with its initial position. This is precisely analogous to the way in which IMF members pay or receive interest on their holdings of SDRs.

Thus with respect to itself the EMS has been operating like a small-scale Bretton Woods arrangement, complete with an equivalent of the IMF in the form of the EMCF. However, par rates are expressed in terms of the components of the system itself through the weighted basket of the ECU instead of with a single currency fixed to gold. The arrangement would be more like a fixed but adjustable exchange rate regime based on an amended SDR.

Experience of the EMS

The EMS has experienced a series of mutually agreed re-alignments of currencies with respect to the central rate. Unlike the behaviour under the snake, all the countries which made the agreement have continued to participate throughout (although the UK has still not joined). There have been six re-alignments thus far since March 1979. These have not been spread evenly over the period. There were no changes at all during the 21 month period between December 1979 and October 1981 and, at the time of writing, there has been no change in considerably more than a year since the last re-alignment in March 1983.

In the re-alignment, the general pattern has been for the Danish krona, the French franc and the Italian lira to fall and for the Deutschmark to rise. Although the guilder has been revalued once and the Belgian franc devalued once, since exchange rate changes are reciprocal, there have been larger and more frequent relative movements in these currencies.

More interesting than the exchange rate changes themselves, which in some respects represent a failure or inability to co-ordinate policies among the EC countries and illustrate the difficulties of achieving a more substantial degree of economic union in the EC, is the extent to which member countries have taken measures to prevent their exchange rates from fluctuating within the EMS at the expense of the objectives of domestic policy. It was clear even from the first few months of the operation of the system that there were conflicts between exchange rate and domestic monetary policy. However, since targets except for monetary policy are not usually explicit it is difficult to judge to what extent domestic monetary policy has been adjusted for exchange rate reasons. To some extent emphasis on the exchange rate aim can be seen by the scale of foreign currency interventions, as in the case of the Bundesbank, but this also is insufficient as the need to intervene except for purposes of smoothing operations is conditioned by the domestic targets that have been set.

Table 7.4: Average Monthly Absolute Percentage Changes in Exchange Rates

Currencies	February 1974–February 1979	April 1979–April 1984
Deutschmark/dollar	1.79	2.31
Pound/dollar	1.60	2.12
French franc/dollar	1.46	2.41
Lira/dollar	1.36	2.23
Dollar/Deutschmark	1.81	2.29
Pound/Deutschmark	1.64	1.93
French franc/Deutschmark	1.36	0.63
Lira/Deutschmark	1.80	0.72

As is clear from Table 7.4, the three main EMS currencies, Deutschmark, the French franc and the lira, have moved rather less against each other than they have moved against the sterling and the dollar. In the previous period between 1974 and 1979 variations in all the exchange rates were fairly similar. Since that date the dollar and sterling have fluctuated more with respect to all other currencies, including each other while the EMS rates have been considerably more stable. In one sense this is an undoubted consequence of the EMS as par rates can move only in steps and not continuously thereby limiting the month to month drift.

However, over the second period both the pound and the dollar have been subject to rather different pressures than have the EMS currencies (in so far as it is sensible to talk about them as a group). The United States has run a large deficit coupled with a tight monetary policy which has led both to high real interest rates and high real economic growth. This in turn has driven up the dollar relative to all other currencies. The UK on the other hand had a very tight fiscal policy after 1979 which contributed to a rapid fall in economic activity and initially helped to raise the value of sterling relative to all other currencies and to lower domestic inflation. This rise in sterling was probably also aided by the continuation of the effect from North Sea oil through rising oil prices. However, since 1981 sterling has fallen along with the EMS currencies against the dollar and its parity with the EMS currencies has remained relatively stable.

The EMS has therefore probably resulted in much smaller short-run fluctuations in exchange rates for the member countries than independent floating would have done. It has also probably resulted in more orderly re-alignments of rates and a reduction in some of the problems of overshooting which were mentioned in Chapter 5. However, this does not imply that extension to other countries, principally the UK, would be beneficial, because the success and stability of the EMS stems to a large extent from the similarity of the members' economic policies and their trade cycles. The UK has been rather out of step and there is no immediate indication that it is returning to more coincident behaviour.

Optimum Currency Areas

The experience of the EMS and the snake raises a question which has been widely posed (see Mundell, 1961; Grubel, 1970) of whether there are optimal types of areas for having single currency. Areas are currently defined as much by history as by economic desirability. Some existing areas may be too big and should be broken up and others may be too small. It is to be determined whether the EC is an example of the latter.

The question at issue is largely whether having different currencies for particular areas enables them to pursue individual policies which are not just non-appropriate for their own areas as well. Thus, for example, the Irish Republic thought it suitable to break its parity with the pound sterling in order to be able to react differently both to the opportunities within the European Communities and to the other influences on the United Kingdom's overseas transactions. One could equally well ask whether Wales and Scotland should have separate exchange rates or perhaps whether the Northern Irish pound should be linked with that of the Irish Republic.

The relative advantages of being a member of a currency area or independent from it are no different from the policy consequences of fixed versus flexible exchange rates spelt out in the next part of the book. The main gain from being a member of the area, other than the avoidance of transactions costs, is, as McKinnon (1963) points out, increased price stability. The larger a currency area the smaller the proportion of external to internal trade and hence the smaller the impact from external price stocks. The desire for stability is widely documented (see, for example, the Report of the House of Lords Committee on Overseas Trade, 1985). It enables more efficient planning of production and enables people to hold smaller precautionary balances against unforeseen expenditures.

The cost is that government loses the instrument of monetary policy as a means of stabilising the economy. The worry therefore is that unemployment may persist in parts of the area while overheating and inflation occurs in others. As indeed has been observed in parts of many countries. Thus in effect what happens is that problems of national adjustment become problems of regional policy. It becomes necessary to make transfer between regions to achieve equilibrium.

The exchange rate mechanism of EMS is a half-way house as it does not use a common currency, indeed currencies can vary from day to day. Thus the system can be viewed as a means of reducing fluctuations but without the rigid requirements on the means of making adjustments which apply to a common currency area.

8   OTHER EXCHANGE RATE REGIMES

For currencies of smaller countries, particularly ones where capital markets are not well developed it may make good sense not to have a freely traded market which can find its own level. Insufficient transactions, discontinuities and poor information may lead to a market which is difficult to manage effectively without distortion to the requirements of domestic policy. Furthermore such currencies usually play a much smaller role in the invoicing of trade. As a consequence it is not surprising that the largest single group of currencies shown in Table 8.1 are those pegged to the dollar. The United States is the largest single trading country and the dollar is the most common currency of invoicing for trading countries not choosing to use their own currencies.

Although there is now fairly free convertibility of the main currencies there are still restrictions on international capital transactions even among the EC countries (see Mayes, 1984, for example) particularly in France and Italy. The UK ended exchange controls only in 1979. Where controls exist it is possible for a country to 'manage' its exchange rate much more closely, particularly when it can stifle the destabilising speculative flows of the funds which are only held for relatively short periods of time. Where the exchange rate is controlled in this manner any rate can be sustained provided that a country can borrow sufficient to meet any short fall caused by trading requirements or is prepared to control trade flows. The increasing deficits of some developing countries reflect how long this process can last and how serious the difficulties can be. In the case of Mexico, for example, continuing trade deficits (shown in Table 8.2) accompanied by large public sector deficits financed by overseas borrowing led to interest payments reaching almost half the value of exports in 1982. Although the borrowing had been built up on Mexico's strength as an oil producer the size of the debt was compounding the difficulty. Price inflation had reached almost 100 per cent in 1982.

The solution, which so far has been remarkably successful, was to abolish the fixed exchange rate with the dollar and create a 'dual exchange rate system' with a controlled rate for exports, vital imports (since extended to all imports) and foreign debt repayments and a free rate for other transactions, principally private sector capital transactions. It is the controlled rate which is shown in Table 8.2. At the same time there was a drastic cut in the government deficit from 18 per cent of GDP

Table 8.1: Exchange Rate Arrangements[1] (30 June 1984)

Currency pegged to:

US dollar	French franc	Other currency	SDR	Other composite[2]
Antigua & Barbuda	Benin	Bhutan (Indian Rupee)	Burma	Algeria
Bahamas	Cameroon	Equatorial	Burundi	Austria
Barbados	C. African Rep.	Guinea	Guinea	Bangladesh
Belize	Chad	(Spanish	Iran I.R. of	Botswana
Bolivia	Comoros	Peseta)	Jordan	Cape Verde
Djibouti	Congo	Gambia (The	Kenya	China P.R.
Dominica	Gabon	Pound	Rwanda	Cyprus
Dominican Rep.	Ivory Coast	Sterling)	Sao Tome &	Fiji
Egypt	Mali	Lesotho	Principe	Finland
El Salvador	Niger	(South	Seychelles	Hungary
Ethiopia	Senegal	African	Vanuatu	Kuwait
Grenada	Togo	Rand)	Vietnam	Madagascar
Guatemala	Upper Volta	Swaziland		Malawi
Haiti		(South		Malaysia
Honduras		African		Malta
Iraq		Rand)		Mauritania
Lao P.D. Rep.				Mauritius
Liberia				Nepal
Libya				Norway
Nicaragua				Papua New
Oman				Guinea
Panama				Romania
Paraguay				Singapore
St. Lucia				Solomon
St. Vincent				Islands
Sierre Leone				Sweden
Sudan				Tanzania
Suriname				Tunisia
Syrian Arab Rep.				Zambia
Trinidad and Tobago				Zimbabwe
Venezuela				
Yemen Arab Rep.				
Yemen P.C. Rep.				

Table 8.1 *contd.*

Flexibility limited in terms of a single currency or group of currencies:

Single currency[3]	Co-operative arrangements[4]
Afghanistan	Belgium
Bahrain	Denmark
Ghana	France
Guyana	Germany
Maldives	Ireland
Qatar	Italy
Saudi Arabia	Luxembourg
Thailand	Netherlands
United Arab Emirates	

More flexible:

Adjusted according to a set of indicators[5]	Other managed floating	Independently floating
Brazil	Argentina	Australia
Chile	Costa Rica	Canada
Columbia	Ecuador	Israel
Peru	Greece	Japan
Portugal	Guinea-Bissau	Lebanon
Somalia	Iceland	South Africa
	India	United Kingdom
	Indonesia	United States
	Jamaica	Uruguay
	Korea	
	Mexico	
	Morocco	
	New Zealand	
	Nigeria	
	Pakistan	
	Philippines	
	Spain	
	Sri Lanka	
	Turkey	
	Uganda	
	Western Samoa	
	Yugoslavia	
	Zaire	

Source: IMF *Financial Statistics.*

Notes
1. Excluding the currency of Democratic Kampuchea, for which no current information is available. For members with dual or multiple exchange markets, the arrangement shown is that in the major market.
2. Comprises currencies which are pegged to various 'baskets' of currencies of the members' own choice, as distinct from the SDR basket.
3. Exchange rates of all currencies have shown limited flexibility in terms of the US dollar.
4. Refers to the co-operative management maintained under the European Monetary System.
5. Includes exchange arrangements under which the exchange rate is adjusted at relatively frequent intervals, on the basis of indicators determined by the respective member countries.

Table 8.2: Mexican Exchange and Payments, 1979–83 ($bn)

	(1) Trade balance	(2) Interest payments	(3) Current balance	(4) Capital balance	(5) Export cover for interest payments (ratio)	(6) Exchange rate peso/$*
1979	−3.2	−3.4	−4.9	4.5	2.6	22.8
1980	−3.7	−4.9	−7.2	11.9	3.1	23.0
1981	−4.5	−7.5	−12.5	21.9	2.6	24.5
1982	6.6	−10.2	−2.7	6.1	2.1	55.0
1983	13.2	−9.5	4.5	−1.9	2.2	120.1

* Period averages as shown in IMF *Financial Statistics*.

Mid-point between average buying and selling rates up to July 1982;
floating rate, August 1982; ordinary rate, September–November 1982;
December 1982–December 1983 mid-point of buying and selling rates in
the controlled market.

in 1982 to 8½ per cent in 1983. The major gain came in a halving of imports while exports remained unchanged. Of course, it is also possible to impose differential price ratios through a system of discriminatory tariffs and subsidies on traded goods instead of through having multiple exchange rates.

The controlled rate of exchange is operated as a 'crawling peg' and in 1983 the Mexican authorities moved it by 0.13 pesos each day relative to the dollar. These steady movements, largely to try to offset rapid price inflation, are the characteristics of the crawling peg which moves by changing the par or central rate by a stated amount at fairly frequent intervals. It is not necessary for the intervals to be uniform nor as short as one day nor for there to be equal sized movements on each occasion. In the case of Peru, for example, the rate was changed monthly with announcement of the size three months in advance. This 'tablita' system allowed the authorities to slow the rate of devaluation as domestic inflation eased.

There is no reason why the authorities should only have two exchange rates for transactions which they can separate out. Egypt, for example, has five. However, in such a highly regulated system it is not surprising that there should also be a flourishing black market. The choice of which transactions to separate can also vary, Belgium, for example, distinguishes a financial franc from its ordinary transactions, the South African rand has also had more than one rate. It depends on the reasons for separating out transactions, whether it is to limit certain forms of capital transaction, say portfolio investment, or to encourage (discourage) trade in particular commodities or with particular countries. At this level the exchange rate is being used as a substitute for tariff or quota restrictions. It may be imposed because that appears the easiest way of administering the restriction and because the relatively limited channels through which transactions operate, say, through major banks mean that changes in rates can be made without any time delays. Clearly the possible and actual variety precludes discussion of the whole range of multiple exchange rate regimes. We therefore examine only one example, that of the UK investment dollar, in the next section.

Other countries, rather than having multiple rates at any one time have tried varieties of different exchange rate mechanisms over the last few years. Australia, for example, fixed its currency to sterling until late 1971 when it switched to fixing it to the US dollar. This decision would have been influenced by the fact that Australia trades much more with the United States than she does with the United Kingdom. However, the A\$/US\$ rate was varied on a number of occasions until in 1974 the pegging was switched to a basket of currencies, perhaps reflecting the rising importance of trade with other Pacific basin countries. The Australian dollar was devalued substantially in both 1974 and 1976 but from then on the authorities preferred to use small but relatively frequent changes with respect to the basket rather than the more traditional step devaluations. Since the end of 1983 the Australian dollar has been floated.

In a world of uneven development and conflict between the objectives of domestic and external policy it is difficult for countries to choose some form of managed exchange rate which best fulfils their objectives. Floating makes the exercise of control difficult because it has to be undertaken by trading in the market or by changing interest rates or, less directly, by changing the overall management of the domestic economy and altering the public sector deficit or the determinants of the trade balance as is explained in the next part of the book. With rates fixed to other particular currencies, unintended movements in relative prices can take place affecting the country's trade balance, unless that currency dominates a country's trade. For example, any country linked to the dollar over the last few years has found its exchange rate rising relative to those of the main European currencies. Fixing to a basket of currencies, except perhaps to the SDR, is a more complex arrangement which makes forecasting and planning more complicated but does ensure closer correspondence between movements in domestic and foreign prices. However, import and export baskets are not necessarily similar. If we take the example of Australia again, as is shown in Table 8.3, export and import

Table 8.3: Export and Import Shares in Australia, 1982/3
(per cent)

	Exports	Imports
Japan	27	21
USA	10	22
UK	5	7
New Zealand	5	3
Other	53	47

Source: Australian Trade Department.

shares are quite different, with exports to Japan being the dominant category and a surplus on Japanese trade aided by raw material exports.

Thus, with a given dollar weighting, a rising dollar, for an exchange rate based on a currency basket, will result in import prices and export prices rising more than the export pattern requires. As for arguments about gradual as opposed to step devaluations and announced and surprise changes, it is clear these operate in different ways (see Chapter 9) and a country's choice depends on its objectives. Major short-run structural changes are clearly best achieved by unannounced devaluations. Orderly changes in exchange rates which attempt to match up the internal rate of price inflation with that abroad are probably best achieved through some form of crawling peg, whether or not the exact size of the change is announced beforehand. The benefits of particular arrangements thus depend very much on the particular country and how well its economic activity is co-ordinated with that of the rest of the world, particularly with its trading partners.

The UK Investment Currency Market

One of the better documented dual exchange rate markets was that operated by the UK after the Second World War, up to 1979, for securities traded in dollars. The market had approximately the same form between 1962 (when two categories of 'dollar' securities were amalgamated) and 1979, although there were several other more minor changes; the most important was the requirement, in force between 1965 and 1978, to surrender 25 per cent of the proceeds of dollar security sales to the fund. The system worked, in effect, by having a fixed pool of dollar securities. The only way for a newcomer to invest in dollar securities was for an existing holder to sell, hence releasing funds, as new funds could not be obtained from the ordinary foreign exchange

Figure 8.1: Effective Investment Currency Premia

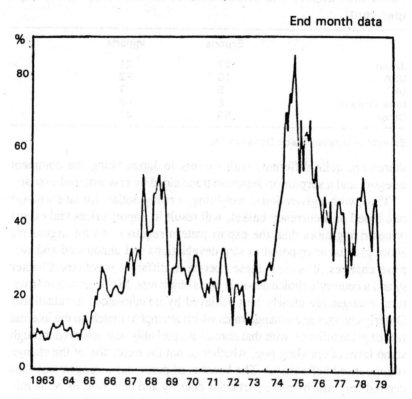

Source: Hughes (1983).

market. The net result of this is that for the whole of the period 1962–79 there was a premium for the investment currency as demand exceeded supply ranging from around 10 per cent at the outset to over 80 per cent at its peak in 1974 (see Figure 8.1). By this means the UK authorities were able to restrict purchases of foreign securities and the consequences for the ordinary exchange rate. The restriction was obviously substantial, whatever the nature of the premium, in the light of the surge of investment as soon as the controls were lifted in 1979 — although some of the out-flow may have represented a re-financing of existing holdings. In 1976 and 1977 there was slight net inward portfolio investment in the UK although 1978 and 1979 both saw an out-flow of some £1 billion. However, in 1980 the out-flow rose to over £3 billion, and thence to £4 billion in 1981 and over £6 billion in 1982 (or some 12 per cent of the value of trade in goods in that year). It would be misleading to attribute all this surge to the ending of controls as it coincided with a period of substantial surplus on the current account which would itself tend to lead to a capital out-flow.

Bilateral Arrangements

Until recently the exchange of goods for goods in foreign trade rather than goods for some international instrument of payment was relatively uncommon for trade with countries outside the Eastern bloc. Currently around 5 per cent of UK trade is in this form of swap or barter, frequently referred to as 'counter trade'. In so far as this trade takes place it eliminates the foreign exchange transaction. It means that there is no need for importers in developing countries to find foreign exchange. It also means that very different 'rates of exchange' may be operated at the same time in different deals. One firm may have good connections which may allow it to dispose of, say, sugar in return for machinery, perhaps even within another division of the firm itself while another firm will merely have to sell the sugar in the open market and thereby have to accept a much bigger discount.

The former firm may therefore be prepared to accept rather less sugar in exchange than the latter one would. The number of developing countries adopting this approach is quite large and it is prevalent in countries like Brazil, Iran, Nigeria, and Indonesia. However, it is not restricted to lower income countries and is practised, for example, by Australia. In the main it is countries with serious payments problems whose trade credit is unlikely to be advanced where such transactions are most popular. It is wrongly characterised as pure barter and can take several forms. Among them are 'buy-back' or 'off-take' where the constructor of a capital project agrees to take future production from the plant he is constructing in payment. Another is 'offset' whereby a proportion of the work is undertaken in the client's country to try to keep down the foreign exchange cost. In dealings with Eastern bloc countries it is common not to match up individual deals but for the countries to set up a clearing account so that when one exports to the other it gets a credit in that account which is used to finance trade in the opposite direction at a later date thus avoiding any foreign exchange transaction in 'hard' currency.

One of the most well-known examples of this last arrangement is trade between Finland and the Soviet Union which accounts for around a quarter of Finland's total trade. Finland has an agreement to buy products such as oil, coal and timber from the USSR in return for which she can ship a much more general range of products to the USSR. Since these products which Finland agrees to import have a world price, usually expressed in dollars, the price of the goods which can be exported in return is related to it. Thus when the price of oil rose, Finland was immediately able to export more to the USSR, so that the USSR gained from the improvement in its terms of trade and Finland was immediately able to have non-inflationary expansion in the face of rising oil prices. Elsewhere with unrelated trading transactions this combination of events would have tended to result in a recession. The more recent fall in oil prices, however, works the other way round and Finland has run up a considerable credit in the Soviet Foreign Trade Bank, which although it is interest-bearing is not convertible. Finland, operates a fixed but adjustable exchange rate pegged to a basket of currencies reflecting trade weights, see Table 8.1, but the USSR, although the largest trading partner, is excluded from this calculation because its currency is not convertible. Counter trade reduces the need for exchange transactions.

Part 2: Further Reading

There are several histories of how the exchange rate system has evolved: those by Argy (1981), Strange (1976) and Solomon (1982) are among the best known but Yeager (1976) will also give a wide background to the arrangements. Many other books have been written advocating particular reforms to the international monetary system but they do not all cover the ground in a purely explanatory manner.

The debate between different exchange rate mechanisms has occurred over a long period of time but Artus and Young (1979) is a useful summary. In so far as this debate has then been extended to optimum currency areas, Grubel (1970) and Ishiyama (1975) provide a useful exposition although Mundell (1961) and McKinnon (1963) show the debate at an earlier stage. More interesting perhaps are the discussions of the European Monetary System, both in prospect — Ingram (1973); Krause and Salant (1973) — and subsequently — Trezise (1979); MacKinnon (1980). Further studies on the relation between exchange rates in theory and practice are given in Klein and Krelle (1983); Bilson and Marston (1984).

PART 3

THE EXCHANGE RATE AND ECONOMIC POLICY

Since commitments to fixed exchange rates were abandoned and the UK decided to float its currency, debates about exchange rate policy have — almost paradoxically — been continuous. The chapters in this part of the book consider the connections between the exchange rate and macroeconomic policy from the point of view of an individual country. Chapter 9 deals mainly with the role of exchange rate management in securing full employment and balanced trade. Until about ten years ago that was where the analysis usually stopped. The experience of the 1970s demonstrated the general relationship between countries whose currencies were depreciating and countries with high inflation rates. This commonplace observation prompts the question of whether, now that governments are not bound by the need to maintain by explicit exchange rates, they might exploit this relationship as an anti-inflationary device. This forms the subject of Chapter 10.

Early discussions about exchange rate policy tended to presume that the mechanics of obtaining the desired exchange rate were straightforward and hardly worthy of analysis. Government dealing in the foreign exchange market would set the price of foreign exchange with the reserves acting as a buffer stock. The sustainability of such a policy depended not only on government policy being so arranged that the chosen exchange rate would not involve continuous changes of reserves in either direction but also on the adequacy of reserves to meet normal fluctuations in supply and demand. Although the IMF system means that countries can supplement their reserves by borrowing, albeit with increasing requirements of conditionality, the progressive freeing of the international capital market rendered even those resources inadequate. Increasingly governments came to rely on the manipulation of interest rates to control their exchange rates. At the same time they were hoping to use interest rates to control money supplies. The conflicts between exchange rate targets and monetary targets revealed the always latent conflicts between various related policies. These issues are discussed in Chapter 11.

The final chapter examines the effects of the exploitation of North Sea oil on policy in the UK. Theoretical models strip away detail irrelevant to the problem at hand. Of course there is often disagreement about what is important and what is not — which accounts for the multiplicity of models. Abstraction is a pre-requisite for understanding, but in practice problems do not arrive one by one to be dealt with and then forgotten. Often important empirical facts are known only with great uncertainty, if they are known at all. Normally the interests of different groups in society do not coincide. Policy making and prescription benefit enormously from hindsight.

Notation

In Parts 3 and 4, it is convenient to measure the exchange rate in units of foreign per unit of domestic currency, and it is denoted by e. Thus a rise in e indicates an appreciation of the domestic currency (and vice versa). The *proportionate change* in variable, for example the exchange rate, is denoted by ê.

9 THE EXCHANGE RATE AND THE REAL ECONOMY

Introduction

In this chapter we consider the use of the exchange rate as an instrument of government policy in a fixed exchange rate system. We discover that most discussions of exchange rate policy differ not in their hypotheses about exchange rate determination but over the policies which are assumed to accompany the exchange rate change or the events which, in a floating rate system, cause the exchange rate to change in the first place. At the end of the day much disagreement in fact depends on value judgements concerning the relative importance of competing policy objectives.

As a preliminary to our discussion it will be helpful to consider some of the accounting relationships that *necessarily* hold between the balance of payments and domestic output and expenditure. As is shown in Equation (9.1) the current balance B measured in domestic currency equals the volume of exports of goods and services X *times* the average price of these exports P_x *less* the volume of imports of goods and services M *times* their average price P_m *plus* net receipts of interest, dividends, profits and unrequited transfers from abroad R; thus

$$B = P_x X - P_m M + R \tag{9.1}$$

In most of what follows we will assume R is constant and zero. This is the current account balance as set out in Table 2.1. However, the important addition here is that instead of dealing entirely in the current values of trade in goods and services we are distinguishing volumes and prices so that we can examine the effects of variations in these two components separately.

All goods (and services) produced in the home country are either exported or consumed internally; similarly all goods consumed in the economy must be either imported or produced domestically. Let Q be the volume of goods both produced and consumed domestically and let P_q be their average price. Then, if Y is the total value of production in the economy and E is the total value of expenditure in the economy, we have

$$Y = P_qQ + P_xX \qquad\qquad (9.2)$$

$$E = P_qQ + P_mM \qquad\qquad (9.2')$$

From this it follows that the current balance exactly equals the difference between the value of production and the value of expenditure:

$$B = P_xX - P_mM$$
$$\quad = P_xX + P_qQ - P_qQ - P_mM = Y - E \qquad (9.3)$$

The difference between the value of production and the value of expenditure is a measure of the country's saving. The economy as a whole can save only by accumulating financial claims on the rest of the world in return for its *net* exports of goods and services. To distinguish national savings from the more familiar notion of personal sector saving, we shall often use the term 'hoarding' to emphasise that the economy is accumulating assets.

Before examining various models which have been constructed to explain the role of the exchange rate it is worth considering just in terms of this identity the effects of changes in the components under certain sets of assumptions.

The Effect of an Increase in Exports at Constant Prices and Expenditure

Since prices are to be constant it is possible, without loss of generality, to make all prices equal by suitable choice of units so that the identity becomes

$$B = X + Q - Q - M = Y - E. \qquad\qquad (9.4)$$

Since expenditure is to be constant the identity can be further simplified,

$$B = X + Q - E = Y - E. \qquad\qquad (9.5)$$

Consider a change in X when E is constant. If production for home demand, Q, is not affected then both B, the current balance, and Y, production, increase by the same amount as X. But suppose that to produce an increase in exports an equal amount of production for domestic use has to be given up. In this case the sum $X + Q$, the value of production, is not changed and, since expenditure is constant, the current balance is unchanged. Since E is constant but Q has fallen domestic residents have had to increase imports to maintain their expenditure at the required level.

The Effect of an Increase in Prices at Constant Levels of Real Expenditure and Production

Suppose that all prices increased by δ per cent. Then the new current balance is

$$B' = (\frac{100 + \delta}{100}) (P_x X + P_q Q - P_q Q - P_m M)$$

$$= (\frac{100 + \delta}{100}) (Y - E). \tag{9.6}$$

In other words, the new balance is just $(100 + \delta)/100$ times the old balance. Of course nothing real has changed — X, M and Q are as they were. If the current balance was initially in surplus then a rise in prices with all real quantities fixed increases the current surplus. This raises the possibility that X could fall and the current balance could still improve. If ΔX is the change in X then the new balance is

$$B' = (\frac{100 + \delta}{100}) [P_x(X + \Delta X) + P_q Q - P_q Q - P_m M] \tag{9.7}$$

$$= (\frac{100 + \delta}{100}) B + (\frac{100 + \delta}{100}) P_x \Delta X$$

$$B' - B = (\frac{\delta}{100}) B + (\frac{100 + \delta}{100}) P_x \Delta X.$$

It is easy to show that the balance will improve as long as

$$\Delta X > \frac{B}{P_x} (\frac{-\delta}{100 + \delta}).$$

Since B and δ are both positive, this means that an improving current balance is certainly compatible with a fall in export volumes. When prices are changing, the change in the current balance is no longer a reliable indicator of changes in the real economy. For this reason it is useful to consider also the real current balance. In the case cited above it is clear that the real current balance should be obtained by adjusting all nominal quantities by the uniform rate of inflation δ. In this case it is clear from Equation (9.6) that the real balance is unaffected by pure inflation. Similarly any fall in X will reduce the real balance. Consequently it is necessary to specify whether any changes discussed are to the real balance or to the nominal balance (or, equivalently, to real hoarding or nominal hoarding). The real and nominal quantities may well be changing in opposite directions.

Exchange Rate Policy under Fixed Exchange Rates

In this section, exchange rate policy is described in a world in which it can be assumed that the exchange rate is fixed by the dealings of the domestic monetary authorities on the foreign exchange market. In particular the authorities are prepared to buy or sell foreign currency, that is, to accumulate or shed foreign exchange reserves, in such a way that the announced exchange rate is in fact the price at which the foreign exchange market is cleared. This may be called *direct* policy.

Although this section deals with exchange rate policy, it is important to remember that much of the relevant economic literature was written in the Bretton Woods period when it was widely believed that governments could, by means of demand management, control quite precisely the level of output or demand in the economy. Consequently assumptions of fixed output or fixed demand are freely made. As discussed above, variations in these background assumptions alter the apparent effects of changes in the exchange rate and we will attempt to indicate such sensitivity where it is important.

The Simplest Case: The Small Country Producing a Single Good

This very simple model illustrates most of the problems of government policy under a regime of fixed exchange rates. It is, however, seldom analysed — perhaps because, at first blush, there is no role for exchange rate policy. By a small country is meant a country that faces perfectly elastic foreign demand curves for the goods which it exports and perfectly elastic foreign supply curves for its imports. A direct implication of this is that the price of the export good relative to the price of the import good is independent of domestic supply and demand. In Figure 9.1 the output of the home country's export good — the only good in production — is shown on the vertical axis. Maximum output of the good is at the point X. The quantity of the import good is shown on the horizontal axis. Because the relative price of exports and imports is fixed, export goods can be exchanged for import goods at a constant rate. M is the quantity of import goods that can be purchased by exchanging the entire maximum output of export goods. Obviously,

$$P_m M = P_x X. \tag{9.8}$$

Any point on line XM also entails the same level of national expenditure. Suppose that the economy consumes the combination of goods at point A. Then OB of the domestically produced good is consumed along with OC of the imported good. Given the relative prices, imports of OC (=

Figure 9.1

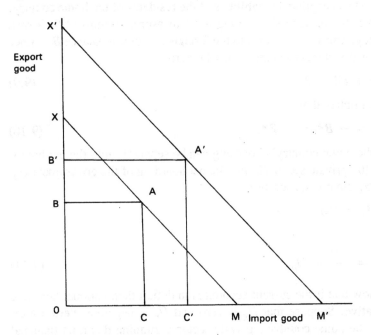

BA) are exactly paid for by *BX* of exports. Measured in units of the home produced good, production and expenditure are both equal to *OX*; there is no hoarding; and the current balance is zero.

Suppose that instead of consuming at *A* the economy chose the combination of goods *A'*. Consumption of the home produced good is *OB'* and of the imported good *OC'*. Because the country is 'small' the change in expenditure does not affect the relative prices at which the home produced good can be exchanged for imports. The new level of imports now costs *B'X'* in terms of the home good. Expenditure now exceeds production by *XX'* and the home country must be running a current account deficit — that is running down its claims on non-residents.

Is there any reason for the government to intervene? It has been assumed that domestic production is at capacity output. If foreign currency prices are stable then, given the assumption of the fixed exchange rate, domestic prices must be stable too. Thus the only macroeconomic problem — if problem it be — is the current account deficit. If the exchange rate is constant then it must be the case that the demand for foreign currency by residents of the home country — that is the current balance, *B*, *times* the exchange rate, *e*, must equal the supply of foreign currency by foreigners. This supply is, of course, the result of their own (net) desires to accumulate assets which in the aggregate they can only achieve by accepting the liabilities of the residents of the home country. Suppose the foreigners' hoarding is Z^* measured in units of their own currency. This must be equal to the foreigners' current balance B^*. Since the world's current balance must be zero

$$B^* + eB = 0 \qquad (9.9)$$

which implies that

$$eB = -B^* = -Z^*. \qquad (9.10)$$

Now the home country's hoarding can be separated into the net hoarding of the private sector H_p and the net hoarding of the government H_g. Then by simple substitution

$$e(H_p + H_g) = -Z^*$$

or

$$H_g = \frac{-Z^*}{e} - H_p \qquad (9.11)$$

We know that if the current account is in deficit then national hoarding is negative. Suppose that H_g is zero and H_p is negative. Period after period the home country's private sector is running down its financial assets while the foreign sector is increasing its own. Now if assets denominated in domestic and foreign country were perfect substitutes this process could continue as long as each sector agreed about their rates of asset accumulation — although if expenditure were directly related to wealth we might expect this situation to be self-stabilising so that in the end both countries attain a stable level of wealth[1]. A necessary condition for the perfect substitutability of assets is that the exchange rate should be universally expected to be irrevocably fixed. Clearly under these circumstances there is no role, by assumption, for exchange rate policy.

Continuous dishoarding by the home country's private sector must lead to an increase in the proportion of home-currency denominated assets in the foreign sector's portfolio. But such home-country assets derive their value from their fixed rate of exchange against the foreign currency (in which, it will be recalled, the price of goods is fixed). Foreign asset holders' confidence can be sustained only as long as the home country's government stocks of foreign assets are believed to be sufficient to meet all demands for currency exchange. This belief is less credible the greater the outstanding stock of domestic assets relative to the foreign exchange reserves. (Note that this fear affects the domestic private sector just as much as the foreign sector.) At some stage asset holders may wish, in spite of the 'fixed' exchange rate, to increase the proportion of foreign currency denominated assets in their portfolios by exchanging home-country assets for foreign-country assets with the home country's government. Under the current assumptions this *must* lead in the end to the exhaustion of the government's foreign exchange reserves. The realisation that this is the only outcome will make asset holders all the more anxious to effect the exchange.

If its foreign exchange reserves are exhausted the home-country government will lose control of the exchange rate altogether. A devaluation, however, brings about a one-shot capital loss to all holders of domestic assets (see Chapter 11 below for a fuller discussion). In so far as the devaluation was unanticipated and does not generate expectations of further devaluations, the only other effect of the exchange rate adjustment is to reduce the proportion by value of home-country assets in portfolios. Since by assumption nothing has happened to affect the desired proportions of domestic and foreign currency assets in portfolios, the process can recommence and the foreign sector can again begin to increase its holdings of home-country assets. However, it is hard to imagine a policy of repeated partial repudiations of debts in this manner being possible without leading to some reassessment of the desirability of holding home-country assets. If asset holders eventually decide to abandon home-country assets altogether, the policy merely brings about that which it was designed to prevent — namely the loss of control over the exchange rate.

The alternative polar case arises when the private sector is in continuous equilibrium ($H_p = 0$) and the current account deficit reflects dishoarding by the government ($H_g < 0$). Such a policy is ultimately unsustainable because the government may either run out of reserves or find increasing difficulty in persuading non-residents to accept its liabilities for those reasons discussed above. *Any* policy that succeeds in reducing the government's deficit without inducing a private-sector deficit will eliminate the current account deficit. Different policies will, of course, have different implications in a more complex model, but we may note here one possible reason for pursuing a policy of exchange rate devaluation. If the government's policy in respect of its rate of dishoarding (which is the same as its financial deficit) is drawn up in nominal or cash terms then a devaluation will increase the price level and thus reduce the real financial deficit and its value in foreign currency. Thus if, for institutional reasons, the government's nominal targets for expenditure or receipts are difficult to adjust, real changes could be effected by manipulating the exchange rate. Once again the chance of such a policy being successful must depend on whatever factors made the financial deficit inflexible not reappearing after the devaluation.

The Exchange Rate and Employment. This very simple model appears to offer no straightforward role for discretionary exchange rate changes in a fixed rate system. We shall now consider two ways in which a scope for policy may be introduced — by relaxing in turn the assumptions that output is given and that the country is small. The simplest alternative arises if it is assumed that domestic output of the exported good depends on the amount of labour employed. Let labour be the only variable input and output depend on labour input with a diminishing marginal product of labour. If the money wage, W is given to firms then the product wage W/P_x is also given, since the small country assumption ensures that the product price depends only on the foreign price and the exchange rate. Under these circumstances profit maximisation implies that the derived demand for labour varies inversely with the product wage. The diagram already used can easily be amended to allow for a labour market which does not clear. In Figure 9.2 the north-eastern quadrant remains just as before. The north-western quadrant shows the relation between output on the vertical axis and the product wage on the horizontal axis. At an heuristic level, it is clear that if the product wage rises desired output will fall. If it is assumed that marginal product of labour is indefinitely large when employment is zero and approaches zero as employment increases, then, for any given product wage, there will exist some positive level of output and employment that is optimal as far as firms are concerned. Suppose that initially the product wage is ϱ (which gives output A), and employment is below the (arbitrary) full employment level. Since it is assumed that the country is small, variations in the level of domestic demand have no effect on the level of domestic output or employment. This is because domestic demand is so small that variations in demand do not affect world prices and so do not affect the product wage. But variations in the product wage, or profitability, are what is required to induce variations in supply. Assume that the government controls real expenditure to keep it at C. In this case there will be a current account deficit. Consider the effect of an increase in the price level at given nominal wages. The product wage would fall and employment and output would rise. Full employment is achieved at A'. If the authorities maintain expenditure at C the current deficit will be eliminated. The only problem appears to be managing the price level. But the small country assumption that prices are fixed in foreign currency makes this

Figure 9.2

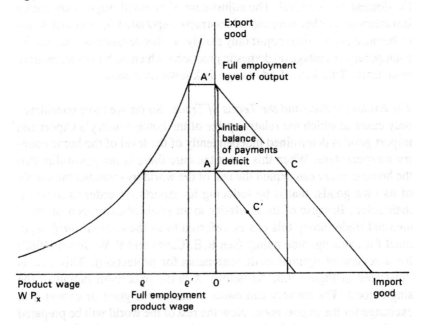

easy. Devalue the currency: the price level in domestic currency will rise and so will employment and output. A case for exchange rate policy to promote employment has been found.

It is important to note that we have assumed that by maintaining expenditure at *C*, the government is pursuing a policy that is sustainable in the long run as long as the labour market can be made to clear. While the real wage is too high, the country will be running a current account deficit. In the absence of exchange rate policy (or some other means of reducing the real wage) expenditure would in the end have to be reduced. Balance of payment equilibrium or 'external balance' would be achieved if absorption were at *C'* where the associated price line passes through *A*. Under these circumstances the economy would have accommodated itself to the high real wage and the resulting unemployment — 'internal balance' would not exist. The motivation for exchange rate policy can be identified from the constraint on the economy that it relaxes.

We may call this *employment oriented* exchange rate policy, and the function of the exchange rate is to manage the real wage. As such it depends for its efficacy on the rigidity of nominal wage levels. If, however, nominal wages adjust following the exchange rate change so as to keep real wages fixed, the change in output will not occur and, maintaining the assumption that the government acts to hold real expenditure constant, the only effect of exchange rate policy is to alter the domestic price level. The adjustment of nominal wages may not be instantaneous either because of contracts negotiated in nominal terms or because expectations adjust only slowly, so that devaluation may confer a temporary advantage on domestic producers which is, however, reduced over time. This loss of advantage is known as *erosion*.

The Exchange Rate and the Terms of Trade. So far we have considered only cases in which the relative price of the home country's export and import good is determined independently of the level of the home country's expenditure. When this is not the case there is the possibility that the home country can exploit the rest of the world by reducing the supply of its own goods, that is by reducing its exports, in order to drive up their price. Because of its similarity to an established branch of international trade theory this can be referred to as the *optimal tariff* argument for exchange rate policy (see R.E. Caves and R.W. Jones (1983) for a review of optimal tariff arguments for protection). This case is illustrated in Figure 9.3. As before, X is the maximum output of the single good. The country can either consume the good or export it in exchange for the import good. Now the rest of the world will be prepared to offer more units of the import good in exchange for the first unit of the export good than for the second, and more for the second than for the third, and so on. Thus by considering what the rest of the world will offer for given quantities of the home country's export good we can trace out the foreign country's offer curve which is the home country's trade possibility curve. By a similar argument the home country's offer curve must be similar to XY. There is a single point common to both curves at which there is agreement about the relative price of the two goods: KX units of the export good are exchanged for Km units of the import good. Suppose that the home economy were able to obtain Km' units of the import goods for the same amount of the export good. Other things being equal, since such an exchange permits at least the same consumption as before of both goods, it would be preferred. A new, higher, relative price would have been established. But m' is not on the foreign offer curve and so does not represent a feasible option for the home country. If the home country wishes to trade at this price it will have to accept $K'm''$ ($< Km < Km'$) units of the import good in exchange for $K'X$ ($<KX$) units of the export good.

It is not possible to say, *a priori*, whether consuming at m'' is better than consuming at m as more of one good and less of the other is consumed at m'' than at m. However, for the moment, we are concerned

Figure 9.3

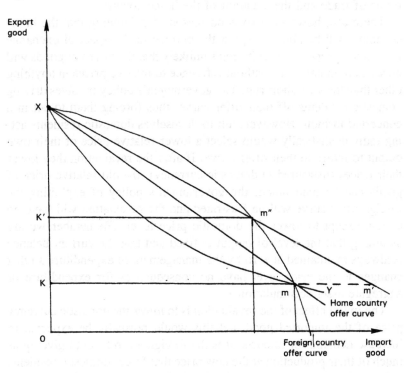

with whether the point is attainable rather than whether it is desirable. Suppose that the home economy comprised a single individual. In this case he would not have an offer curve but, if he knew the foreign offer curve, he would merely select that point on it that suited him best, knowing that the foreign offer curve represented the best deal he could get from the rest of the world. If he selected *m"* he would merely put *K'X* units of the export good on the world market and consume the rest of the production himself.

In a competitive economy there is no alternative mechanism to permit concerted action by the home country's residents to get to the point that they collectively consider to be best in the way that a single individual can. But from the point of view of policy analysis matters are easier since it is the government that decides, *de facto*, which point to select.

Suppose that the price of the imported good is fixed in units of foreign currency and that the price of the domestic good is fixed in units of home currency. In this case a change in the exchange rate amounts to a change in the relative price of the goods. In particular, if the currency is revalued the relative price of the home country's good will rise, improving the terms of trade and the situation of the home country.

There are, however, two good reasons for doubting that the home economy will be able to exploit the optimal tariff aspect of exchange rate policy properly. First it seems unlikely that the prices of goods will be set in nominal terms without reference to relative prices in anything other than the very short run. The government's policy involves driving domestic residents off their offer curve, thus forcing them to act in a concerted fashion. However, left to themselves domestic residents acting individualistically would select a lower relative price of their own output to return to their offer curve. If after the revaluation they lower their prices (measured in domestic currency), the old relative price of goods can be maintained, the government's policy of exploiting the foreign offer curve will be frustrated and the revaluation will have no effects except to lower the domestic price level. (Remember we are assuming that the level of output is fixed and that the current balance is always maintained at zero by the management of expenditure so that changes in the price level have no consequences for expenditure or aggregate asset accumulation.)

The initial effect of the revaluation is to *lower* the domestic currency price of the imported good and this would normally be expected to increase demand for imports: it is the foreigners' refusal to give up as much of their production at the new price that forces domestic residents collectively to the new, preferred point. In this respect a tariff is a superior instrument for changing the international terms of trade since the imposition of a tariff *increases* the relative price of the import good as far as domestic consumers are concerned, leading them to reduce their demands for imports and thus their offers of exports for exchange. The reduction in the supply of exports improves the national terms of trade — the relative price at which goods are actually being exchanged — although the internal terms of trade, the relative price of goods inside the home country (inclusive of tariffs), will be worse than before as far as domestic residents are concerned.

The second problem with the optimal tariff argument applies equally to exchange rate or tariff induced changes to the terms of trade — namely the possibility of retaliation. After the revaluation it may be in the interest of the foreign country to revalue also in order to regain a part of what it has given up. There is no guarantee that at the end of a round of competitive revaluation the home country will be better off than it was before the policy was first applied.

The Implications of Producing more than one Good

The previous section examined the possible payoffs from an active exchange rate policy within a fixed exchange rate system for a country producing a single good. In this section we examine what modifications are required when two goods are produced. We shall introduce the important distinction between traded and non-traded goods. Goods may not enter into international trade either for technological reasons or because of prohibitive transport costs. A country's production and consumption of non-traded goods must necessarily be equal. Non-traded goods include some services — for example, construction, internal transport, theatre and cinema performances, restaurant meals and so on — which, by their very nature have to be consumed at the point of production, as well as some low-value high-bulk goods. In the past, for example, the transportation costs of coal were so high that the production of coal in Britain and America were not in competition with each other.

Traded Goods

We shall first examine the implications of the production of two goods for exchange rate policy on the assumptions that both goods produced are traded goods in which the home country has such a small share of world markets as both producer and consumer, so that the prices of these goods do not vary with the rate of domestic production or consumption. The previous diagram is easily amended. In Figure 9.4 the vertical axis shows levels of production and consumption of the country's exportable good X, but now the horizontal axis shows levels of production as well as absorption of the importable good, M. Whereas before the production of the economy was confined to the X axis, now the economy can produce either X or M and it is now constrained to produce somewhere in the area bounded by the axes and the curve $X'M'$.

The general shape of this curve — the production possibility frontier — depends on the factors of production having positive but diminishing marginal products. Suppose the economy is producing x units of the exportable and m units of the importable at P. At P the exportable industry is using L_x units of labour and K_x units of another factor which we will call capital for the sake of convention. Similarly, the importable industry is using L_m and K_m units of the factors. If a_x is the *average* productivity of labour in the exportable industry and b_x is the *average* productivity of capital, then

Figure 9.4: The economy's production possibility set

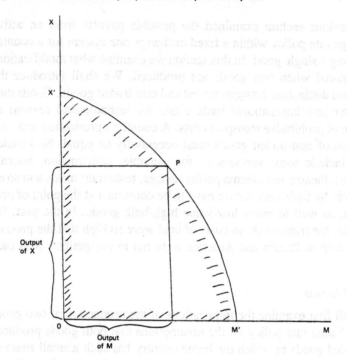

$$x = a_x L_x = b_x K_x \tag{9.12}$$

$$m = a_m L_m = b_m K_m \tag{9.13}$$

$$L = L_x + L_m \tag{9.14}$$

$$K = K_x + K_m \tag{9.15}$$

Since the production possibility frontier encloses all possible combinations of x and m that can be produced with a given availability of factors of production, we want to find out what is the smallest amount of m that has to be given up for a given increase in x. Suppose that the increase in x is q units of output. If the industry uses the same average productivities then this new level of production will require new rates of factor utilisation as follows

$$x' = x + q, \tag{9.16}$$

$$L'_x = \frac{1}{a_x}(x') = \frac{1}{a_x}(x + q) = L_x + \frac{q}{a_x}, \tag{9.17}$$

$$K'_x = \frac{1}{b_x}(x') = \frac{1}{b_x}(x + q) = K_x + \frac{q}{b_x}. \qquad (9.18)$$

Now q/a_x units of labour could produce $(a_m/a_x)q$ units of m if sufficient capital were available, and q/b_x units of capital could produce $(b_m/b_x)q$ units of m with the help of sufficient labour. Since the extra production of x requires both the extra capital and the extra labour, the loss of m must be the larger of $(a_m/a_x)q$ and $(b_m/b_x)q$ and there will be some of one factor left idle. We will suppose that $(a_m/a_x)q$ is greater than $(b_m/b_x)q$ so that some capital is left over.

In terms of Figure 9.5 we assume that to begin with no exportables were produced at all and that production was at m. Since the amount of importables given up per unit of exportable product is a constant, either (a_m/a_x) or (b_m/b_x), the production possibility frontier must be a straight line, the inner one of mx and mx_1. At all points on mx the total amount of labour is fully utilised whereas the total amount of capital would only be fully utilised if enough labour were available to make mx_1 the production possibility frontier. But suppose that the average factor productivities in the importable industry were not fixed; in this case the 'spare' capital could be used to produce importables as long as the marginal product of capital was positive. This establishes the commonsense result that the possibility of factor substitution must widen the production possibilities open to the economy. We may suppose that instead of importable production being m' when q of exportables is produced, it is m''. By repeating the experiment for different values of q we can trace out the production possibility frontier on the assumption that substitution is possible only in the importable sector. This is the curve $mm''Gx$. By a similar argument it is clear that the possibility of factor substitution in the exportable sector must further extend the possibilities of production.

In general the form of the production possibility frontier depends on the number of goods and the number of re-allocatable factors of production as well as in the production technology in each sector. See, for example, R.W. Jones (1974).

When the country is small it is easy to discover the combination of outputs of exportables and importables that maximises the value of output in terms of either exportables or importables. Suppose in Figure 9.6 the economy is producing P where output of importables is Om_1 and of exportables Ox_1. Under the small country assumption the relative price of exportables and importables is independent of the country's outputs. Suppose that relative prices are such that Ob units of importables

Figure 9.5

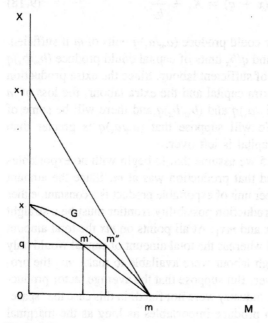

Figure 9.6

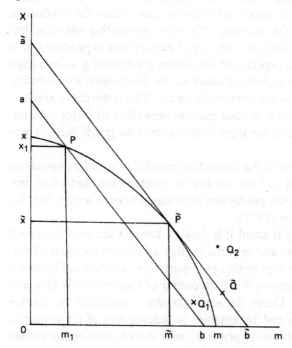

can be exchanged for Oa units of exportables. Then, as ab passes through P, the country's output of importables, Om_1, could be exchanged for x_1a units of exportables.

The country's own output of exportables is x_1 so the value of output is a. Similarly if measured in terms of importables the value of output is b. Since the relative price of goods is independent of home production, the value of output for any point can be assessed by examining where a straight line through the production point and parallel to ab cuts the axes. Clearly the value of output is maximised when the relative price line just touches the production possibility frontier as at $\bar{P}$.

The logic is straightforward. The slope of the line ab measures the rate at which goods can be exchanged for each other on world markets; the slope of the production possibility frontier measures the rate at which the goods can be transformed into each other by re-arranging the uses of fixed quantities of factors of production. At P importables can be produced much more favourably, in terms of exportables foregone, by increasing domestic production than by exchanging exportables on world markets. So if the intention is to maximise the value of output, it pays to increase production of importables (and replace, if desired, the lost exportables by international trade). This argument holds for all points between P and $\bar{P}$. At $\bar{P}$ the rate of transformation of the two goods by international trade equals the marginal rate of transformation obtained from domestic production, so there are no further gains to be had. Normally any change in the relative price of goods obtaining on world markets requires some re-organisation of production if the value of output is to be maximised.

It is worth noting briefly two special cases. First, suppose that production of each good has no opportunity cost in terms of production of the other good. This would occur if the factors used to produce each good were 'specific' and could not be re-employed in the other sector. In this case the production possibility frontier is rectangular — as $\bar{x}$ $\bar{P}$ $\bar{m}$ in Figure 9.6. Output is always maximised at $\bar{P}$, whatever the relative prices. Secondly, suppose that the mix of factors in each sector is fixed. In this case, as we have argued above, the production possibility frontier is a straight line — as mx in Figure 9.5. In this case only when relative prices are given by the slope of mx can the output maximising production point involve the production of both goods. If importables are any cheaper, it will pay to produce only exportables; if they are any more expensive it will pay to produce only importables. Note that if relative prices are given by the slope of the production possibility frontier, all production points have the same value.

We can use Figure 9.6 to analyse the effects of a devaluation. Let the relative prices be given by the slope of $\bar{a}\ \bar{b}$. Then production is maximised at $\bar{P}$. This may be brought about either by the free play of perfect competition with profit maximising firms or by planning or by some other hybrid method. Suppose domestic absorption is at Q_1. At Q_1 domestic consumption of exportables is less than their production and domestic consumption of importables exceeds their production. The value of expenditure at Q_1, assessed in the same way as the value of production as described above, is clearly less than the value of production, so the economy is running a current account surplus. At Q_2 the value of expenditure exceeds the value of output so the economy is running a deficit. At $\bar{Q}$ expenditure and output have the same value — the economy consumes more importables than it produces but pays for these by producing more exportables than it consumes and selling the excess abroad.

To make it interesting suppose that the economy is consuming at Q_2. Given that the country is small a devaluation will not lead to any change in relative prices so that the production point $\bar{P}$ will still be the mix of outputs that maximises the value of output. So the devaluation will only reduce the deficit if it succeeds in reducing the real absorption of the economy. But this is exactly the same as in the one good case and the arguments for and against devaluation as a process of reducing the deficit require no further elaboration. This is a very general result which depends on the invariance of relative prices to the outputs and demands of the home economy. Since the production pattern that maximises output depends only on relative prices, the pattern is not affected either by the devaluation or by variations in domestic demand.

Moreover it should already be clear that the case for devaluation based on increased employment is no stronger when the economy produces two traded goods than it was when only one was produced. Instead of defining a unique production possibility frontier suppose that for each level of employment a separate curve is defined. Two are shown in Figure 9.7. Without more explicit assumptions about the technologies in each sector it is difficult to say much about the forms of each curve except that they must have the same general shape and that the curve for each successively higher level of employment must lie outside the previous one. In fact, given that relative prices are fixed all we need to know is the output expansion path, the locus of points of tangency between relative price lines and the various production possibility curves, for this particular relative price. Now, even though absorption may remain stubbornly at Q_2, devaluation will eliminate the deficit if it increases employment and shifts the economy up the output expansion path OZ

Figure 9.7

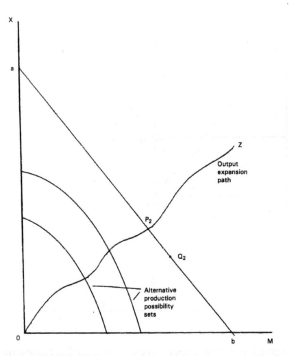

as far as P_2. This could occur if the devaluation succeeded in reducing the product wage. This is precisely analogous to the case described in the section above on the simplest case of exchange rate policy under fixed exchange rates.

The addition of an extra good holds out the hope that employment may be increased by a change in relative prices that favours expansion in the labour intensive sector (possibly relative rather than absolute expansion) but in the small country case such a shift in relative prices is not possible so that the only way that devaluation can increase employment is by cutting the product wage in each sector leading to increased demand for labour by producers. Given that this involves a cut in the real wages received by labour it is again hard to see why devaluation should have any more than a temporary effect. Again the addition of the extra traded good does not lead us to modify our previous argument.

Traded and Non-traded Goods

In the previous section we have shown that there is not much to be gained by distinguishing between different *traded* goods when the country is small. In this section we assume that all traded goods can be lumped

Figure 9.8

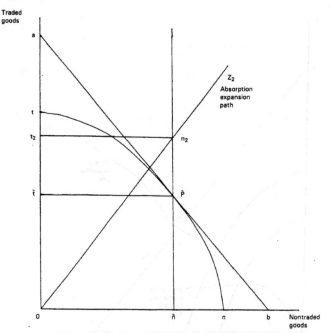

together and treated as a single good. We distinguish this composite traded good from another good which does not enter international trade. In Figure 9.8, the output of traded goods is shown on the vertical axis, and of non-traded goods on the horizontal axis. The previous discussion of the shape of the production possibility frontier remains sound and the frontier is shown by the curve in Figure 9.8. Suppose that the relative price of traded and non-traded goods is given by the slope of *ab*. (For the moment assume that this relative price is exogenous.) The value of output is maximised at $\tilde{P}$ where $\tilde{n}$ of non-traded and $\tilde{t}$ of traded goods are produced. Since, by definition, the domestic supply and demand for non-traded goods must be equal, realised domestic demand for non-traded goods must also be $\tilde{n}$ so that the economy must both produce and consume on the vertical line through $\tilde{n}$. We know from our previous arguments that if it consumes at some point above $\tilde{P}$, say n_2, the country will be running a balance of payments deficit on current account, as the absorption of traded goods t_2 exceeds their production $\tilde{t}$. Conversely consumption at points below P will produce a current surplus.

Suppose that the proportion of expenditure on each good depends on the relative price but not on the level of expenditure. Corresponding to each relative price there is a ray which may be called the absorption expansion path. The precise position of the economy's consumption point depends on the level of expenditure which, it is assumed, is controlled by the government. The absorption expansion path corresponding to the relative price given by ab is OZ_2. When the relative price of non-traded goods is lower than that implied by ab the absorption expansion path will lie below OZ_2 — that is, the proportion of non-traded goods in consumption will be higher. If the government wants the market for non-traded goods to clear in such a way that both producers and consumers fulfil their plans, it will have to manage the level of expenditure so that at the prices given by ab, the economy consumes at n_2. We know that this is a sustainable policy as far as producers are concerned — their decision to produce at $\bar{P}$ depends only on relative prices as long as demand for the non-traded output is forthcoming. However, the policy involves running a current account deficit and reducing the home country's net foreign assets. If it is the private sector's assets that are falling, then eventually its net wealth must become negative and before then the private sector will want to reduce its expenditure, and retreat down the OZ_2 ray towards the origin. Their demand for the non-traded goods will fall below $\tilde{n}$, the quantity which firms wish to supply at the given relative price. In the absence of sufficient demand firms will reduce their output resulting in unemployment. This can be avoided if the private sector's wealth is held constant. But this means that the government must bear the entire national dishoarding at n_2. It is not necessary to assume that the government itself absorbs traded and non-traded goods, merely that its net transfers to the private sector are equal to the current account deficit.

In practice, because of the way fixed exchange rate systems have been controlled, the country's loss of net foreign assets will normally be reflected in a decline in the government's own net foreign assets. How can the government eliminate this drain on its assets while at the same time keeping the economy at the same level of factor utilisation — that is maintaining the production point on the frontier tn? If net income transfers to the private sector are reduced, expenditure will be lower but consumption of non-traded goods will tend to fall below $\tilde{n}$. What is needed is an accompanying policy to increase the proportion of non-traded goods in expenditure (and possibly reduce their supply). The home currency price of traded goods is fixed by the exchange rate and the world price of traded goods. Suppose that the price of non-traded goods is fixed in domestic currency. In this case changes in the exchange rate will lead to equiproportionate changes in the relative price of traded and non-traded goods. In particular a devaluation will increase the domestic currency price of traded goods and increase the price of traded goods relative to non-traded goods. The devaluation will also increase the domestic price level, cutting real wealth and probably reducing the private sector's expenditure. It is assumed here that this temporary second round effect on expenditure is met by an appropriate adjustment to the government's policy on net transfers.

An increase in the relative price of traded goods will cause the home economy to shift to a new absorption expansion path below OZ_2 which involves a higher proportion of expenditure on non-traded goods. The higher relative price of traded goods means that the production point will shift to the left. So a combination of a fall in expenditure and a change in the exchange rate is required to shift the economy from a position of chronic and ultimately unsustainable current account deficit to one of balance of payments equilibrium if full employment is to be maintained. The before and after positions are illustrated in Figure 9.9.

The introduction of non-traded goods into the description of the economy has been very important because it re-establishes a role for exchange rate policy for small economies even when, as was generally presumed during the 1950s and 1960s, the government is deemed to have control over the level of expenditure in the economy. The importance of non-traded goods was first stressed by W.E.G. Salter (1959). It was generally assumed that the *ex ante* equilibrium in the market for non-traded goods was equivalent to, or, at the very least, analogous with, the concept of full employment in income-expenditure models. If, *ex ante*, there was excess demand for non-traded goods, this would lead to upward pressure on their price and so to an incipient inflation; if, *ex ante*, there was excess supply of the good, realised supply would be less than desired supply and this margin of supply would not in fact be produced, leading to unemployment in the non-traded sector. These dire alternatives could be avoided in principle by the continuous careful application of expenditure controlling policies and accompanying exchange rate policy so that the economy could be maintained in a position of neoclassical equilibrium at which the rigidly fixed price of non-traded goods turned out to be the equilibrium price.

While the recognition of the existence of non-traded goods is a valuable insight, the simple account given above may be thought inadequate on at least two counts. First the assumption that the economy's problems are caused by the rigid money price of non-traded goods is unrealistic: it is generally believed that it is rigidity in labour markets not product markets which is important. The implications of assuming that wages are not fully flexible are considered below. Secondly while the description

Figure 9.9

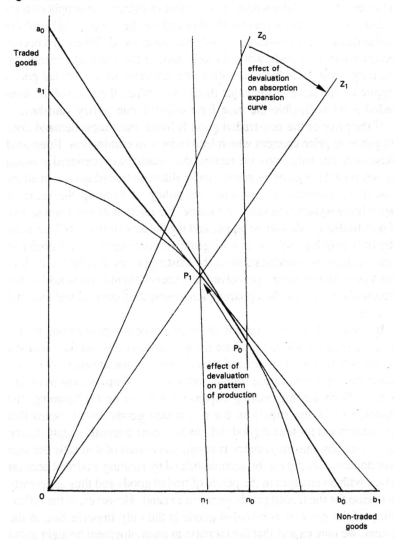

Curves indexed 0 refer to pre-devaluation position.
Curves indexed 1 refer to post-devaluation position.

shows how exchange rate and expenditure policy should be combined in order to attain continuously internal and external balance, it contains no discussion of what would happen if the economy were not in internal balance. Suppose, for example, there is an *ex ante* excess demand for non-traded goods. If the price of the non-traded good did in fact increase, while the authorities maintained a policy of managing demand to keep the value of expenditures equal to the value of output, the supply of non-traded goods would increase while demand for them would fall until the excess demand for non-traded goods was eliminated. When this occurred the balance of trade would be zero too, as the value of expenditure and output are equal by assumption and the value of non-traded goods supplied is the same as the value demanded. When the price of the non-traded good is flexible the case for exchange rate policy vanishes.

If the price of the non-traded good is fixed, the excess demand does not generate price changes which lead to its own elimination. Frustrated consumers may either save the income they would have preferred to spend on non-traded goods or switch the expenditure to traded goods. In either case if the government maintains its policy of keeping the value of expenditure equal to the value of income, the realised demand and supply of non-traded goods will be equal, and the balance of trade will be zero. The only problem will be that disgruntled consumers would prefer to consume more non-traded goods at the existing prices. It is hard to believe that a government would perceive this excess demand and would rather congratulate itself on the apparent achievement of internal and external balance.

If, on the other hand, there is an *ex ante* excess supply of non-traded goods, producers will not produce the unwanted goods and their realised supply will be less than desired supply, and, in the absence of a com-pensating expansion in the traded goods sector, employment must fall as well. Such a compensating expansion will not be forthcoming: the existence of excess supply in the non-traded goods sector means that desired demand for traded goods will exceed their domestic supply. Given the assumption that the country is small, this excess of domestic demand over domestic supply can be accommodated by running a current account deficit with no changes in the prices of traded goods and thus apparently no reason for the traded goods sector to expand. However, if the inflex-ibility of the price of non-traded goods is the only imperfection in the system, we may expect that the increase in unemployment brought about by the failure of the output of non-traded goods to reach its desired level will result in a fall in the wage level. This increases the desired level of output in both sectors, but since the non-traded sector is already in a state of excess supply, employment will not be increased here. But in the traded goods sector extra output can always be sold at the given price on the world market. Consequently as long as the wage falls to clear the labour market the fall in employment in the non-traded goods sector will all be absorbed in the traded goods sector. Furthermore, since the demand and supply of non-traded goods must necessarily be equal *ex post*, if the government controls expenditure to keep the value of output equal to the value of expenditure, the current account will be in balance. The final position this time is one in which consumers are satisfied with the quantity of non-traded goods and traded goods they receive, the economy is at full employment (thanks to the flexible wage) and producers of non-traded goods are dismayed at not being able to find buyers for the output they would be prepared to supply. Under these circumstances it is not obvious that governments would realise they had a problem at all.

The appeal of exchange rate policy in this case depends very much on the accompanying budgetary policy. We can consider the role of devaluation when, rather than fixing the level of expenditure, the government varies expenditure to maintain equilibrium in the balance of payments. Clearly there is no case for exchange rate changes for balance of payments reasons. Our previous analyses suggest that we may find a motive for exchange rate intervention arising from short-run wage rigidity so that the exchange rate may affect employment. In the ensuing analysis we assume that the price of non-traded goods is completely flexible so that excess supply or demand for non-traded goods is always zero; and also that demand is managed to keep the value of expenditure equal to the value of output, so there is always equilibrium in the balance of payments. Furthermore suppose that the nominal wage is fixed, and that there is substantial unemployment of labour and of other factors. This last assumption means that an increase in the output of one sector does not entail a fall in the output of the other since the level of unemployment may fall. Suppose now that the exchange rate is devalued. The price of the traded good rises in equal proportion so that the product wage in the traded sector falls. Therefore output in this sector must increase. Given our assumptions the increase in output must lead to an increase in expenditure, part of which is reflected in an increase in demand for non-traded goods. Even without this increase in expenditure the demand for non-traded goods would have risen because of the decline in the price of non-traded goods relative to the price of traded goods. So for two reasons the pre-devaluation output of the non-traded sector is now inadequate. The price of non-traded goods rises which tends to check the increase in demand from the relative price side. Output of non-traded goods rises. If the elasticity of supply in the non-traded sector is very high, output will rise substantially with little change in prices, while if the elasticity is low, the effect will be felt mainly in the form of price changes. At worst, however output will have risen to the extent that output in the traded goods sector has increased. Thus using this more natural notion of internal balance, we see again that the exchange rate can potentially be used to manage the level of employment.

In earlier sections we have been sceptical about the potential for exchange rate changes affecting employment in the long run because of *erosion* brought about by the fixity of real wages. These conclusions are unaffected by the introduction of non-traded goods. Suppose first that wages are fixed in terms of traded goods. After the devaluation both the price of traded goods and the nominal wage increase in the same proportion. So there is no change in the product wage in the traded goods sector and no change in output in the traded goods sector. If the price of non-traded goods is fixed in the short run, the relative price of non-traded goods will have fallen and so demand for non-traded goods will have increased. But output will have fallen in this sector because the product wage in terms of non-traded goods has risen. In order to eliminate the excess demand the price of non-traded goods will have to rise to neutralise the change in relative prices and the rise in the product wage. The final position is with unchanged output but a higher price level.

If, however, wages are fixed in terms of non-traded goods, it is the output of the non-traded goods sector that is fixed. After the devaluation output in the traded goods sector expands in the usual way. But the increase in the demand for non-traded goods is not met by increased supply. Prices rise in the non-traded goods sector, dragging the wage upwards, equilibrium is regained and the prices of non-traded goods and the wage have risen just enough to offset the effects of the devaluation. Thus, whichever good is the wage good, erosion is just as much a problem in the presence of non-traded goods as it is in their absence. (It is straightforward to generalise this result to the case where the wage is a weighted average of goods prices.)

A Special Model: Devaluation in the Income Expenditure Model

The previous account of the effects of devaluation has concentrated on identifying motives for devaluation in models which assume efficient behaviour by firms. The income-expenditure framework, used for example by all the main forecasting groups in the UK, is built around the extended income-expenditure identity

$$Y = C + I + G + X - M$$

where Y is income, C is consumption, I is investment, G is government consumption, X is exports and M imports. All variables are measured in volume terms. Generally exports are considered a function of a world activity variable and some indicator of competitiveness with imports a function of a domestic activity variable and an alternative measure of competitiveness. Thus typically[2]

$$X = X(WT, RPX)$$

$$M = M(D, RPM)$$

where WT is world trade, D is final demand $(D = C + I + G + X)$ and the RPX and RPM are the relative prices of exports to some world index of export prices and of imports to some measure of domestic prices respectively.

The export equation then is essentially a model of world demand for the goods produced by the home economy. It is implicitly assumed that world trade (particularly in manufactures) is characterised by, at the very least, monopolistic competition so that the home economy has some control over the relative price of its output and thus over the sales it secures. The world trade variable is analogous to the level of (real) income variable in consumption functions. Since no domestic variables are considered, other than the domestic component of the relative price term, it is implicitly assumed that exports are never reduced because firms are unable or unwilling to produce or because domestic demand is so high that goods which would otherwise have been exported are diverted to the home market. In terms of reconciling this system with the earlier discussion it would be sufficient to assume that, at the ruling factor prices, firms are always prepared to supply more goods at the given output prices — in other words, a situation of generalised excess supply exists.

The import equation, on the other hand, attempts to model domestic demand. As imports are unaffected by variations in domestic production, it must be assumed that there is no local production of importables. Again, this is an extreme view. However, once appropriate assumptions have been made about the structure of production and demand, the analysis of the effects of exchange rate changes on output and employment is as straightforward as before.

One advantage of considering this rather special model is that variants of it have often been estimated econometrically. The analysis of the effects of exchange rate changes has often concluded that they are at best temporary. To make such statements we have had to assume that the temporary increase in exports (say) does not generate any increase in investment (say) so that a temporary stimulus may be more generally spread throughout the economy with domestic expenditures taking over the role of engine of growth as the competitive advantage is eroded. If the induced investment reduces the costs of producing traded goods the loss of competitiveness might be slowed or avoided. Certainly, in the short run, expansion of output normally reduces average unit labour costs. Even if the increase in exports is only temporary the beneficial effects on employment and output may be prolonged by the induced effects on domestic expenditure. It clearly makes a great deal of difference whether it takes twenty years or two months to return to the original equilibrium. The only way of investigating the quantitative persistence of devaluation is by examination of the large macro models of the economy which in principle include all the second round effects. Simulation results from macro models must be treated with circumspection if not downright suspicion because of the known inadequacies of data, estimation techniques and model structure. Nevertheless they provide a starting point which practical discussions of exchange rate policy must take account of.

Table 9.1 (a) sketches the effects of a ten per cent devaluation on the main macroeconomic variables in the National Institute's Model 6. As anticipated the devaluation stimulates exports by improving competitiveness. In the National Institute's model the effect is greatest after two years and thereafter starts to decline. Consumers' expenditure is reduced in the first two years as real wages are initially reduced. As real wages improve and as the economy starts to expand consumption increases. The overall effect is to smooth out the effect on GDP which is greatest after three years. The general pattern of erosion of the gain to competitiveness is quite marked. It is reported that immediately after the devaluation export price competitiveness is improved by eight per cent but that by the end of five years only about two per cent of the gain remains so that presumably the stimulus from exports will in due course be extinguished.

Panel (b) of Table 9.1 shows the effects of a five per cent revaluation in the Treasury model. Making due allowance for the differences in sign and size of the exchange rate changes in the two simulations, we see that the effects on GDP are much the same initially in both models, but the effect in the Treasury model dies away in the fourth year while that in the National Institute, though declining, is still substantial.

One point to note in the National Institute simulation is that the current account of the balance of payments actually deteriorates at first, contrary to the usual expectations of exchange rate policy. This is the so-called *J*-curve which arises from the much slower adjustment of quantities than prices. Following a change in relative prices it takes some

Table 9.1: Exchange Rate Policy in Models of the UK Economy[a]

(a) *Effect of a 10 per cent devaluation in the National Institute's Model 6*

End of year	GDP	C	X	M	CB	RW	$\dot{P}$
1	0.4	−0.3	2.4	0.6	−358	−0.6	2.1
2	1.0	0.0	3.3	0.3	−53	+0.8	1.5
3	1.2	0.2	2.5	−0.6	−35	+1.6	0.7
4	1.0	0.2	2.2	−0.7	232	+1.2	1.2

(b) *Effects of a 5 per cent revaluation in the Treasury Model*

Year	GDP	$\dot{P}$
1	−0.2	−0.5
2	−0.5	−1.2
3	−0.5	−1.0
4	0.0	−1.5

Sources: (a) S. Brooks and S.G.B. Henry (1983). The figures for *RW* and $\dot{P}$ may be inferred from their Table 10.5. (b) HM Treasury (1982).

   a. Figures given are percentage deviations from base except for *CB* which is the deviation in £m at current prices.

Notation:
GDP = Gross domestic product (£1980m)
C = Consumers' expenditure (£1980m)
X = Exports of goods and services (£1980m)
M = Imports of goods and services (£1980m)
CB = Current balance (£m)
RW = Real wage (averge earnings per man ÷ consumer price index)
$\dot{P}$ = Inflation rate: consumer price index in (a); retail price index in (b).

time for firms to adjust production and establish new contracts with customers; similarly importers may not be able to switch their demand from foreign to domestic sources of supply. Adjustment will be all the more sluggish if it takes time for the new relative prices to be perceived and trusted. In the very short run export and import quantities may not change at all. However, export and import prices measured in domestic currency have increased. In the 'small country' case both prices will have increased in the same proportion as the devaluation. Thus if the balance of trade was in deficit before the devaluation, that deficit will have increased in the same proportion as devaluation as well. In the economic models discussed above the situation is even worse as it is generally assumed that the UK is much 'smaller' in terms of import markets than export markets. For example in the National Institute model import prices in sterling rise in exactly the same proportion as the devaluation (Brooks, 1983); export prices rise by much *less* as firms pass on most of the devaluation to their customers in the form of lower foreign currency prices — in fact, as mentioned above, competitiveness improves by eight per cent at once, implying a two per cent rise in export prices measured in sterling.

The adverse effect on the balance of trade is purely a price effect as in the short run quantities exported and imported are unchanged. In subsequent periods, as the relative price changes start to work, exports increase and imports decline which improves the balance both in real and nominal terms. The decline in imports is offset by the increase in import demand resulting from higher domestic expenditure which offsets the competitiveness effect. Somewhat paradoxically the balance in nominal terms improves as competitiveness is eroded and export prices rise faster than import prices. When discussing the effects of exchange rate changes on the balance of payments it is vital to distinguish the real from the nominal effects.

In this chapter the usefulness of the exchange rate as a policy instrument has been predicated on the assumption that at least in the short term variations in the exchange rate can lead to relative price changes with implications for output employment and the balance of payments. Under favourable circumstances exchange rate policy can be used to manipulate the product wage, competitiveness, the terms of trade, the relative price of traded and non-traded goods. Normally the policy has effects on the general price levels which have been neglected often by the assumption that, if such changes would have affected real expenditure, government fiscal policy would have shifted to prevent this. But the simulation results cited above show that, at least in the short term, by raising the price level, devaluation also increases the rate of inflation. Given the policy effort devoted to the control of inflation *per se*, we turn to the analysis of this topic in the next chapter.

Notes

1. The wealth adjustment hypothesis and the preferences of asset holders are discussed more fully in Chapter 11.

2. See, for example, Brooks (1983), HM Treasury (1982), London Business School (1984). Occasionally attempts have been made to allow for the pressure of domestic demand as a dampening effect on exports and the availability of domestic output as a dampening effect on imports.

10 EXCHANGE RATE POLICY AND THE RATE OF INFLATION

Imported Inflation

The previous chapter considered how manipulation of the exchange rate may permit control over some *real* quantity, with particular attention focused on employment and the balance of payments. In this chapter we turn to two related problems.

(1) Can exchange rate policy be used as an anti-inflationary policy?
(2) Through what channels might such a policy operate?

The very simplest model is used to examine this question: only one good is produced; a portion of the output of this good, the exportable, is exchanged for imports; production is characterised by diminishing returns to scale in the only variable factor of production which is labour; output is produced by competitive firms or, at least, by profit maximising firms whose output is small relative to world output; the country's consumption of importables is small relative to the world's output of importables. The discussion of the effects of devaluation in the previous chapter is sufficient to indicate the effects of departures from these assumptions.

The Arithmetical Relationship between Exchange Rate Changes and Inflation

The 'small country' assumption means that, as usual, the home country's price of exportables P_x and of importables P_m are given by the foreign prices and the exchange rate:

$$P_x = P_x^*/e$$

$$P_m = P_m^*/e.$$

If the composition of the home country's expenditure depends only on the relative price of exportables and importables, then the home country's price level P is similarly equal to the foreign price level divided by the exchange rate:[1]

$$P = P^*/e$$

where:

$$P = \lambda P_x + (1 - \lambda) P_m \quad 0 < \lambda < 1$$

$$P^* = \lambda P_x^* + (1 - \lambda) P_m^*.$$

Consider the proportional change in P between two periods, the home country's rate of inflation. Now, using the relation between foreign prices, the exchange rate and domestic prices, $e_t P_t = P_t^*$, the change in foreign prices is just $e_{t+1}P_{t+1} - e_t P_t = P_{t+1}^* - P_t^*$. After some tedious manipulation, the basic relation between exchange rates and the price levels can be derived:

$$\frac{P_{t+1} - P_t}{P_t} + \frac{e_{t+1} - e_t}{e_t} + \frac{(e_{t+1} - e_t)}{e_t}\frac{(P_{t+1} - P_t)}{P_t} = \frac{P_{t+1}^* - P_t^*}{P^*}$$

If $\hat{x}$ is used to denote the proportional change in x, then this can be written as:

$$\hat{P} + \hat{e} + \hat{P}\hat{e} = \hat{P}*$$

or

$$\hat{P} = (\hat{P}* - \hat{e})/(1 + \hat{e}).$$

This relation is exact. For small changes it may be approximated by

$$\hat{P} = \hat{P}* - \hat{e}.$$

In words, the rate of inflation equals the foreign rate of inflation less the proportionate increase in the exchange rate. Suppose that the foreign rate of inflation is five per cent per annum, if the home country's government could engineer an appreciation of five per cent there would be no inflation at all in the home country. So exchange rate management is, potentially, an anti-inflationary policy. Note at once that a policy of influencing the rate of inflation by means of the exchange rate involves continuous appreciation or depreciation. A once and for all change in the exchange rate will affect the price *level* and thus the rate of inflation measured over a short period. But if thereafter the exchange rate is fixed the domestic rate of inflation will be coupled to the world rate of inflation. For this reason an active exchange rate policy directed at the rate of inflation is incompatible with a commitment to maintaining fixed exchange rates and thus has only become an important issue in the past fifteen years or so. This change of practice is discussed more fully in Chapter 6.

However, it is also true that *any* policy that generates a five per cent appreciation will lead to price stability even though this policy does not consist exclusively of direct intervention in the foreign exchange market. Normal usage attributes an 'exchange rate policy' to any government which considers the exchange rate implications of other policies although the exchange rate is in this case more like a constraint on policy than a policy instrument itself. For the rest of this chapter, intervention in the foreign exchange market will be referred to as *direct* exchange rate policy, all other actions undertaken at least partly with the intention of affecting the exchange rate will be called *indirect* policies. Under the current system of 'managed' floating most exchange rate policy is indirect and it is necessary to consider in some detail the links between exchange rates, asset accumulation and interest rates.

Inflation, Capital Losses and Expenditure at Full Employment: Basics[2]

The easiest case to consider is when the government has only the direct policy available, and money wages are perfectly flexible. In this case, given a constant labour force, real output Y_t will be constant at the full employment level in every period

$$Y_t = \bar{Y}.$$

If there is no taxation or government expenditure, the private sector's disposable income is equal to the value of this level of output. It is convenient to assume that, by suitable choice of units, $P_m^* = P_x^* = P^*$. It follows that disposable income is

$$P_t Y_t = P_t \bar{Y}.$$

Assuming that the share of each good in expenditure depends only on relative prices then since the relative price of exportables and importables is fixed, we can talk of a unit of real expenditure E_t made up of λ units of exportable and $(1 - \lambda)$ units of importable. The price of a unit of expenditure is, of course, P_t. The net accumulation of wealth by the private sector, ΔW, is

$$\Delta W_t = P_t (\bar{Y} - E_t).$$

If the government is not accumulating assets, then ΔW_t is equal to the current balance B_t. Since asset accumulation is allowed, some assumption must be made about the type of assets that are in fact saved. While it would be perfectly possible for the private sector to store goods, it is potentially more realistic to assume that, in fact, they accumulate only financial assets. Remember that in this context the use of the personal sector's savings for investment by the company sector is a transfer within the private sector. What we are considering here is the accumulation of claims on either the government or on foreigners. Such assets may be required to permit consumption when income falls for some reason (a natural disaster or the exhaustion of a natural resource (see Chapter 12), for example). Suppose that the private sector holds its wealth entirely in the form of domestic currency. If it receives foreign currency for the goods it exports and pays for its imports with the foreign currency, it will wish to exchange with the government domestic currency, equal to the value of the current surplus in foreign currency (we assume non-residents do not hold domestic currency).

The accumulation of assets involves foregoing absorption now for the sake of the possibility of absorption in the future, so it is reasonable to suppose that for any given flow of income there is some level of wealth that is considered best. If current wealth is below this level, accumulation is positive, if above this level, negative. If $\bar{W}_t$ is the optimum level of wealth for the full employment level of income at the current price level, the rate of accumulation of assets in nominal terms can be written as

$$\Delta W_t = \theta_t(\bar{W}_t - W_{t-1}) \qquad 0 < \theta_t < 1$$

θ_t is the proportion of the discrepancy between desired and actual wealth that is eliminated by accumulation in the current period. It seems unlikely that, in general, the whole of the discrepancy would be eliminated straightaway. The greater the necessary accumulation, the more current consumption must be given up. On the other hand, if it is desired to reduce wealth, it seems more likely that the extra consumption will be spread over several periods rather than being taken all at once. In the simple case where desired wealth is a multiple of income, this formula reduces to

$$\Delta W_t = \theta_t(\alpha P_t \bar{Y} - W_{t-1}). \qquad \alpha > 0$$

But we know that the change in wealth is the value of the excess of income over expenditure, $P_t(\bar{Y} - E_t)$. Moreover, as the level of real income is fixed, by substituting for ΔW and re-arranging the result, an absorption or expenditure function can be obtained

$$E_t = (1 - \theta_t \alpha)\bar{Y} + \theta_t \frac{W_{t-1}}{P_t}.$$

If, furthermore, the real level of wealth, R_t, is defined as nominal wealth divided by the price level (that is, $R_t = W_t/P_t$) then this expression for real expenditure can be written as

$$E_t = (1 - \theta_t \alpha)\bar{Y} + \frac{\theta_t R_{t-1}}{1 + \hat{P}_t}$$

where as before $\hat{P}_t$ is the rate of inflation, expressed as the proportional change in the price level.

The first term in this real expenditure function is analogous to the familiar consumption function, as comparing countries which have different levels of $\bar{Y}$ but are otherwise identical will yield a 'marginal propensity' to spend of $(1 - \theta_t \alpha)$. An increase of one unit in the level of full employment income increases desired real wealth by α units but since only θ_t of these units are accumulated in the first period, saving will increase by $\theta_t \alpha$ units in real terms, leaving an extra $(1 - \theta_t \alpha)$ units left over for spending.

The second term is important as it includes the channel by means of which *inflation* itself affects real expenditure.[3] An increase in the rate of inflation of 1 per cent reduces expenditure by $0.01 \, \theta_t R_{t-1}/(1 + \hat{P}_t)^2$ units. To see why this is so, suppose that the price level rises by 1 per cent. Then the desired *nominal* level of wealth also rises by 1 per cent, increasing the nominal gap to be closed by asset accumulation. Looked at in real terms, the increase in the price level does not increase the desired level of *real* wealth, $\bar{R}$, but reduces the purchasing power of the existing stock of assets W_{t-1}. The amount of this capital loss depends on the size of the existing stock of assets and the size of the change in price level. The *real* capital loss is just

$$(1 - \frac{P_{t-1}}{P_t})R_{t-1}.$$

Subtracting this from the *real* stock of assets gives the *real* stock of assets after revaluations. It is

$$R_{t-1} - (1 - \frac{P_{t-1}}{P_t})R_{t-1} = R_{t-1} \cdot \frac{P_{t-1}}{P_t} = \frac{R_{t-1}}{1 + \hat{P}_t}.$$

If the rate of inflation were eleven per cent rather than ten per cent the capital loss would be

$$(1 - \frac{1}{1.11})R_{t-1}$$

rather than

$$(1 - \frac{1}{1.10})R_{t-1}.$$

Thus the change in the capital loss is (approximately)

$$(\frac{1.11-1.10}{1.10^2})R_{t-1}.$$

But since only a proportion θ_t of the capital loss is made up in the current period, the difference in expenditure in the two cases would be

$$(\frac{0.1}{1.10^2})\theta_t R_{t-1}$$

as indicated above.

It is also worth noting that as domestic currency is the only means by which saving can be undertaken, 'wealth adjustment' is the same as 'demand for money'. The only amendment necessary is to substitute M_t for W_t throughout. It is the formulation of the wealth adjustment hypothesis as a demand for money equation that has been responsible in part for the confusion between 'monetarism' and the 'monetary approach to the balance of payments': see especially Frenkel and Johnson (1976) for an elucidation of this point.

Equilibrium and Exchange Rate Policy. In this simple model, if the adjustment coefficient θ_t is a constant, full equilibrium is not possible unless the rate of inflation is zero. This is because in equilibrium, real wealth is constant and expenditure equals income. But if expenditure *does* equal income, real wealth cannot be constant if a positive rate of inflation is leading to continuous capital losses. However, a sort of equilibrium is possible at which the rate of asset accumulation is constant and just fast enough to offset the capital losses arising from inflation.

In the pseudo-equilibrium, the private sector is hoarding at a constant rate, in real terms, and accumulating domestic currency at a constant real rate. The government is increasing its reserves of foreign currency at a constant real rate and increasing its liabilities, the domestic money supply issued, at a constant real rate. (Under fixed exchange rates and given a commitment to convertibility the domestic money supply is quite properly a liability of the government because the private sector might wish to exchange domestic currency for foreign currency.) Thus the private sector is accumulating assets while the government's net wealth is constant. It follows that the home country as a whole is accumulating assets and is therefore running a current account surplus.

Suppose instead the government adopts a policy of maintaining a constant level of foreign exchange reserves. In this case domestic residents who receive foreign currency from the proceeds of exports can exchange it for domestic currency only with those domestic residents who need foreign currency to pay for imports. (Remember that we are assuming there is no foreign demand for domestic currency.) Since initially there is a current account surplus, the supply of foreign currency exceeds its demand at the current exchange rate. Competition amongst exporters to get the limited supplies of domestic currency will reduce the price of foreign exchange in terms of domestic currency and so lead to an appreciation. The rise in the exchange rate reduces the domestic price level below what it would have been under the fixed exchange rate. The fall in the price level reduces the capital loss and so reduces the incentive for the private sector to hoard in equilibrium. This reduction in accumulation reduces the excess supply of foreign currency. If competition causes the domestic country's exchange rate to appreciate at the same rate as the foreign rate of inflation, there will be no inflation and no capital losses and thus no incentive to hoard in equilibrium because the domestic price level will be constant. So exports will equal imports and expenditure will equal income.

In this, the simplest case, a *direct* policy aimed at accumulating foreign exchange reserves will hold the exchange rate down, induce a current account surplus and cause foreign inflation to be transmitted directly to the domestic economy via the prices of traded goods. A policy of non-intervention, however, eliminates inflation and generates balance of payments equilibrium. (Remember that full employment is maintained by flexible wages.)

While the structure of this model is very simple, it already contains the basic ingredient of the old-fashioned foreign exchange crisis — a government-owned stock of foreign exchange. If the government intervenes to prevent the exchange rate from rising, it will accumulate foreign exchange without limit; if it tries to prevent the rate from falling the exchange reserves will be exhausted eventually, and the policy will have to be altered. It also demonstrates the link between monetary policy and exchange rate policy. When the exchange rate was fixed, the government assumed an obligation to exchange domestic and foreign currency at a given price and thus surrendered control of the money supply. Increases in its foreign exchange reserves were exactly matched by increases in the money supply. Under floating exchange rates, the government regains control of the nominal money supply although, in this simple model, variations in the nominal stock of money will merely lead to price level changes in equilibrium to maintain the relation between real output and real wealth.

The Effects of Allowing for More Financial Assets. The framework needs to be made more realistic by increasing the number of assets that the private sector can hold and by reconsidering the assumption that the domestic level of output is fixed. Also the assumption that non-residents do not hold domestic assets can be relaxed. In this section we suppose that domestic residents hold a portfolio containing domestic currency, foreign currency, domestic securities (government stock) and foreign securities. The private sector's financial wealth, in units of domestic currency, is

$$W_t = M_t^d + S_t^d + (M_t^f + S_t^f)/e_t$$

where M is the stock of currency held, S the stock of securities, e is the exchange rate and $(\ )^d$ and $(\ )^f$ denote domestic and foreign currency denominated assets respectively.

In this richer model, the change in real wealth R_t is equal to the real excess of income over expenditure, $(\bar{Y} - E_t)$, *plus* interest receipts *less* capital losses arising from changes in the price level and from changes in the exchange rate with both interest receipts and capital losses expressed in real terms. Interest receipts are the sum of income arising from domestic assets and from foreign assets expressed in domestic currency, that is

$$r_t^d S_{t-1}^d + r_t^f S_{t-1}^f/e_t$$

where S_{t-1} is the stock held at the beginning of the period, and r_t is the current interest rate. To obtain the real value of interest flows it is necessary to divide by the domestic price level, P_t. The total capital loss on the beginning-of-period stock of wealth is obtained by subtracting the real value of the beginning-of-period stocks of assets evaluated at the old price level and exchange rate from their real value at current price levels and exchange rates:

$$\text{Capital loss} = \frac{1}{P_{t-1}}\left(M_{t-1}^d + \frac{M_{t-1}^f}{e_{t-1}} + S_{t-1}^d + \frac{S_{t-1}^f}{e_{t-1}}\right)$$

$$- \frac{1}{P_t}\left(M_{t-1}^d + \frac{M_{t-1}^f}{e_t} + S_{t-1}^d + \frac{S_{t-1}^f}{e_t}\right)$$

$$= \frac{W_{t-1}}{P_t}\left(\hat{P}_t + \frac{1}{e_t}\hat{e}_t \, \psi_{t-1}\right)$$

where ψ is the proportion of wealth held in foreign assets. The first part of this expression is the capital loss due to domestic inflation $\hat{P}_t$ which affects the entire portfolio; the second part is the loss due to exchange rate changes, $\hat{e}_t$, which has an effect that depends on the importance of foreign assets in wealth. Note that to avoid having to deal with a further set of capital gains and losses, it has been assumed that government securities are interest bearing deposits rather than negotiable bonds.

Collecting these terms together gives an expression for the change in real wealth

$$\Delta R_t = \bar{Y} - E_t + (\frac{r_t^d S_{t-1}^d + r_t^f S_{t-1}^f / e_t}{P_t}) - \frac{R_{t-1} P_{t-1}}{P_t} (\hat{P}_t + \frac{\hat{e}_t}{1 + \hat{e}_t} \psi_{t-1}).$$

This structure is much more complicated than before. In that case the private sector had only to decide how much to hoard; in this case it must decide what to hoard as well — that is, in what proportions to hold the various assets. It is natural to suppose that the desired proportion of an asset in the portfolio increases as its own rate of return increases, and falls as the rates of return on other assets increase. The nominal rate of return on domestic money is zero as it pays no interest; its real rate of return is approximately *minus* the rate of inflation, $-\hat{P}$, as this is the cost, in terms of expenditure foregone, of holding stocks of money. The nominal rate of return on domestic securities is just the domestic rate of interest, r^d, and the real rate of return is $r^d - \hat{P}$. If exchange rates were fixed the rate of return on foreign money would be zero in nominal terms and $-\hat{P}$ in real terms. But if the exchange rate rises there will be a loss, so to get the overall rates of return the rate of appreciation $\hat{e}$ must be subtracted. The rate of return on foreign securities should now be obvious. It is shown in Table 10.1 below, which also indicates the effects of changes in the various rates of return on the demand for each asset. To obtain the real rate of return it is necessary to deduct the domestic rate of inflation from each of the nominal rates of return. It is important to note that the foreign rate of inflation does not directly effect any of these calculations. In fact the rate of appreciation of the currency is not known at the time that decisions are made: asset holders must decide how to spread their assets on the basis of their expectations about future exchange rates, and these expectations may in part be determined by expectations about the foreign rate of inflation.

Government Policy and the Rate of Inflation at Full Employment. How is the rate of inflation affected by the government's decisions about its own accumulation of foreign exchange reserves and the rate of interest

Table 10.1: Rates of Return and the Demand for Assets

Asset	Nominal rate of return	Effect on demand of a rise in:		
		r^d	r^f	$\hat{e}$
Domestic money, M^d	0	↓	↓	↑
Domestic securities, S^d	r^d	↑	↓	↑
Foreign currency, M^f	$-\hat{e}$	↓	↑	↓
Foreign securities, S^f	$r^f - \hat{e}$	↓	↓	↓

it is offering on its own debts? Suppose as before the exchange rate is fixed by *direct* policy and that as before the economy has achieved some pseudo-equilibrium. The domestic rate of inflation is the same as the foreign rate of inflation. Asset holders experience capital losses to the extent that they hold stocks of currency so that the ratio of money to income will fall unless there is, as before, some hoarding in equilibrium to keep it as its desired value.

If, as before, the government's level of indebtedness is unchanged[4] this hoarding must be reflected in a current account surplus. The only difference from the previous case is that some extra dealing in assets is necessary to keep the asset proportions right. Suppose that the current account surplus accrues initially as foreign currency in the hands of the private sector. Some proportion of this is needed to maintain the real value of the private sector's stocks of foreign currency; the rest is exchanged on the foreign exchange market for domestic currency. As the government is committed to maintaining a fixed exchange rate, it will have to buy all this foreign currency in exchange for domestic currency — which is just what the private sector wanted. Thus the pseudo-equilibrium can be maintained with a constant money to income ratio in the domestic economy, a constant real current account surplus and rising government foreign exchange reserves.

The only differences between this case and the previous one arise from the treatment of interest payments: since the domestic private sector is in receipt of interest payments on its stocks of securities, positive accumulation of financial assets no longer implies that the absorption of goods is less than the value of full employment output, merely that absorption is less than full employment output *plus* interest received.

While the government's policy of maintaining its indebtedness seems one reasonable notion of a 'neutral' background policy, it has the implication that the counterpart to any asset accumulation of the private sector has to be decumulation by non-residents. But how plausible it is to base the analysis on the assumption that the foreign sector will always be accommodating? An alternative neutral assumption is that the hoarding of the private sector finds its counterpart is an increase in the government's indebtedness. In these circumstances the current account must be in balance so that the small domestic economy does not impinge at all on the rest of the world. In particular, suppose that the government's own demand for goods (which may be for distribution to the public as a transfer or which may consist of public goods like defence) is equal to the private sector's equilibrium level of hoarding. The government and the monetary authorities finance these purchases by issuing currency or securities. In the pseudo-equilibrium the private sector is trying to accumulate money, so suppose that the authorities pay for all their purchases by issuing money. A proportion of this will be held by the private sector in order to keep its real domestic money-wealth ratio constant. With the balance the private sector will attempt to buy foreign currency. Since the exchange rate is fixed, the government is obliged to supply this, so that its foreign exchange reserves fall. The higher the proportion of its wealth that the private sector wants to keep as foreign money, the greater the fall in the foreign exchange reserves. Of course the amount of foreign assets held by all residents *including* the government is constant.

In the absence of interest bearing assets it was argued that if the government switched from a policy of maintaining the level of the exchange rate to one of maintaining the level of its foreign exchange reserves, the exchange rate would appreciate steadily and inflation would be eliminated. In the present cases things are rather more complicated. Under the first kind of neutral policy, in which the foreign sector bore the counterpart deficit to the private sector's surplus, the private sector will find that the government is no longer prepared to accept its excess foreign currency. Its efforts to purchase domestic currency bids up the exchange rate as before and reduces the price level: the fall in the price level (relative to what it would have been) reduces the capital loss while the appreciation of the currency increases the proportion of the value of the portfolio accounted for by its domestic assets. Indeed, because the nominal money supply is increased only when the monetary authorities offer domestic currency in exchange for foreign currency, a decision on their part not to increase their own stocks of foreign currency implies that the money supply will not increase either.

Under the second form of neutral policy, when the current account is in balance the effect of the government's change of policy is quite different. In that case domestic residents were prepared to accept domestic money from the government in return for goods and services on the assumption that they could exchange a portion of this for foreign exchange at the going exchange rate. The foreign currency was supplied by the government because it was committed to a fixed exchange rate. If it now decides to keep its reserves constant instead of letting them fall, the private sector will be unable to exchange its excess balances of domestic currency for foreign currency. Its efforts to do so will depreciate the currency. The higher domestic price level and new exchange rate is needed to induce the private sector to hold the excess balances of domestic currency. Thus, in this case, the adoption of a constant exchange reserves target will in fact make inflation worse. Once again the effects of a particular policy action are seen to hinge on the background assumptions.

The reasons for the difference are quite clear but nevertheless generate a useful distinction. In the first case the country as a whole was in current account surplus and accumulating claims on the rest of the world. Because the private sector wanted to accumulate some domestic assets as well as some foreign assets, the role of the government was to accept the unwanted foreign assets in exchange for its own liabilities. Its intervention in the foreign exchange market was, at the risk of oversimplification, *current account motivated*. In the second case, in which the government was a purchaser of goods, the current account was in balance. Its role in this case was to accommodate the private sector's desire for foreign assets *given* the country's overall stock of these assets — in particular to supply foreign exchange for domestic money. The government's decision to fix its own stock of foreign assets is, *given that the national stock is fixed*, equivalent to fixing the private sector's stock. In these conditions the private sector can only increase the proportion by value of foreign assets in its portfolio by depreciating the domestic currency's exchange rate. Given that the current balance was always zero, the government's original intervention policy might be called *capital account motivated*.

Even in the first case not everything is straightforward. A regime of continuous appreciation will lead to continuous exchange rate losses reducing the value in domestic currency of foreign assets held. To maintain the value of foreign assets held there will have to be some hoarding, even when the rate of inflation is zero. Interest bearing assets do not present too much of a problem. When there is a steady rate of appreciation $-\hat{e}$, the rate of return on foreign securities is $r^f - \hat{e}$. Asset holders earn nominal interest at a rate r^f. If instead on repatriating the whole of this they leave a proportion $\hat{e}$ on deposit and draw only $r^f - \hat{e}$ as income, their foreign assets will maintain their value. If no non-interest bearing assets were held, full equilibrium would be attainable if interest receipts were measured as $r^f - \hat{e}$ and income were suitably redefined. In practice the whole of r^f is counted as a current account credit. Thus even if hoarding, properly measured, were zero in equilibrium, current account data would still indicate a surplus on the balance of payments. However, even this expedient is not available for holdings of foreign currency or for cases in which the nominal rate of interest is smaller than the rate of appreciation.

Changes in Interest Rates. Now consider the effect of an increase in the rate of interest paid on domestic securities, first on the assumption that the exchange rate is kept fixed by *direct policy* under neutral government policy of the first kind (in which government indebtedness is constant). The increase in domestic interest rates leads asset holders to attempt to increase the proportion of domestic securities in their portfolios. First, asset holders will exchange a portion of their holdings of domestic currency for holdings of domestic securities. Thus the money supply falls, but this has no implications for the balance of payments as long as domestic residents alone hold stocks of domestic currency. (If non-residents reduce their stocks of domestic currency in favour of domestic securities, interest payments due abroad will increase, reducing the current surplus in the future.)

In so far as there is substitution away from foreign assets, the chain of events is more complicated, but may be thought of as follows. Some foreign securities are converted into foreign currency; asset holders then attempt to buy domestic currency with foreign currency with the ultimate intention of converting the domestic currency into domestic securities. There is an increase in the demand for domestic currency. Because the government is committed to maintaining the exchange rate, it supplies the domestic currency in exchange for foreign assets. The rise in the domestic money supply is only momentary, however, as the newly-won domestic money is straightaway exchanged for domestic securities. In the final position the government's stocks of foreign currency are higher; more domestic securities are held; and fewer foreign assets and less domestic money are held. In so far as domestic residents' holdings of foreign securities have fallen and non-residents' holdings of domestic securities have risen, the current surplus will be smaller in the future.

It is important to note that once stocks of assets have been re-arranged following the change in the interest rate, the government's stocks of foreign exchange reserves will stop increasing. Although the re-arrangement may take some time to achieve, it is nevertheless a once-and-for-all phenomenon. Thus a policy of using the interest rate to replenish the foreign exchange reserves continuously will require steadily increasing interest rates to induce asset holders to keep increasing the proportion of their wealth in the form of domestic securities.

In practice there are qualifications to this view. In order to minimise transactions costs, it may be more profitable to approach the desired asset proportions gradually by investing flows of savings and the proceeds from maturing securities in the desired assets rather than actually selling existing stocks of the 'wrong' assets. This may spread the adjustment over many periods, giving the appearance of a flow effect induced by the interest rate change. Also, the overall desired level of wealth may depend on the rates of interest available on securities. An increase in the rate of return on domestic securities means that, even without the re-arrangement of assets, the rate of return on accumulation has increased. If the desired level of financial assets depends positively on the average rate of return available, then, on our previous assumptions, asset accumulation will increase. Again, given our assumption that the level of output is maintained by flexible factor prices, this extra accumulation is accomplished by reducing expenditure and running a balance of payments surplus. Since the government is committed to maintaining the exchange rate, its foreign exchange reserves will increase if the domestic private sector's hoarding generates excess supplies of foreign currency relative to its desired holdings of foreign currency.

The preceding analysis has been only sketched out. It is extremely complicated, mainly because both *direct* policy (a decision about the rate at which the government should increase or reduce its own foreign exchange reserves) and *indirect* policy (interest rate management) have been combined in pursuit of a single objective — exchange rate stability. We have already moved away from thinking of the exchange rate as a policy instrument in the way that the rate of value added tax is a policy instrument. It is more like an intermediate target which may be more or less tightly controlled by a variety of other policies.

When the background policy is of the second kind, in which the government is purchasing goods and services from the private sector and the current account is in balance, a decision to raise the interest rate will have similar effects. The increase in the domestic interest rate will induce substitution away from domestic money and foreign assets in favour of domestic securities. Under fixed exchange rates, asset holders would, at the end of the day, have exchanged some of their foreign assets for domestic securities, so that the government's foreign exchange reserves will be at a higher level relative to their previous path.

Consequently, if there is no commitment to maintain the exchange rate, an increase in the domestic interest rate will inhibit the private sector's desire to accumulate foreign assets and so reduce the downward pressure on the exchange rate that would occur in the pseudo-equilibrium. Indeed, a sufficiently large increase in the interest rate could reverse the fall in the exchange rate at least in the short run by encouraging asset holders to switch into domestic assets to such an extent that the chronic excess demand for foreign assets is at least temporarily offset.

The logic of this particular case is quite clear. When the current account balance is zero and the government is purchasing goods and services, the private sector's rate of hoarding is consistent with its wealth adjustment plans. But the hoarding all takes place in domestic currency. While the government is committed to a fixed exchange rate, the private sector can obtain foreign exchange on demand. When the government gives up this commitment, the only way the private sector can increase the value of its holding of foreign assets is by generating an exchange rate decline. When the interest rate is higher, the private sector wants to increase its holdings of domestic assets, so the excess demand for foreign currency does not arise.

So far in this section we have considered mainly the responses of *residents* to change in the government's policy and the implications for the exchange rate and thus for the price level. We have not considered the part played by non-resident asset holders who may hold domestic assets in their portfolios. Non-resident asset holders will hold the same kinds of assets as residents, and will be subject to the same influences as residents. For example, if the government increases the rate of interest paid on its own securities, non-resident asset holders will be induced to re-arrange their portfolios in favour of domestic assets. Under the fixed exchange rate system this will augment the government's foreign exchange reserves as it accepts the foreign currency in exchange for domestic securities. Thus for most purposes the foreign sector can be treated as enhancing the response of capital flows to changes in rates of return. The most important difference is that, whereas the relationship between domestic policy and the desire to hoard of residents is strong, it does not make much sense to assume that the desire to hoard of the rest of the world is affected by the actions of the government of such a small country.

To summarise the response of asset holders to variations in the rates of return, we may note the basic conclusion that by varying the rate of interest available on domestic securities, the government can generate short-term capital flows which may lead to variations in the exchange rate. In addition, we have considered the effect of variations in the exchange rate on the rate of inflation. However, in order to keep the analysis fairly straightforward, we have assumed that output was always at the full employment so that implicitly all the inflation experienced was the result of the exchange rate failing to adjust to compensate for the foreign rate of inflation. In this sense all the inflation was imported. The idea that there is no domestic component to inflation is absurd and this subject is treated in the next part of this chapter where, again for ease of exposition, we shall economise on the description of asset holders' behaviour.

But first it is worth considering in this simple model the issue of 'confidence'. In Table 10.1 the rate of return on foreign securities was shown to be $r^f - \hat{e}$. For non-residents the rate of return on domestic assets, measured in their own currency, is $r^d + \hat{e}$. As we have noted, these are *ex post* concepts. Decisions to invest are made at the beginning of the period and, either because of contractual obligations or because of transactions costs, have to be held to for some time. Resident asset holders must make decisions on the basis of the expected rate of return, which is $r^f - \hat{e}^e$, where ( )^e denotes an expectation. Asset holders are uncertain about what the future exchange rate will be, so that the expected depreciation is just the mean of a probability distribution of outcomes. Suppose that there is a shift in expectations so that the expected rate of depreciation increases. Other things being equal, this increases the attractiveness of foreign securities for residents and reduces the attractiveness of domestic assets to non-residents. Both groups will attempt to increase the proportion of foreign assets in their portfolios and the demand for foreign exchange will rise. Unless the government is controlling the exchange rate, it will now fall to clear the market. Thus an exogenous change in expectations may well bring about the change that was anticipated in the first place.

A more subtle issue, the full discussion of which is beyond the scope of this volume, arises when the expected value of the future exchange rate is unchanged but asset holders' views about the possible spread of outcomes around this mean changes. Although the expected outcome of investment abroad has not changed, foreign assets are now perceived to be more risky. As such they become less attractive to risk-averse asset holders and substitution away from these assets will take place. Thus in a fixed exchange rate system an increase in the perceived riskiness of holding domestic assets will lead to a drain on the government's foreign exchange reserves. In a flexible rate regime the substitution away from domestic assets will lead to a fall in the exchange rate. If, as assumed, the expected value of the future exchange rate is unchanged, the fall in the current exchange rate increases the expected appreciation in the future. Thus we may expect an equilibrium at which the higher riskiness of domestic assets is just balanced, at the margin, by the higher anticipated return. If, however, the expected future exchange rate depends largely on the current exchange rate, then it is not clear that the stability of such a process can be established without making further simplifying assumptions.

This confidence effect suggests that the government may influence asset holders' behaviour by affecting their mean expectation of the future exchange rate, their confidence in this expectation, or by changing the costs and benefits to asset holders of their own inaccurate forecasts.

Domestically Generated Inflation

In the previous section inflation was generated externally and, modified by exchange rate changes, was transmitted to the home economy via goods prices. As real wages were assumed to be sufficiently flexible to clear the labour market, there was no scope for inflation to be generated internally, associated with changes in the tightness of the labour market. Phillips curve theories of inflation and their elaborations were developed in a period of fixed exchange rates in which the feedback from wage inflation onto itself via its effects on the exchange rate could be ignored. It seems likely that the wage-price spiral will be more severe under floating exchange rates, but also that manipulations of the exchange rate may allow an extra lever to be applied for inflation control. These topics are the subject of this section.

The Small Country Case

In the simplest framework, suppose that the country is still economically 'small'. For the time being it is assumed that by some suitable fiscal policy the level of real expenditure of the domestic private sector is held constant. In this case variations in the supply of traded goods must be reflected directly in the trade balance. Thus, if any exports are sold at all, the home country's export price must be the same as the world price, and the rate of inflation of domestic traded goods' prices must be the same as the rate of inflation of world prices less the rate of appreciation.

Now suppose that *all* goods are produced at constant marginal cost. For production to take place at all prices must exceed variable costs by at least the margin necessary to generate normal profits. Although the marginal costs of traded and non-traded goods may differ, the assumption that marginal costs are constant means that their relative cost (including allowance for normal profit) is constant and that their relative price will be constant in equilibrium. The price level is a weighted average of the prices of traded goods and non-traded goods. Thus the rate of inflation will be the same as the rate of increase of traded goods' prices. If production does take place, output is limited by either the size of the labour force or by available capital. When output does take place, then, in equililbrium,

$$\hat{P}_t = \hat{W}_t$$

where W_t is the wage in period t. If this condition is not met then eventually either wages or profits will exceed the value of output.

Finally let us suppose that the rate of wage inflation depends only on the level of output — the old fashioned Phillips curve —

$$\hat{W}_t = f(Y_t) \quad f' > 0.$$

Output equals the sum of the output of the traded good, Q_t, and of non-traded goods, N_t. It is illuminating to write the identities together,

$$\hat{P}_t^* - \hat{e}_t = \hat{P}_t = \hat{W}_t = f(Q_t + N_t).$$

The first equality is concerned with the state of international competitiveness; the second with the state of profitability; the third with domestically generated or local inflation.

Suppose an equilibrium has been established such that $\hat{W}_t = \hat{P}_t$. Suppose the government wishes to achieve a new lower rate of inflation. Given that the rate of inflation in the rest of the world is unaffected by this decision, this implies a new faster rate of appreciation. One method of achieving this inflation target might to be intervene directly in the exchange market. Firms are in a dilemma: unless they reduce the rate of inflation of their prices they will lose all their foreign customers; but if they reduce their rate of price increases while the rate of wage inflation is unchanged, costs will exceed prices and normal profits will no longer be earned. If they choose to maintain the margin of price over cost, for demand and output of domestic traded goods falls. This reduces the rate of wage inflation and thus the rate of domestic price inflation. A new equilibrium may be established at which the level of output is lower, the domestic rate of inflation is lower and the rate of appreciation is higher.

An alternative policy is to reduce the level of output of non-traded goods directly. This will reduce the rate of wage inflation leading in the short run to higher profits. If, however, the previous level of real wages (W/P) is re-gained, eventually domestic price inflation must fall too. Then, in order to maintain the relationship between domestic and foreign prices, the rate of appreciation will increase.

The final position is the same in each case.[5] However the policies differ in which sector bears the short-run cost of reducing the rate of inflation. When policy is directed at the exchange rate, the pressures are on profits and output in the traded goods sector; in the other case the pressures are initially on output in the non-traded goods sector and on wages. Although this analysis is deficient in many respects, the essential fact that the difference between *direct* and *indirect* policies lies in the distribution of the adjustment costs will remain largely unaltered.

It is also worth considering the determination of inflation and output under a fixed exchange rate in this model. In this case, if traded goods are produced at all, the identity is amended to read

$$\hat{P}_t^* = \hat{P}_t = \hat{W}_t = f(Q_t + N_t).$$

As before commodity arbitrage ensures that the domestic and foreign prices of traded goods change at the same rate. Suppose there is an exogenous fall in the demand for non-traded goods. Initially the rate of wage inflation falls, reducing the product wage in the traded goods sector. Demand increases and output expands increasing the rate of wage inflation and so increasing the product wage. Assuming that no capacity limits are reached, the process can continue until a new equilibrium is reached at which the real wage is at its original — the only difference being that the traded goods sector will have expanded while the non-traded goods sector will have contracted.

If in the fixed exchange rate regime the government arranges a devaluation, the product wage falls in the short run as the domestic price level is increased. Output expands which increases the rate of wage inflation. A new equilibrium will be established when wages have caught up with prices. The process is shown schematically in Figure 10.1. So far, however, we have discussed only comparative statics without specifying the rates of adjustment of the product wage, employment and output.

Downward Sloping Demand Curves, Inflation, Output and Exchange Rate Management

It is more realistic to suppose that, at least in the short run, domestic producers of traded goods face downward sloping demand curves. It may be difficult for their customers to adapt instantaneously to new sources

Figure 10.1

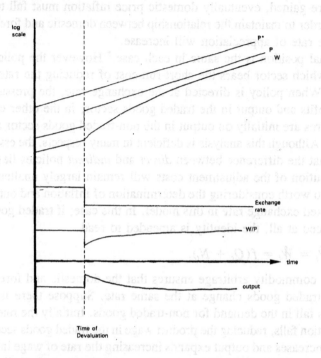

of supply and to switch to products which differ slightly in specification. Even in the long run, product differentiation may be sufficient to permit the exercise of some monopoly power by producers. In these conditions, producers have discretion about price setting as not all their sales will be lost if prices are increased above the prevailing level of world prices of similar goods. In fact as we shall see the choice of a price relative to the world price will determine output and thus, via the Phillips curve, the rate of inflation. If firms are profit maximisers and if their costs are outside their control, then the mark-up of export prices over marginal costs depends on the elasticity of demand. More generally if marginal costs are not constant, the optimum price will depend also on the elasticity of marginal costs with respect to output.

If we assume that world income is unaffected by events in the home economy we can write export demand X^f as a simple function of relative prices, measured in a common currency.

$$X^f = X^f[P/(P^*/e)]. \qquad X^f_1 < 0$$

Similarly home demand for domestic traded goods X^h depends on relative prices but also on the private sector's real expenditure E.

$$X^h = X^h[P/(P^*/e), E] \qquad X_1^h < 0, X_2^h > 0.$$

So total demand for traded goods which, in the absence of supply constraints, will equal the supply of traded goods is Q where

$$Q = X^f + X^h.$$

The demand for non-traded goods is the sum of private sector demand and government demand.[6] Because the price of non-traded goods is rigidly linked to the price of traded goods by our assumption concerning technology, the private sector's demand also depends on the relative price of domestic output and on expenditure,

$$N^p = N^p[P/(P^*/e), E] \qquad N_1^p < 0, N_2^p > 0.$$

The government's demand is exogenous:

$$N^g = \bar{N}^g.$$

Total demand for non-traded goods is the sum of private and government demand and is also equal to the production of non-traded goods:

$$N = N^p + N^g.$$

Imports are equal to the private sector's demand for foreign traded goods, Q^m. They are thus equal to total expenditure less the private sector's expenditure on exportables and on non-traded goods. Thus

$$\frac{p^*}{e} Q^m = PE - P(X^h + N^p)$$

where, by suitable choice of units, we have imposed the condition that the prices of domestically produced traded goods and non-traded goods are equal.

Total output of the domestic economy is $Q + N$, so using the simple Phillips curve described above, the rate of wage inflation is given by,

$$\hat{W} = f(Q + N)$$
$$= f\{X^f[P/(P^*/e)] + X^h[P/(P^*/e), E]$$
$$+ N^p[P/(P^*/e), E] + \bar{N}^g\}.$$

Thus the choice of a price of domestic output, relative to foreign output, determines the rate of wage inflation by determining the level of demand for domestic goods. An increase in the price of domestic output reduces export demand, reduces home demand for domestically produced traded goods and reduces the demand for non-traded goods by the private sector.

Thus the demand for imports will have increased. The higher the price of domestic output relative to the price of foreign output, the lower the rate of wage inflation. But as we discussed above, the price of domestic output will be set by reference to costs (wages) and to demand curves. Given that the level of real domestic expenditure is being held constant at E by government policy, this means the demand conditions can be completely described by the price of foreign output expressed in domestic currency, P^*/e. Suppose, for simplicity, that prices are set as a geometrically weighted average of costs and foreign prices:

$$P = W^\alpha (P^*/e)^{(1-\alpha)} \quad (0 < \alpha < 1).$$

Using this formula the relative price of domestic output can be written as

$$P/(P^*/e) = W^\alpha (P^*/e)^{(1-\alpha)}/(P^*/e) = [W/(P^*/e)]^\alpha.$$

Substitute this into the Phillips curve to get

$$\hat{W} = f[\tilde{X}^f (\frac{W}{P^*/e}) + \tilde{X}^h (\frac{W}{P^*/e}) + \tilde{N}^p (\frac{W}{P^*/e}) + \bar{N}^g]$$

where $\tilde{X}^f(Z) = X^f(Z^\alpha)$, etc. and the arguments in E (which is being held constant) are omitted. We can infer from this equation that, for a given level of government demand, $\bar{N}^g$, the higher the real wage in terms of the cost of imports, $W/(P^*/e)$, the lower will be the rate of wage inflation as a higher real wage implies a level of domestic output. This relation is shown in the *NW* quadrant of Figure 10.2 as the curve aa'.

In order for the rate of inflation to be constant, it is necessary that the real wage in terms of imports should be constant. This means that the rate of domestic wage inflation $\hat{W}$ must equal the foreign rate of inflation $\hat{P}^*$ *less* the rate of appreciation $\hat{e}$. This relation is shown for a given rate of foreign inflation in the *NE* quadrant, as a downward sloping 45° line whose intercept on the $\hat{W}$ axis is the foreign rate of inflation. Finally in the *SW* quadrant the relationship between the real wage and output is shown.

A macroeconomic equilibrium is described by points indexed 1 in the figure. The real wage is at r_1 which implies a level of output Y_1, a rate of inflation $\hat{W}_1$ and a rate of appreciation $\hat{e}_1$. Suppose the rate of exchange rate appreciation were controlled by the government. If it could be increased to $\hat{e}_2$, the new equilibrium would involve a lower rate of inflation $\hat{W}_2$, a higher real wage r_2 and therefore a lower level of output Y_2. Given our assumptions about the conditions of production, this implies a lower level of employment and thus a higher rate of unemployment. It is important to note that by virtue of the Phillips curve there

Figure 10.2

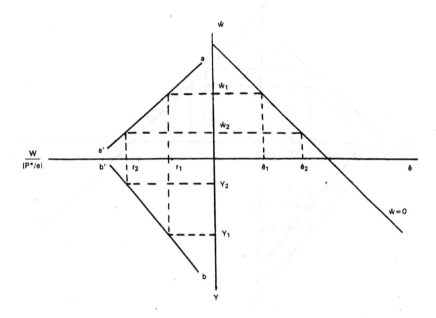

is a unique association between rates of inflation and levels of output: to select one is to select the other.

The diagram shows the relationships between equilibrium rates of inflation, appreciation, output and real wages, and the framework we have described has been wholly static. We can, however, suggest the chain of events leading to the lower rate of domestic inflation. When the rate of exchange rate appreciation is increased, the domestic price level falls below what it would otherwise have been so that the wage relative to the price of foreign traded goods tends to rise. The price of domestic output is adjusted and the prices of domestic traded goods and non-traded goods rise relative to the price of foreign traded goods. This leads to substitution towards foreign produced traded goods, which in turn leads to lower domestic output. The lower level of output reduces the rate of wage inflation. In the end the rate of wage inflation is reduced enough to keep the real wage constant and a new equilibrium is achieved as shown in the diagram.

Consider now the effect of a fall in the government's purchases of non-traded goods, which may be thought of as being similar to a fall in public sector employment. The fall in the government's demand does

Figure 10.3

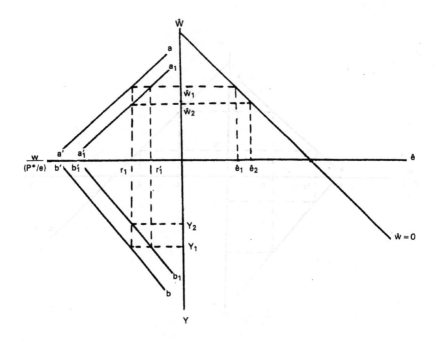

not affect other consumers of domestic output, so now each real wage will be associated with a lower level of output than before and the output-real wage curve in the *SW* quadrant of Figure 10.3 will be shifted upwards from *bb'* to b_1b_1'. For similar reasons the inflation:real wage curve in the *NW* quadrant will shift downwards. When government demand is reduced at a given real wage, output falls, so, by virtue of the Phillips curve, the rate of wage inflation falls. This shift is shown as a movement from *aa'* to a_1a_1'. The initial equilibrium is shown as before with output at Y_1, the real wage at r_1, wage inflation at $\hat{W}_1$ and the rate of appreciation at $\hat{e}_1$. When government demand falls, output declines at once to Y_2. Under our assumption about technology there is no reason for the real wage to change, but the lower level of output means that the new equilibrium rate of inflation is $\hat{W}_2$, lower than $\hat{W}_1$. For this change to be accommodated the rate of appreciation must increase to $\hat{e}_2$.

Suppose, however, that the rate of appreciation remains at $\hat{e}_1$. In this case when the rate of inflation is only $\hat{W}_2$, the real wage will be falling, permitting an increase in the sales of domestic traded goods. This tends to offset the fall in output and to increase the rate of wage inflation. This process continues until the fall in government purchases of non-traded goods is entirely made up by increased sales of traded goods. The final position is wage inflation of $\hat{W}_1$, output at Y_1 but the real wage at r'_1 which is less than the initial real wage. Thus the extent to which the restrictive government policy succeeds in reducing the rate of inflation depends on the rate of exchange rate appreciation being sufficiently flexible.

The Expectations Augmented Phillips Curve. This formulation of the macroeconomic problem has often been criticised for implying that it is only nominal wage changes that matter to workers. One way around this is to re-formulate the Phillips curve by arguing that the change in wages depends in part on the expected rate of inflation and in part on the level of demand. Thus wages must rise in proportion to the anticipated change in prices to compensate for inflation. Only the margin over this is responsive to the state of demand. We re-write the Phillips curve to include the expected rate of price inflation $\hat{\varrho}^e$

$$\hat{W} = f[\tilde{X}^f(R) + \tilde{X}^h(R) + \tilde{N}^p(R) + \tilde{N}^g] + \hat{\varrho}^e$$

where $R = W/(P^*/e)$.

The price level relevant for workers' decisions is a weighted average of domestic prices P and import prices P^*/e, with the weights reflecting the relative importance of the two goods in consumption:

$$\varrho = P^\beta(P^*/e)^{(1-\beta)} \quad (0 < \beta < 1).$$

But we know that P is itself an average of wages and foreign prices:

$$P = W^\alpha(P^*/e)^{(1-\alpha)}.$$

It is easy to show that these two equations imply

$$\hat{\varrho} = \alpha\beta\hat{R} + \hat{P}^* - \hat{e}.$$

This is a sensible result. It says that the home country's rate of inflation is equal to the rate of increase of import prices $(\hat{P}^* - \hat{e})$ plus a term in $\hat{R}$ which allows for the fact that domestic costs (wages) may be increasing at a different rate from import prices.

Suppose that workers have perfect foresight — analogous here to the assumption 'rational expectations'. In this case we can replace the expected rate of price inflation with the actual rate of inflation, so that the Phillips curve becomes

$$\hat{W} = f[g(R) + \tilde{N}^g] + \alpha\beta\hat{R} + \hat{P}^* - \hat{e}$$

where $g(R) = \tilde{X}^f(R) + \tilde{X}^h(R) + \tilde{N}^p(R)$.

As we know that in this case the expected rate of inflation is the same as the actual rate of inflation, we can subtract the rate of import price inflation, $\hat{P}* - \hat{e}$, from both sides to show how the rate of change of real wages (in terms of imports) depends on the level of the real wage R and the level of exogenous demand $\bar{N}^g$:

$$\hat{R} = \frac{1}{1 - \alpha\beta} \cdot f\,[g(R) + \bar{N}^g].$$

On reasonable assumptions about the forms of the Phillips curve and the demand curves for domestic output, this means that for any given level of government demand for non-traded goods there is a single real wage at which the real wage is constant. We call this, the long-run equilibrium real wage (in terms of imports), R^*. Corresponding to this equilibrium real wage is an equilibrium level of output, Y^*. Obviously, the rate of wage inflation itself is a function of R and the rate of appreciation $\hat{e}$:

$$\hat{W} = \frac{f\,[g(R) + \bar{N}^g]}{1 - \alpha\beta} + \hat{P}* - \hat{e}.$$

This means there is now a family of 'short run' Phillips curves, one for each value of $\hat{e}$. Figure 10.4 introduces three of these curves labelled e_1, e_2, e_3 in the *NW* quadrant and shows R^* and its corresponding level of output, Y^*. Suppose that the economy is initially at equilibrium with rate of inflation $\hat{W}_1$ and rate of appreciation $\hat{e}_1$. Output and real wages are of course at their equilibrium levels. Suppose now that the rate of appreciation increases to e_2. If price expectations were fixed the new equilibrium would be found to the left of R_1^* on the e_1 curve and would involve higher real wages, lower output and a lower rate of inflation. But price expectations are not fixed. The effects of the higher rate of appreciation on the domestic rate of inflation both directly via import prices and indirectly via the effects on domestic costs and prices are perceived by workers and the rate of wage inflation is adjusted accordingly. The economy moves directly along the R^* line to R_2 with no change in real wages or output but lower wage inflation to compensate for the higher rate of appreciation.

   In between the case in which expectations of future prices are completely inflexible (and so may be ignored) and the case in which all new information is incorporated immediately lie a mass of expectations generating assumptions which allow new information to be incorporated only slowly. The delay may result from the difficulties of collecting new information or uncertainty about how to process it. One *ad hoc* way of representing such a situation is to suppose that the expected rate of

Figure 10.4

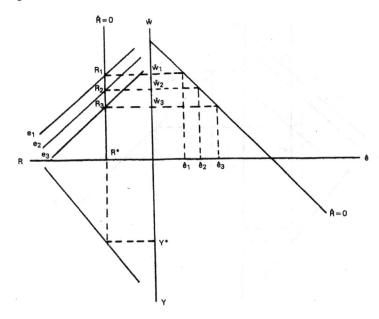

inflation is a weighted average of past rates of inflation. If the weights sum to unity then, if the actual rate of inflation changes, this change will in due course be reflected exactly in a change in the expected rate. A simple example of this is when the rate of inflation is expected to be the same as it was in the previous period. So the Phillips curve is now

$$\hat{W} = f[g(R) + \bar{N}^g] + \hat{\varrho}^e_{-1}.$$

In an equilibrium with a constant rate of inflation, $\hat{\varrho}^e_{-1}$ will be the same as $\hat{\varrho}^e$, so that the previous perfect foresight case describes the equilibrium. The R^* line can now be interpreted as the long-run curve. Once again there is a family of short-run curves positioned according to the expected rate of inflation. These are shown in Figure 10.5.

We are now in a position to describe a sequence of events as inflation is reduced. In the initial equilibrium wage inflation is $\hat{W}_1$ and the rate of appreciation is $\hat{e}_1$. Real wages and output are at their equilibrium levels. Suppose the rate of appreciation is increased to $\hat{e}_2$. This combination of appreciation and wage inflation shifts the economy off the constant real wage line in the *NW* quadrant from R_1 to R'_1. The higher rate of appreciation means that the prices of foreign goods measured in domestic currency are falling below what they would have been. Taking nominal wages as given, firms re-calculate the prices of domestic goods which

Figure 10.5

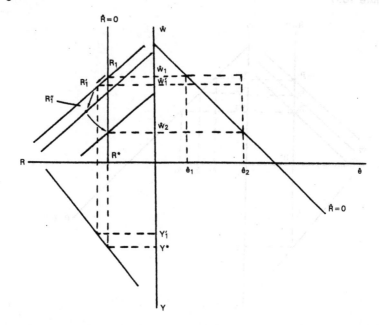

are reduced to offset partially the decline in competitiveness. Output is reduced somewhat, which reduces the rate of wage inflation and so makes nominal wages in the next period lower than they would otherwise have been.

Attention now shifts to the next period. Nominal wages have already been determined. The Phillips curve has shifted downwards because the rate of inflation in the previous period turned out to be lower than in the period before that. Thus in the next period the movement of the economy will involve a shift from one curve to the other as well as some movement along the curve. Now the rate of import price inflation will be constant at its new lower level. But the price of domestic output relative to foreign output can be reduced because the rate of nominal wage inflation has fallen. This fall in relative inflation will generate lower wage inflation in the subsequent period. The process continues until a new equilibrium is established when the rate of wage inflation has fallen to $\hat{W}_2$, at which point the rate of wage inflation and the rate of exchange rate appreciation are consistent with constant real wages. The precise path of approach depends on the parameters of the system. One possibility is arrowed. The important point to note about this process is that the exogenous slowing of the rate of import price inflation sets off a domestic wage-price spiral. Until domestic price inflation has converged on import price inflation, the relative price of domestically produced goods to imports will be higher than in equilibrium, so that exports will be low and thus output will be low. As the home country's rate of inflation converges on the rate of import price inflation, output and real wages will return to their equilibrium levels. Thus the cost of reducing inflation may be measured by the output foregone during the period in which the home country's products are relatively uncompetitive.

Government Expenditure and the Exchange Rate. The analysis of a change in government expenditure in this framework is quite illuminating. If government purchases of non-traded goods fall, then the amount of output that firms can sell at any given price of domestic output relative to the price of imports is reduced. Since relative prices depend directly on real wages, this means that the output sold at any given real wage also falls. This in turn means that the long run equilibrium real wage falls. This can be seen directly from the Phillips curve

$$\hat{W} = f[g(R) + \bar{N}^g] + \hat{\varrho}^e.$$

Starting from a position of equilibrium with $\hat{W} = \hat{\varrho}^e$, consider a small change in $\bar{N}^g$ compensated by a change in R in such as way as to keep $f[g(R) + \bar{N}^g)]$ constant. The fall in $\bar{N}^g$ must be offset by a rise in $g(R)$; but, as $g(R)$ varies inversely with R, this means that R must fall. An alternative, somewhat heuristic way of arriving at the same conclusion is to suppose that, at equilibrium, employment and the real wage are determined by the intersection of labour supply and demand curves. In Figure 10.6 the labour demand curve slopes down. The fall in government expenditure shifts the labour demand curve to the left. From the Phillips curve we know that there is a unique level of output, and thus employment,[7] consistent with constant real wages. If this level of employment is given by the vertical line L_1, the new equilibrium real wage is R_2, below R_1.

These various shifts in our basic diagram are shown in Figure 10.7. When government expenditure is reduced the equilibrium real wage in the *NW* quadrant shifts to the left; at the same time the output curve in the *SW* quadrant shifts upwards so that the long-run equilibrium output is just maintained. The entire family of short-run Phillips curves in the *NW* quadrant shifts downwards. Initially the economy was in equilibrium with output of Y^*, real wage R_1, inflation $\hat{W}_1$, and a rate of appreciation of $\hat{e}_1$. After the change in government demand a real wage of R_1 is too high and it starts to decline towards R_2. This is achieved by wage inflation falling below price inflation for a time. After the change in

Figure 10.6

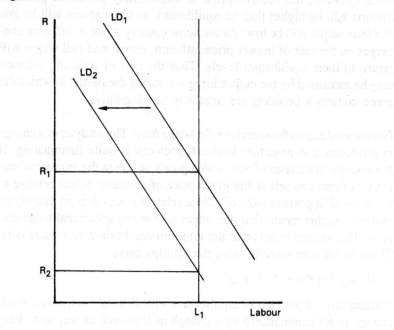

Figure 10.7

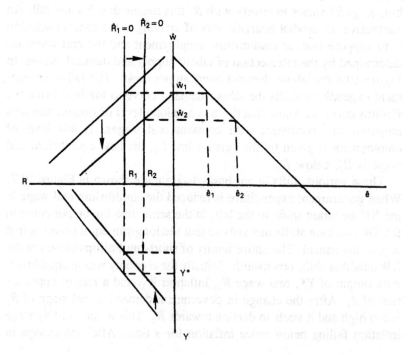

government policy the new equilibrium is such that output is again at Y^* but now the real wage R_2 and the rate of inflation $\hat{W}_2$ are both lower than before, while the rate of exchange rate appreciation at $\hat{e}_2$ is higher than before.

Conclusions

The relationships between exchange rates, interest rates, inflation and output lie at the very core of current macroeconomic problems. The progressive freeing of capital movements since the Second World War has meant that short-run movements in the exchange rate are determined by the views of asset holders about rates of return after making due allowance for risk and, where necessary, about what is likely to happen in the future. Variations in the exchange rate are required to ensure that the outstanding mix of securities and currencies of different denominations is willingly held. Much econometric research has been undertaken to try to discover a robust relationship between interest rate changes and exchange rate changes with rather little success (Chapter 13) and it seems unlikely that reliable numerical guides will be discovered.

But exchange rate policy has implications for real markets as well as for financial flows. Reducing inflation by a policy of currency appreciations imposes output costs on the traded goods sector, so that the benefit of the lower rate of inflation has to be weighed against the output foregone. Whether the output costs persist indefinitely depends in part on the speed with which wage-setters adjust their expectations.

Notes

1. Note that the home country expenditure weights are used to construct the foreign price level.

2. The simplest model used in this section was first popularised by R. Dornbusch, 1973a, b.

3. We assume that agents treat capital gains and losses in exactly the same way as they treat other changes in income. There is a considerable literature investigating the empirical validity of this assumption: see, for example, K. Cuthbertson, 1982.

4. Assume that the government's net interest receipts, that is interest earned on foreign exchange reserves *less* interest paid on its own securities, is zero.

5. As long as there is never excess supply in the non-traded goods sector.

6. It is assumed here that government consumption consists only of non-traded goods. By far the largest proportion of government consumption in the UK is accounted for by the wages and salaries of government employees. Making an allowance for government consumption of traded goods would be straightforward but would add little to the analysis.

7. We assume for exposition purposes that labour:output ratios are the same in each sector.

11 THE INTERACTIONS OF EXCHANGE RATE POLICY WITH OTHER POLICIES

Exchange rate policy is almost a misnomer. The government cannot decree that the exchange rate will from a given Sunday in March stand at such and such a level in the way it can organise the start of British Summer Time. What it can do, at least over limited periods, is instruct government departments, including the central bank, to arrange their affairs so that the exchange rate follows a given path. The *direct* policy of market intervention is an instruction to buy or sell foreign exchange in the market to prevent the exchange rate from moving away from its target path. The exchange rate is not unique in being amenable only to indirect control — interest rates are equally determined by the authorities' willingness to buy or sell securities in response to market pressure. Because the exchange rate is not set by decree, the way that other macroeconomic policies are conducted will often have implications for the path of the exchange rate, and a decision to influence the exchange rate in some way may restrict the choice of paths for other policies. When policy instruments are selected in a co-ordinated fashion which allows for their interactions no particular problem arises, apart from the formidable practical one of assessing just what the strengths of the interactions are. When policy is promulgated as a series of rules for individual policy variables problems of consistency may arise if the rules were not fully co-ordinated in the first place or, more reasonably, if circumstances change to bring previously consistent rules into conflict. This chapter examines the relationships between some policy instruments and the exchange rate.

Exchange Rate Policy and Fiscal Policy

In Chapter 10 we developed a simple apparatus for considering the relationship between exchange rate policy and output and inflation on the assumption that the level of real expenditure was fixed. This useful device enabled us to abstract from another set of considerations that would arise if expenditure were free to vary endogenously. Implicitly we required that fiscal policy should so affect the private sector's disposable income as to stabilise expenditure. However it is also of interest to

226

consider what would happen if fiscal policy were characterised by constant tax rates. First we must reconsider the fixed expenditure case in an alternative framework.

The private sector's hoarding equals $PY - T - PE$, the value of output, PY, less taxes paid to the government, T, less the value of expenditure, PE. Government hoarding is the excess of tax receipts over its own expenditure, $T - P\bar{N}^g$. As we are assuming that the government buys only non-traded goods, government expenditure is just $P\bar{N}^g$. National hoarding H is the sum of private sector hoarding and government hoarding. Thus

$$H = (PY - T - PE) + (T - P\bar{N}^g) = P(Y - \bar{N}^g - E).$$

Taxes are eliminated from the definition of national hoarding as they are merely a transfer from the private sector to the government. We have shown how the level of output depends partly on the wage in terms of import prices, R, and partly on the exogenous level of government expenditure (see Chapter 9) and can be written as

$$Y = g(R, E) + \bar{N}^g.$$

As we have seen an increase in wages relative to import prices (that is an increase in R) reduces output at a constant level of expenditure because the prices of domestically produced goods rise relative to imports leading to a fall in demand for domestic output. Substituting this expression for output into the hoarding function allows us to write hoarding as a function of R and E only.

$$H = P[g(R, E) - E].$$

Government demand for non-traded goods $\bar{N}^g$ has disappeared from the formula because it adds equally to output and expenditure and thus contributes nothing to national hoarding.

In Figure 11.1 the relationship between national hoarding and R is shown on the right hand side and the relationship between output and R on the left hand side. The latter is familiar from our previous analysis; the former is a downward sloping curve because a high real wage means lower output of traded goods and thus lower national output and lower hoarding when expenditure is fixed. The point at which the hoarding function cuts the R axis is the real wage compatible with zero national hoarding and therefore equilibrium in the balance of payments. As we have already seen a fall in government purchases reduces the level of national output attainable at a given wage so that the output schedule shifts inwards. It follows that if the change in government expenditure

Figure 11.1

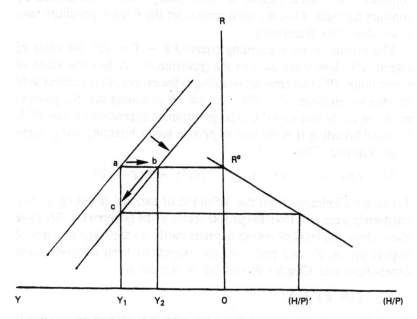

is accompanied by continuous equilibrium in the balance of payments, the level of income must fall — in the case drawn, from Y_1 to Y_2. But we argued in the previous chapter that under certain circumstances the operation of the Phillips curve would lead to some equilibrium level of output being maintained. If the economy were to succeed in re-gaining Y_1, the wage would be lower (as already described) but the country would be running a continuous balance of payments surplus of $(H/P)'$. It is the conflict between these two notions of equilibrium that generates the anti-inflationary appreciation of the exchange rate.

What happens is this. Suppose the government's purchases of non-traded goods are reduced, while, for the moment, prices and taxes are held constant. The government's rate of hoarding increases; the private sector's income falls by the same amount. But the fall in private sector income is likely to lead to falls in expenditure. However, the government can forestall this by reducing its taxes by the same amount as it reduces its purchases of non-traded goods. In this way the private sector's disposable income is unchanged, so there is no reason for it to reduce its expenditure. In these circumstances both government and private sector hoarding are unchanged after the reduction in the government's purchases of non-traded goods, so national hoarding is unchanged as well. In the first instance output has fallen by an amount equal to the reduction in government demand, and the economy has shifted from *a* to *b* in Figure 11.1.

The reduction in output will next reduce wage inflation via the Phillips curve and thus reduce the price of domestic output relative to imports. This will generate secondary real income gains for the private sector as output expands in response to increased demand from exports and as a result of domestic residents switching expenditure in favour of domestically produced goods. If real expenditure is positively associated with real income, the government will have to increase taxes to prevent real *disposable* income rising and then leading to extra expenditure. Thus although private sector output expands, this benefits only the government. (Furthermore, the fall in the price level, relative to what it would have been, will generate extra expenditure in so far as the private sector treats capital gains as income. These gains too will have to be taxed away.) In order to keep the private sector's real expenditure constant, the government has to keep its real disposable income constant. *A fortiori*, private sector hoarding will be constant. But we know that the current balance has moved into surplus because output of traded goods has increased, while expenditure on imports has fallen. As the relative price of exports has fallen, we require that foreign demand for home country exports and domestic demand for imports are sufficiently elastic for a fall in the relative price to generate a surplus.[1] So national hoarding has increased but all of this is reflected in an increase in government hoarding.

The new equilibrium output is at *c* in Figure 11.1, where output of traded goods is higher than at *a* to compensate for the lower demand for non-traded goods. If the economy could attain *c*, it would be running a current account surplus in which the private sector is accumulating foreign currency, by way of international trade. But the private sector is not increasing its wealth as the extra earnings are needed to pay the government's tax demands. The private sector has somehow to convert its foreign currency into domestic currency in order to pay its taxes. As the government is, by assumption, not prepared to supply the domestic currency, competition amongst the private sector leads to upward pressure on the exchange rate. The increase in the exchange rate worsens the competitiveness of domestic output and thus tends to reduce private sector income and the need for the government to levy taxes.

While the economy is adjusting, output is always below its equilibrium level so that the rate of wage inflation falls continuously. The general rate of inflation falls continuously too. This result is not very surprising. We know that if output is to return to its previous level following the change in government behaviour, the output of goods to other buyers must increase. This is generated by a fall in the relative price of domestic output, which, with domestic expenditure fixed, must lead to a current account surplus. But if the government is not prepared to accept its higher hoarding in the form of foreign currency, this incipient change in relative prices is frustrated by the appreciation of the exchange rate. The rate of inflation will decline continuously as output is held below its natural rate.

Suppose the government were to adopt the opposite policy of accepting all the extra taxes in the form of foreign currency. In this case the extra output of traded goods on the part of the private sector would not generate any upward pressure on the exchange rate. The rate of increase of import prices measured in domestic currency will remain just what it was before. The rate of wage inflation and of domestic price inflation will be temporarily lower while output is below its natural level in order to bring about the change in the ratios of wages to import prices and of domestic prices to import prices which are necessary to increase output from Y_2 to Y_1. As output recovers the real wage stops falling. As a constant real wage requires that wages and domestic prices increase at the same rate as import prices, it follows that the inflation will in the end return to its former rate. We may conclude that the less inclined the government is to accumulate foreign exchange reserves, the more successful the policy of reducing expenditure will be in reducing the rate of inflation, but the more costly it will be in terms of output foregone. If output is to regain its natural level consistent with stable inflation the government must be prepared to accumulate some foreign exchange reserves.

Consider now the case in which the government's taxation policy, instead of being geared to holding private sector expenditure constant, is so arranged as to keep government hoarding, and therefore government borrowing, the same before and after the change in government expenditure when measured in units of domestic output. This corresponds to the simple 'balanced budget multiplier' analysis of the closed economy.

As before we can write down the hoarding schedules of the private sector and the government:

$$H_p = PY - T - PE$$

$$H_g = T - P\bar{N}^g.$$

Since we are assuming government hoarding is constant, we can re-arrange the hoarding schedule to give the level of taxes as a function of the government's demand for non-traded goods and then this can be substituted into the private hoarding schedule to get

$$H_p = PY - \bar{H}_g - PP\bar{N}^g - PE.$$

Where H_g is the rate of real government hoarding. Income Y depends on relative prices and on the level of expenditure as well as on government demand for non-traded goods; substituting this into the expression for H_p gives

$$H_p = P[g(R, E) + \bar{N}^g - \bar{H}_g - \bar{N}^g - E]$$

$$= P[g(R, E) - \bar{H}_g - E].$$

Equilibrium in the balance of payments requires that total national hoarding is zero, that is that

$$H_p + H_g = P[g(R, E) - E] = 0.$$

The combinations of R and E that yield national hoarding of zero are shown in the right hand side of Figure 11.2. Suppose that all prices are constant and that expenditure increases. The extra expenditure will generate extra income. However, the extra income will be less than the extra expenditure because some part of expenditure goes on imports. Thus when E increases R must fall in order to generate higher sales of domestic goods if the current balance is to be zero. The left hand side contains the familiar relation between output and the real wage for a given level of expenditure and of government demand.

After the change in government expenditure but before prices change output falls from a to b as the output curve shifts inwards, as before. In order to maintain its level of hoarding the government cuts taxes in line with its expenditure and, as we saw before, this is enough to keep expenditure constant. Now the differences begin. As output has fallen wage inflation slackens and the price of domestic output falls relative to the price of imports. At the initial level of expenditure a surplus now arises as residents shift away from imports and the economy starts to move vertically downwards towards E_1 on the right hand panel of Figure 11.2. This time the secondary rise in income is allowed to generate extra expenditure. This has two effects: first on the right hand side of the diagram expenditure increases which tends to reduce the current surplus; secondly, on the left hand side, the extra expenditure increases the demand for domestic output and this causes the output schedule to shift part of the way towards its old position (broken line). If the system is stable the current balance will be eliminated as the national level of output is re-gained at c. Expenditure at E_1' has to be higher than it was

Figure 11.2

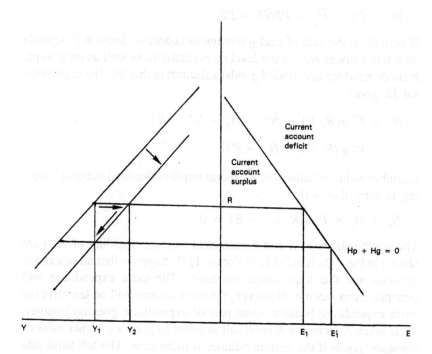

originally as private sector expenditure has to compensate for the reduction in government demand.

On the approach to the new equilibrium the current account is generally in surplus unless the private sector always spends its entire disposable income. In the latter case the economy moves from E_1 to E_1' along the curve in the diagram. Normally we would expect some hoarding in the short run as a result of the higher level of disposable income.

As before, the hoarding is reflected in an excess of exports over imports and in receipts of foreign currency. But it is unlikely that the private sector will want to hold the whole of the increment in its wealth in the form of foreign currency and so it attempts to exchange a portion of it for domestic currency. But there are no willing sellers of domestic currency. Competition drives up the price of foreign currency relative to domestic currency — that is, it leads to an appreciation.

To summarise the differences, we note that a commitment to holding the private sector's expenditure constant involved taxing away the secondary gains in income resulting from the fall in the relative price of domestic output. This generates a chronic surplus and strong reasons for the currency to appreciate. But when government policy is to balance its budget, the secondary increase in disposable income is allowed to take place so that in the short term there is a greater increase in output. During the transition the private sector is likely to increase its hoarding and thus generate an appreciation of the currency. However we would expect that in the end expenditure would increase to match income and the pressures for appreciation of the currency will be eliminated.

Exchange Rate Policy and Monetary Policy

So far we have argued that *direct* policy with respect to the exchange rate may be used to influence the development of price inflation in the domestic economy and that *indirect* policies have implications for the exchange rate that must be allowed to occur if such policies are to be successful. In particular we have considered in some detail the implications of changes in public expenditure on the exchange rate and on domestic inflation. However, the problem usually considered is that of a possible conflict between exchange rate policy and monetary policy. In considering this problem it is important to bear in mind that domestic money can get into circulation in a variety of ways.

(a) Money-financed Deficits. If the government runs a deficit with unchanged outstanding stocks of interest bearing assets and foreign exchange reserves, the supply of (high-powered) money must increase. If the government's expenditure exceeds its tax receipts, then like any other agent it must be running down its wealth and must either increase its borrowing or run down its assets. The government is, however, in a unique position in that it can, to all intents and purposes, borrow from itself by obliging the central bank to purchase unlimited amounts of its securities. In return for these securities the central bank grants the government credit. In the simplest case the central bank gives the government cash in return for securities: that is it 'prints money' — literally. However, since the central bank is really part of the government sector these transactions are largely fictitious and we may accept that deficits not financed by borrowing from the (non-bank) private sector or by running down foreign exchange reserves must be financed by increasing the amount of money in circulation.

(b) Changes in the Amount of Government Securities Held by the Private Sector. Suppose, with the government deficit fixed, the private sector can be induced to hold more government debt. Because the government

deficit is unchanged the net wealth of the government and of the private sector are unchanged. The private sector exchanges some of its holding of domestic money for government securities. Thus the amount of money in the hands of the private sector falls. Combining this result with that of (a) above we may conclude that if an increase in the government's deficit is accompanied by an equal increase in sales of government debt to the private sector, then the money supply will not increase.

(c) Changes in the Level of the Government's Foreign Exchange Reserves.
If, with the government deficit unchanged and sales of debt to the private sector unchanged, the government increases its foreign exchange reserves, what happens to the money supply? Once again there is no change in any sector's wealth, just changes in composition. In order to achieve the increase in its foreign exchange reserves, the government must offer something in exchange — domestic currency. Thus an increase in the foreign exchange reserves will be accompanied by an increase in the money supply.

An important case to consider is when the government is keeping the exchange rate fixed by *direct* policy, and the private sector is accumulating assets with the government sector in balance. In this case the country is running a current account surplus. To the extent that the private sector wishes to hold domestic rather than foreign assets, it will exchange foreign currency for domestic currency with the government. Thus the surplus will be associated with an increase in the money supply. If the government succeeds in offsetting this increase by increased sales of government debt, the surplus is said to have been *sterilised*.

These then are the ways that money gets into asset holders' portfolios. Before considering the relation between exchange rate policy and money supply policy we should note that there are several different ways of measuring the money supply:

   (i)   residents' holdings of domestic money;
  (ii)   residents' and non-residents' holdings of domestic money;
 (iii)   residents' holdings of domestic money and foreign money.

The first measure is most similar to the standard IS-LM concept. It is worth remembering that much of the earlier literature was developed in an era in which exchange control inhibited residents from holding foreign currency. The second measure views the money supply as being the counterpart of the government's monetary liabilities. The final measure is concerned with the degree of liquidity of the private sector.

Let us now consider the effects of a change in the government's deficit that is to be entirely money financed. We have in fact covered this case extensively in our account of the effect of changes in public expenditure on the exchange rate. Rather than repeat the analysis, we may look at it in a rather different way. Suppose the government arbitrarily decided to reduce its deficit and thereby to reduce that rate of increase of the stock of domestic money in the portfolios of asset holders (both resident and non-resident). As far as these asset holders are concerned the supply curve of domestic money has shifted. If their demand for domestic money is unchanged, the market can only be brought into balance by a rise in the exchange rate which satisfies the demand for domestic money by revaluing asset holders' stocks. It follows at once that if the government's money supply policy is accompanied by an exchange rate policy, conflict is inevitable unless the policies have been selected to be consistent. If the government attempts to hold the exchange rate down by buying foreign exchange, then as explained in (c) above, the money supply will rise.

The second case arises when, for a given government deficit, the government attempts to manage the money supply by manipulating the interest rate. Suppose for example it is desired to reduce the money supply. The government raises the interest rate on securities to encourage asset holders to substitute interest-bearing assets for money in their portfolios. However, an increase in domestic interest rates also encourages asset holders to switch from foreign denominated securities in favour of domestic interest-bearing assets. The sale of foreign securities for conversion into domestic assets puts upward pressure on the exchange rate since, in the absence of government intervention, the demand for domestic assets has increased. Once again, by revaluing assets, the change in the exchange rate brings about the desired change in the proportion (by value) of assets held as domestic securities. Again there is a straightforward conflict between money supply policy and exchange rate policy.

Commercial Policy and the Exchange Rate

It is sometimes argued that protection is the only feasible way of eliminating unemployment in an economy with inflexible real wages and a high marginal propensity to import. In the UK this view has been associated with a group of economists centred on the Department of

Applied Economics in Cambridge. Opponents of this view argue either that the widespread adoption of such a policy would lead to a collapse of world trade, leaving most countries worse off than before, or that, even in the absence of retaliation, the policy would fail to work. We agree with both these points. However, it is important to note that the standard arguments for free trade — namely that tariffs or quotas introduce a distortion preventing the attainment of Pareto equililbrium — are simply not applicable as the policy is only advocated when involuntary unemployment is chronic so that, in the absence of tariffs or quotas, the economy would still be inefficient.

We will consider the effects of introducing a tariff at the rate t on imports in a country that can buy all the imported goods it requires at a given price. If the world price, measured in units of domestic currency, is $(P*/e)$, then the price to residents after the imposition of the tariff is $(1 + t) (P*/e)$ although, of course, the foreign exporter still receives $(P*/e)$ — the balance goes to the government. Domestic producers who compete directly with imports will also increase their prices to $(1 + t) (P*/e)$ but as they do not have to pay the tariff their production becomes more profitable, encouraging them to increase output. If they have upward sloping supply curves they will move along them; if they were producing under constant costs with production limited by capacity the extra profits will encourage the installation of more capacity; if production under constant costs was not profitable because the price of imports was not high enough to permit normal profits to be earned, the higher price available may encourage new firms to enter the market. Thus if expenditure on the import good is unchanged, it is likely that more of the demand for it will be satisfied from domestic sources.

If the resources used in the production of these extra goods would otherwise have been unemployed, the extra output must be counted as a gain to the economy. The policy succeeds on employment grounds and also, assuming that expenditure is unchanged, on balance of payments grounds.

The tariff has the same effect on the output of importables as a devaluation and is susceptible to the same criticism: the tariff works by cutting real wages. If subsequently real wages rise to offset the rise in market prices, the benefit to domestic producers of importables is eroded. More than that, as wages rise, the competitive position of those sectors *not* benefiting from the tariff actually becomes worse than in the pre-tariff state. In the special case in which the wage is fixed in terms of the quantity of importables it can purchase, the tariff has only harmful effects as there is no gain to suppliers of importables but there are losses of competitiveness to suppliers of other goods.

But suppose the exchange rate itself were to move in response to the imposition of a tariff. This would lead to further changes in competitiveness which would have to be superimposed on those already described. In particular, if the exchange rate were to appreciate, the beneficial effects would be attenuated. Suppose that the private sector's rate of hoarding is zero both before and after the imposition of the tariff — so that its demand for foreign assets is unchanged. Part of the private sector's expenditure now accrues to the government in the form of tariff revenue. If the government's own expenditure and its other receipts remain the same before and after the imposition of the tariff, then government hoarding will have increased. This extra hoarding is the counterpart to the increased current account surplus.

While the government acquires tariff payments in domestic currency, the current account surplus will accrue as an excess of foreign currency. The exchange rate will rise in an attempt to clear the foreign exchange market. Thus commercial policy will have implications for the exchange rate when the exchange rate is not fixed. In particular tariffs are likely to lead to a high exchange rate.

Note

1. This is the Marshall Lerner condition.

12 THE IMPACT OF NATURAL RESOURCE DISCOVERY ON EXCHANGE RATES: THE CASE OF NORTH SEA OIL

The exploitation of oil reserves in the British part of the North Sea transformed the indigenous oil extraction sector. Before 1975 its output, based on a few tiny onshore fields, was negligible; by 1984 it accounted for 6 per cent including natural gas of GDP and 16 per cent of exports of goods.

The Historical Background and Prospects for the Future

The exploration of the North Sea got underway in the mid-1960s but it was not until the discovery of the important Forties Field in 1970 that the possibility of extraction on a large scale was established. Exploration was further stimulated following the first oil price shock of 1973 when the OPEC cartel succeeded in quadrupling the nominal oil price — the first significant exports of crude oil from the North Sea were recorded in 1975. Production increased from 1.6 million tonnes in 1975 to 80.5 million tonnes in 1980 and to 126 million tonnes in 1984. Although the oil sector has grown rapidly it is unlikely that it has absorbed resources that would otherwise have been used for the production of other kinds of output. Employment in the sector, never more than 30 thousand, is small both in terms of the overall level of employment (about 21.4 million in 1984) and unemployment (about 3 million). Capital expenditure has been very high relative to the value added. Initially most of the plant and machinery was imported although the proportion manufactured in the UK has been rising. Total imports of capital equipment into the UK are large. It seems unlikely that the output of the non-oil sector has been constrained because investment goods have been diverted to the North Sea. For much of the period under discussion capacity utilisation in capital goods industries has been rather low. Overall it is reasonable to consider that the oil sector has no physical opportunity cost in terms of production of non-oil goods foregone. Table 12.1 gives the physical data for the oil sector.

The oil sector is more or less a 'free gift' in terms of production in the sense that oil production does not compete directly for physical

238

Table 12.1: The UK Oil Sector

	1975	1980	1984
Output of crude oil, tonnes	1.6	80.5	125.9
Value added at 1980 prices by extraction of oil and gas (£M)	26 (0.01)[a]	8,809 (4.4)[a]	12,958 (6.2)[a]
Exports of crude oil, million tonnes	.8	38.6	75.8
Exports of crude oil at 1980 prices (£M)	87.8[b]	4,234 (8.9)[b]	8,314 (15.6)[b]
Employment in extraction of oil and gas sector, thousands	—	19	33
Employees in employment, million	22.7	23.0	21.4
Unemployment, million	2.8	3.0	3.0
Investment in extraction of mineral oil and natural gas at 1980 prices (£M)	2,687 (6.5)[c]	2,399 (5.8)[c]	2,910 (6.4)[c]

Sources: *United Kingdom National Accounts* (1985); *Monthly Review of External Trade Statistics* (various); *Monthly Digest of Statistics* (various); *Annual Abstract of Statistics* (various); *Economic Trends Annual Supplement* (1985); *Department of Employment Gazette* (various issues).

a. As a percentage of GDP (1980 prices)
b. As a percentage of UK exports of goods (1980 prices)
c. As a percentage of total investment (1980 prices)

resources. The distribution of income arising from oil production is also quite uncharacteristic of the rest of the economy. Much of the development has been undertaken by foreign firms or at least by firms with a substantial degree of foreign ownership. Consequently a large proportion of the profits accrues to non-residents and appears as a debit item in the invisible balance. Secondly the price of oil is currently far above the level necessary to keep resources in the sector. Some estimates put the proportion of this rent in the price as high as 60 per cent. Although this figure is likely to decline as the larger and low cost fields are exhausted and replaced by more costly sources of supply, the high proportion of rent helps to explain why the rate of extraction has not been very sensitive to the marked swings in the real price of oil (that is the price of oil relative to the average price of other goods) that have been experienced since 1975. Since this rent is not required to maintain production (or investment) it is available for distribution and the UK government has been fairly efficient at extracting most of it through a complicated flexible tax system. The importance of taxes on the oil sector in government revenues has grown dramatically, accounting for about 6¾ per cent

Table 12.2: The Approximate Distribution of Oil and Gas Revenues in 1983 (£ billion)

Output (value of sales)	18.3		
Less purchases of goods and services from other sectors	2.1		
Value added by sector		16.2	
Less Income from employment[a]		0.4	
Gross trading profits			15.8
Less UK taxes[b]			8.5
Less Profits due abroad			3.0
Profits of UK companies[c]			5.5

Sources: *United Kingdom National Accounts* (Blue Book), CSO, 1985; *Development of Oil and Gas Resources of the United Kingdom* (Brown Book), Department of Energy, 1985.

a. Income from employment in extraction of mineral oil and natural gas.
b. Estimate based on taxes paid in 1982/3 and 1983/4 financial years.
c. After taxes, but before depreciation and interest charges.

of total receipts in 1983/4. Not only is the oil sector a 'free gift' in terms of production, but most of the profits accrue directly to the government. The distribution of the value of the oil product is shown in Table 12.2.

Since the oil available on the UK Continental shelf is finite, eventually the economy will have to do without it. But there is enormous uncertainty about just how much oil there is. Exploration on the Continental shelf and on the islands themselves is far from complete; furthermore technical advances may increase the degree to which fields are exploited — at present only about 30 per cent of the oil is recovered. What is less controversial is the view that the rent available from future exploitation of the oil fields is likely to be smaller as production shifts from large fields to smaller, more marginal sites.

Whatever the level of physical production, the value of the oil to the UK depends on the real price of oil in terms of non-oil goods. The oil-producing states in the OPEC have not been able to restrict entry into the oil-producing industry and of course the high prices set by the cartel has led to a fall in OPEC's share of the world market. If the original members of OPEC seek to maintain the real price of oil they must be prepared to reduce their outputs. At the time of writing, the cartel is having great difficulty in getting members to keep to their quotas and prices are tending to fall. Thus the uncertainty about how much oil it will be profitable to produce and, from the government's point of view, about what level of taxation will maximise its revenues is added to the uncertainty about the physical quantity of oil underneath the North Sea.

The Static Effects of Oil on the Non-Oil Economy under Fixed Exchange Rates

The oil sector has little direct effect on the non-oil economy; most of its impact comes through expenditure effects and exchange rate effects. The income (value added) of the oil sector comprises the remuneration of the labour force, the profits of the oil companies and taxes paid to the government. The profit earned by foreign companies is repatriated abroad and so does not contribute directly to expenditure in the UK; the remuneration of the labour force and the earnings of UK oil companies will contribute to UK expenditure. For the time being we will assume that the exchange rate is fixed. If the extra expenditure all goes on traded goods then we know from our previous analysis (Chapters 9 and 10) that:

   (i) (net) imports will rise;

   (ii) employment and output in the non-oil traded goods sector will be unchanged;

   (iii) employment and output in the non-traded goods sector will be unchanged.

The important conclusion here is that the output of the non-oil traded goods sector is unchanged. It follows directly from the analysis in Chapter 9. The price of traded goods is determined by world prices and the exchange rate which are both fixed. Employment in the oil sector is negligible so it does not affect the real product wages paid in the non-oil sector. There is thus no reason for firms in the traded goods sector to change their supply of output. Clearly this argument depends crucially on the assumption that prices are wholly determined abroad. We reconsider this below.

If the extra expenditure all goes on non-traded goods the first round effects are that:

   (i) output and employment in the non-traded goods sector increases;

   (ii) output and employment in the non-oil traded goods sector is unchanged;

   (iii) (net) imports are unchanged.

In this case there are further effects to consider. The extra demand for non-traded goods bids up prices, thus inducing firms to increase output and employment. This increase in output and employment generates extra income which, when it is spent, will lead to second round effects tending to increase demand for all goods (traded and non-traded) and to increase net imports.

So far all the effects of increased expenditure have been beneficial or, at worst, neutral. But the increase in the output of non-traded sector may lead to a rise in the level of wages. This may occur partly because the price of non-traded goods has risen, thus reducing the purchasing power of wages, and partly because the extra demand for labour may lead to an increase in the wage demanded. To the extent that the wage rises, the increase in the output of the non-traded sector will be checked, but the output of the traded goods sector — which has not had the benefit of a price rise — will fall unless production is under constant marginal costs.

It is now easy to see what will happen if the expenditure goes on goods which are exported and consumed internally but over the price of which domestic producers have some control. The extra domestic demand leads producers to increase prices and expand output. However, the increase in prices will lead to a fall in foreign demand and thus in exports. The increase in domestic demand is thus met partly by switching existing supplies away from foreign markets and partly by increasing output.

Overall the effect of increased expenditure at a fixed exchange rate must be to increase employment, output and prices in the non-traded sector, or at worst, leave them unchanged. In the fully-traded sector, where prices are wholly determined abroad, output and employment are unaffected unless the increase in demand for non-traded goods increases wages and so reduces profitability. Where the prices of traded goods are variable, output and employment are increased to the extent that there is an increase in domestic demand but reduced if competitiveness deteriorates, thus reducing exports and also the incentive to supply. In the special case where the wage is constant, the increase in expenditure is unambiguously beneficial in terms of output and employment.

The effects of the exploitation of oil also depend on how the government allocates its receipts of taxes from the oil companies. The greater the extent to which the government increases expenditure either directly by increasing its own expenditure or indirectly by reducing other taxes the greater will be the effect on the non-oil sector. As the UK government is such an important beneficiary it is worth considering the special case when all the income earned (except that due to foreign oil companies) accrues to the UK government. This leads to the following conclusion: if the government's own spending and its non-oil tax receipts are unchanged, then the exploitation of oil (at a fixed exchange rate) has no adverse effects on the non-oil sector.

Paradoxically it has no benefits either. With domestic expenditure unchanged, the exploitation of oil — a traded good *par excellence* — must increase the current surplus; the increase in tax receipts and the consequent fall in the government's borrowing are the counterparts to this current account surplus. Effectively the stock of oil is being transformed into a stock of foreign financial assets owned by the government. These assets yield a return in the form of interest payments. Thus if exploitation of oil is concentrated in only a few years, the strategy of building up foreign exchange reserves allows the benefits to accrue over a longer period. Moreover since domestic expenditure is unchanged (unless the government distributes the interest received) the non-oil sector does not suffer any temporary dislocation associated with oil.

The Effects of Variations in the Exchange Rate

Overall, when the exchange rate is fixed, the exploitation of oil probably benefits the non-oil sector in that expenditure on non-oil goods is increased. Indeed since the government is the chief beneficiary of the exploitation in terms of revenue created and since the government has control over the level of expenditure, it is hard to see why the exploitation of oil should make matters worse. If the government manages the economy so that the level of expenditure is unchanged, it can ensure that the non-oil sector is just as well off as before. But suppose that the exploitation of oil were associated with an appreciation of the exchange rate. From our previous analysis we know that as long as domestic costs — in particular wages — are unchanged, then competitiveness of the traded goods sector would be worsened, reducing output and employment. In so far as this means that less income is generated in this sector, any consequent decline in expenditure would be transmitted to the non-traded goods sector. The increase in oil production in the UK coincided with a sharp appreciation of the exchange rate in 1979 and 1980, and much has been written about whether this was an unavoidable consequence of the exploitation of oil (see below and Chapter 13).

In the UK the proposition that the non-oil sector had to suffer a relative decline in its output is often referred to as the Forsyth-Kay argument (Forsyth and Kay, 1980). Although there are several variants, the general style of the argument is as follows. The exploitation of oil represents a free gift to the economy. In the short run increased oil exports or lower oil imports lead to a current account surplus and an increase in the income of domestic residents. Suppose that the government's fiscal policy is conducted in such a way that oil taxes are redistributed to the private sector. The private sector wishes to spend part of its resources on traded goods and part on non-traded goods. Thus resources will have to enter the non-traded goods sector. This could come about as follows. If the private sector succeeds in spending only a portion of its extra income on traded goods, the increase in net imports of non-oil goods would not be enough to offset completely the surplus generated by the increase in (net) exports of oil. The exchange rate rises, worsening the competitiveness of the traded sector and thus leads to declines in output in this sector. This eliminates the current account surplus and simultaneously releases the resources required in the non-traded sector.

This argument has two major deficiencies. First it depends on the assumption that the level of employment is constant (presumably at the 'natural rate'). As such it may have little to say about short-run behaviour, especially as there is no compelling reason for believing that employment was any equilibrium level to start with. Secondly the exchange rate is a *deus ex machina* arriving on stage at the crucial moment. There is no explanation of why the exchange rate may change, only a recognition that it must.

This latter point can be understood by returning to our basic premise that the exchange rate is determined by the decisions of various parties as to which assets they wish to hold and in what quantity they want to hold them. The increase in oil exports increases the net holdings of foreign assets of the private sector in the short run. But we have seen that the counterpart of the surplus is higher *government* hoarding resulting from its increased receipts of taxes from the oil companies. These taxes are due in sterling. If the monetary authorities do not wish to accumulate foreign exchange reserves, the oil companies will have to attempt to obtain the necessary domestic currency from other asset holders. The process of competition will increase the prices of domestic currency relative to foreign currency — that is, will generate an appreciation of the exchange rate.

Apart from its effects on the exchange rate through alterations in the quantity and pattern of hoarding in the domestic economy, the mere possession of oil may affect the relative attractiveness of sterling denominated assets and thus lead asset holders (both residents and non-residents) to increase the proportion of such assets in their portfolios. As we have seen (in Chapter 5), an improvement in 'confidence' will generate a short-term increase in the exchange rate. The increase in oil output and the appreciation of sterling in 1979 and 1980 took place when oil prices were rising sharply. As a producer of oil the UK's real national disposable income was less affected than those of other countries. As much of the increased revenues would end up with the government, it was in a position to use expansionary policy to offset the contractionary effects on the private non-oil sector of the sharp rise in the relative price of oil and expand without resort to deficit finance. In other words, government policy was less likely to involve running down the foreign exchange reserves than in other countries and output was more likely to be stable. In these circumstances wealth holders might suspect that the exchange rate would tend to rise in the future. In order to appropriate the capital gain it is necessary for them to move before the rise in the rate takes place. This re-arrangement of portfolios will help to generate the rise in the exchange rate.

The Quantitative Importance of Oil in the UK Economy and its Estimated Effect on the Exchange Rate

Armchair theorising about the possible effects of oil on the exchange rate is all very well but what is wanted is a quantitative estimate of the various effects. This is not an easy task as many other aspects of the economy were changing at the same time as the oil sector was increasing its output. For example, in mid-1979 a new government was elected and set about raising interest rates. Thus it is hard to know *a priori* how much of the rise in the exchange rate was due to an oil effect and how much due to interest rate changes. Some (notably Richardson, 1980) have argued that the appreciation of sterling at this time was mainly due to non-oil factors, but this view is not held by everybody. While the large macro-models of the economy are very imperfect, they do offer the only fully articulated accounts of the reaction of the economy to oil. Two such accounts of the quantitative effect of oil on the economy are available, one by a group of economists working at the UK Treasury, 'Byatt' [Byatt, Hartley, Lomax, Powell and Spencer (1982)], and another by a group working at the National Institute, 'Atkinson' [Atkinson, Brooks and Hall (1983)].

Both groups attempt to estimate the effect of the exploitation of oil on the UK's exchange rate. (For a survey of views about the effects of North Sea Oil on the exchange rate see Vernon (1985), and Chapter 13.) The analysis in Byatt is mainly in terms of the effects of changes in oil prices on the UK's balance of payments which serves to bid up the exchange rate by affecting the supply and demand for foreign currency.

On the basis of their calculations they estimated that some 10–15 per cent of the 25 per cent increase in the *real* exchange rate (that is, of the 25 per cent loss of competitiveness) between early 1979 and February 1982 might be accounted for by North Sea oil. Atkinson's estimates are drawn from two sources. First of all they conducted a 'partial equilibrium' analysis based on the calculations of various terms in their exchange rate equation. (The equation itself is discussed more fully in Chapter 13.) They distinguish two effects. First there is the direct balance of payments effect which takes account of the beneficial effect on the balance of payments of the exogenous increase in the output of the traded good, oil. They estimate that without this contribution the effective exchange rate in 1982 would have been more than 25 per cent lower. The second effect is a confidence effect associated with the real value of the UK's reserves of oil. Atkinson and his colleagues reckon that this was worth a further 10 per cent in 1982. The authors are inclined to treat this estimate with caution, partly because it neglects second round effects of changes in the exchange rate on domestic prices and on the non-oil current balance. Alternative results are presented based on a simulation of the National Institute of Economic and Social Research macro-econometric model in which the group attempted to calculate what would have happened to the UK if the exploitation of the oil had not in fact taken place. On this basis they estimate that the *nominal* exchange rate would have been some 15 per cent lower in the absence of oil.

Atkinson also considers the effects of oil on private sector hoarding. In the model they are using, savings in the private sector depend on the distribution of income between companies (profits) and the personal sector (mainly wages and salaries). Redistributing income to the company sector reduces expenditure for a given level of income. The lower exchange rate in the without-oil case is associated with a higher price level and, because wages lag behind prices, with lower real personal sector income. In the without-oil case, the effect is to depress expenditure on and thus the output of non-traded and less-than-perfectly traded goods, so that overall non-oil output is actually lower in the without-oil case than in the with-oil case. This is of course the reverse of the Forsyth and Kay proposition and depends on the assumption that expenditure is determined within the system rather than being constrained by some constant expenditure or output assumption. This is a good illustration of the importance of setting out what is to be held constant and what is allowed to vary when discussing alternative economic scenarios. The details of the Atkinson simulation are shown in Table 12.3.

The Atkinson simulation is based on the assumption that government

Table 12.3: The Atkinson Simulation: State of the Economy in 1982 with and without Oil

		History	Assuming oil was never exploited
GDP	(1975 = 100)	105.8	100.1
GDP excluding oil	(1975 = 100)	101.5	100.1
Manufacturing output	(1975 = 100)	88.3	84.0
Exports of goods and services	(£m, 1975 prices)	32,500	30,450
Imports of goods and services	(£m, 1975 prices)	35,550	34,850
Consumers' expenditure	(£m, 1975 prices)	72,650	69,200
Effective exchange rate	(1975 = 100)	90.7	78.3
Unemployment	(millions)	2.9	3.6

Source: Atkinson, Brooks and Hall (1983).

expenditure would have been the same whether or not it collected any oil taxes. This is as if the tax revenue had been saved, for, if it had been assumed that it had been spent in the with-oil case, government expenditures would have had to have been reduced in the without-oil case to keep real government saving the same in each simulation. Atkinson gives some information about what might happened if the government had spent on extra amount equal to the oil revenues: the group estimates that in 1982 output would have been some 3 per cent higher than was actually the case — but the exchange rate would have been about 10 per cent lower.

Overall then the effect of oil on the UK economy, and on the exchange rate in particular, is shown to be qualitatively similar to what our *a priori* discussion suggested although the effects seem rather smaller than anticipated. While this may be partly due to the slow response of the economy to the shock and partly to the endogenisation of domestic expenditure, it also reflects the more cautious view of the groups on the dominance of the traded sector. It is important to get the relative sizes of the various sectors in perspective. For example, the manufacturing sector, so much the focus of attention, accounts for about one-quarter of UK output but for about two-thirds exports of goods. The Byatt study examines the effect of a 10 per cent change in competitiveness in a highly disaggregated model of the UK economy. The categories in their 'most seriously affected' group are all parts of the manufacturing sector — but even here output has only to be reduced by more than half a per cent at the end of ten years to qualify. After ten years the effects on the rest of the economy — more than 80 per cent of the total — are classed as minimal. Included here are public utilities, transport and communications, construction and public administration and defence which together make up 25 per cent of UK output. Many sectors suffer in the short run, but soon benefit from higher domestic expenditure. This work to some extent fleshes out the Atkinson study, suggesting that, although the depressing effect on the non-oil economy, working through the exchange rate, may well be offset by changes in expenditure, sub-sectors within the non-oil economy may well have divergent experiences consistent at least in direction with those predicted by Forsyth and Kay.

Conclusions

A brief review of the effects of North Sea oil on the UK economy is of interest in its own right. For our present purposes it demonstrates the usefulness of the tools we have developed in previous chapters for organising our thinking about a 'live topic'. We can see that at a qualitative level the outcome has been in rough accordance with our expectations. But we know that our abstractions can only throw light on the main influences and in particular have little to say about the relative magnitudes of various effects. The authors of the more detailed macro-economic studies qualify their figuring with injunctions for the reader not to place too much reliance on the precision of their estimates. The difficulties of verifying theories by an appeal to the 'facts' must make us cautious in applying too simplistically the implications of abstractions. Nonetheless, even in a fog a map is of some use.

Part 3: Further Reading

Exchange rate policy is macroeconomic policy in open economies. It encompasses international trade theory, monetary economics and 'ordinary' macroeconomics. For an introduction to international trade, see Caves and Jones (1974). For a British audience the best treatments of monetary economics are Goodhart (1975) and (1984). For the classic statement of macroeconomic policy in open Keynesian models, see Stern (1973); von Neumann Whitman (1970) is an important survey paper which well conveys the concerns of the fixed rate period. For accounts directed to more recent issues consult Turnovsky (1977) and Dornbusch (1973a, b). The non-traded goods model was introduced into the literature by Salter (1959): the article is still worth reading.

PART 4

FORECASTING

13 FORECASTING THE EXCHANGE RATE — A SCEPTICAL VIEW

In previous chapters we have discussed the factors that are likely to affect the determination of the exchange rate and the effects of changes in the exchange rate on the economy, and we have reviewed the turbulent history of exchange rates in recent years. The exchange rate is clearly important, both to countries and to individuals, yet the ability of economists and others to forecast it has not been impressive. Publicly available forecasts of the economy are always careful to stress the uncertainty about future developments; one highly respected international organisation, the OECD, always presents its forecasts on the assumption of fixed rates of exchange; governments themselves refuse to publish their own forecasts of exchange rates and interest rates for fear of market reaction. In this chapter we review the methods that have been employed by those involved in preparing publicly available forecasts of the UK economy, as well as less formal methods sometimes used in financial institutions. Although some of the approaches are statistical, we will not get involved in complicated econometric discussions; instead we will explain why forecasters have adopted a particular course of action and what are its likely weaknesses.

Econometric Equations and Econometric Models

There are in the UK several 'quasi-public' bodies at least partly financed from public funds which publish regular economic forecasts based on econometric models. The two most well known are the London Business School (LBS) and the National Institute of Economic and Social Research (NIESR). In recent years other teams at universities have developed their own models and have produced short-term forecasts (Liverpool, City University Business School). Since the Treasury maintains its own model, a version of which is publicly available, others have produced forecasts based on this model. The models used by all these groups have been built mainly at public expense and details of their construction are publicly available. Other groups in the private sector (whose models are not generally made freely available) probably also use similar techniques (Philips & Drew, DRI, Wharton).

In this section we shall evaluate exchange rate sectors that have at one time or another appeared in the models of the LBS, NIESR and HM Treasury. The models described have been selected to illustrate particular aspects of the problems involved and to illustrate the logic behind different approaches.[1] We have singled out these models because they use quarterly rather than annual data which seems more likely to be appropriate for exchange rate analysis. Typically the teams using these models publish forecasts of the whole economy showing quarterly paths of variables for horizons from two to five years ahead. In general the forecasts concentrate on the effective exchange rate, which is a weighted average of individual bilateral exchange rates, and have little to say about development in individual cross rates. Such forecasts are particularly valuable because they take a view of future developments which looks at the whole economy and thus in principle allows for interactions between the various sectors of the economy. However by their very nature they are likely to be of little use for predicting day-to-day or week-to-week movements. The rest of this section considers the methods used in constructing exchange rate sectors of models. It must be said that all teams currently find their own exchange rate sectors unreliable — we shall see why — and the econometric forecast is normally helped along with generous amounts of off-model judgement.

Econometrics is the quantitative branch of economics and is concerned with the isolation of the regular patterns of behaviour in the myriad economic and other statistics published by governments and other organisations. Econometric models are maintained and used by most of the organisations involved in the preparation of integrated forecasts of the macroeconomy. The building blocks of such models are econometric equations which formalise the explanation of the relationship in question. Such equations are written (for example),

$$e = a_0 + a_1 r + a_2 r^* + a_3 m + a_4 m^*.$$

In this example, e, the exchange rate, is termed the dependent variable and is assumed to depend on the values taken by domestic interest rates, r, foreign interest rates, r^*, and domestic and foreign money supplies, m, m^*. The effect of changes in the value of each independent variable on the dependent variable is determined by the a's, which are called parameters. The two tasks of the applied economist are to decide what variables to include as independent, or explanatory, variables, and to assign values to the parameters so that the equation can be made operational. Economic theorising and institutional knowledge suggest relationships that might be expected to hold — we know, for example, from previous chapters that a close relationship might be expected to hold between exchange rate movements and interest rate changes. Calculating estimated values for the parameters is a statistical exercise. While we will not comment on the various statistical methods adopted in a particular case, we will discuss the conditions that have to be met before such an exercise can be undertaken as doubts about the extent to which these conditions are met affect one's judgement about the reliability of the parameter estimates. Although we have described the applied economist's task as consisting of two separate activities, in practice the poor statistical performance of one embodiment of theory leads to a re-evaluation of the theoretical part of the job as the economist attempts to isolate from the many possible influences those (few) which are important quantitatively.

Problems of Econometric Equations

(i) Frequency of Observation. The econometric models we will review all attempt to relate the average value of the effective exchange rate over a whole quarter to the average quarterly values of the explanatory variables. Even if such an equation works very well, it is not much help in explaining very short-term movements. In Chapter 5 we discussed the possibility that an exchange rate might move suddenly if expectations were revised on the receipt of new information. Such movements are normally lost in the quarterly averaging so that econometric equations are little help in deciding precisely when such movements will occur.

The choice of quarterly forecasts is partly determined by the desire to use the equation as part of a large macroeconomic model and partly determined by the availability of statistics. While interest rates and exchange rates are available almost continuously and certainly daily, other variables are available at best monthly — as is the case in the UK with the visible trade figures and the retail price index — and often only quarterly and then some time in arrears, as is the case with figures for invisible trade. Such problems are conveniently and properly ignored in theoretical discussions. In practice, what is available will often play an important role in shaping the final equation.

(ii) Forecasting Explanatory Variables. By their very nature econometric equations provide predictions of the exchange rate for given values of the explanatory variables. If you do not have any method of forecasting the explanatory variables, this is not much help for exchange rate prediction. The problem is exacerbated if you are unable to take a view on the likely values of the explanatory variables without previously having

formed a view of the exchange rate. The forecasting teams use other equations to supply values for the explanatory variables and thus forecast all the variables simultaneously. For this reason macroeconomic forecasters set great store in producing a forecast that hangs together. When assessing the errors made by an econometric equation it is therefore vital to consider the extent to which the error has arisen out of failure to predict, for example, a government's interest rate policies and the extent to which the underlying econometric relationship is inaccurate.

This problem is to some extent relieved if the equation does not contain any contemporaneous explanatory variables. Such an equation might be of the form

$$e_t = a_0 + a_1 r_{t-1} + a_2 r_{t-1}^* + a_3 m_{t-1} + a_4 m_{t-1}^*.$$

In this example the exchange rate reacts to changes in the explanatory variables that occurred in the previous period. This means that if we know the current period's values of interest rates and money supplies, we can use the equation to form a forecast of the exchange rate for the next period. If, however, we require forecasts further than one period ahead, we will still have to forecast interest rates and money supplies.

Although this approach can be useful in some areas of applied economics, it is not likely to be useful in exchange rate forecasting because we anticipate that the contemporaneous expected relative rate of return on assets of different currency denominations will be important. A special case of using lagged variables is the univariate time series model which is discussed below (under Non-econometric Methods).

(iii) Technical Estimation Problems. Given the specification of the equation, its usefulness depends on the confidence we can place on the estimated values of the parameters. Discussion of estimation problems is beyond the scope of this book, but it is worthwhile to note the underlying conditions that have to be met if the parameters are to be considered at all reliable.

The most important of these is the assumption of structural stability. The estimates of the parameters are normally chosen to make the divergence between the equation's predicted values of the exchange rate and the observed values of the exchange rate as small as possible over the estimation period taken as a whole. (Often the intention is to minimise the sum of the squared prediction errors.) Such a procedure only makes sense if the underlying 'true' values of the parameters are constant. Suppose in our example a_1 was really 1 in the first part of the period and 0 in the second part. If we assumed that there was no distinction between the two parts, we might end up with some intermediate value, 0.6 say. Given that the true value, assuming that the future will be like the recent past, is 0, the equation is likely to produce poor forecasts.

It is not at all obvious that the floating rate period can be considered homogeneous in the sense required. Sterling was floated in 1972, but floated more or less alone until 1973, when the other major currencies joined it. As we have discussed in Chapter 6, there is good reason to believe that it took some time for participants in the markets to learn how to operate the new system. Perhaps there is a case for ignoring the first eight or ten quarterly observations after June 1972 on the grounds that the underlying exchange rate determining mechanism had not yet settled down. In the UK the system of exchange control was dismantled in 1979 — was behaviour in the exchange market significantly affected or not? During the floating rate period the European countries have experimented with a variety of exchange rate systems culminating in the EMS — have these arrangements had any implications for sterling's exchange rate? If any of these factors affected the relationship between the independent variables and the exchange rate in a way not allowed for in the specification of the equation, the emerging estimates have little claim to statistical support. Careful analysis may indicate where the likely structural shifts are. It may be the case that the relationships have been disturbed significantly so often that there is too little data available on the current relationship to permit estimation. While applied economists seek to make objective as much as possible, the decision about which estimates are best is a matter of judgement, not of science.

Interpreting Econometric Equations

In this section we review two econometric equations that have been used at one time or another in two of the more well-known and long-established models of the UK economy. The equations have been chosen to contrast with each other; we examine their similarities and differences. Subsequently we consider some evidence that suggests that econometric equations provide no guidance at all for exchange rate forecasting.

(i) The National Institute's Model 6 Equation. The equation is set out in Table 13.1 and fully described in Hall (1983). The derivation of the equation is eclectic and Hall's account makes it clear that his intention was to estimate a relationship in which relative interest rates (G), relative inflation rates $\Delta(P^*/P)$ and the current balance should all have a chance to operate. He did not view his equation as embodying any single theory of exchange rate determination. The equation is unusual in that it is

Table 13.1: Econometric Exchange Rate Equations Contrasted

National Institute Model 6

$$\left\{ \frac{eP}{P^*} - \frac{e_{-1}P_{-1}}{P^*_{-1}} \right\} = 0.348G + 0.506(Q - Q_{-2}) + 50.8\Delta(\Delta(P^*/P))$$
$$(12.6) \qquad (3.2) \qquad\qquad (0.8)$$

$$- 116.0\,\Delta\,(\Delta(P^*_{-2}/P_{-2})) + 0.00162\,\Delta\,OR$$
$$(2.0) \qquad\qquad\qquad (2.2)$$

where

$$G = (r - 100\,\dot{P} - r\dot{P}) - (r_{US} - 100\,\dot{P}_{US} - r_{US}\dot{P}_{US})$$

$SEE = 3.57$; $DW = 1.9$; $BP(16) = 16.2$; $LM(8) = 5.2$;
estimation period: 1972 Q1–1982 Q2.

London Business School (1981)

$$\ln e = 0.2699 + 0.5453\,\Delta \ln RMG - 0.465\,\Delta \ln RMG_{-3}$$
$$(3.2) \qquad (3.0) \qquad\qquad (2.9)$$

$$- 0.1968\ln(e_{-2}RMG_{-3}) - 0.0182\sum_{i=1}^{t-1}\ln(e_{-2}RMG_{-3})_{-i}$$
$$(4.5) \qquad\qquad\qquad (3.5)$$

$$+ 0.939\,\Delta \ln R_{-1} + 0.6666\,\Delta \ln R_{-3}$$
$$(3.3) \qquad\qquad (2.4)$$

$$+ 1.7065\,OIL + 0.0143\,\Delta\,OIL2_{-1} + 0.0089\,\Delta\,OIL2_{-3}$$
$$(6.1) \qquad\quad (2.2) \qquad\qquad (3.0)$$

$$+ 0.3896\,\Delta\,B - 0.00306\,TIME + dummy$$
$$(2.4) \qquad\quad (2.8)$$

where

$$RMG = \frac{M/M^*}{GDP/GDP^*}$$

$$R = 1 + \frac{(r - r^*)}{100}$$

$SEE = 0.0169$; estimation period: 1979 Q1–1979 Q4.

Figures in parentheses are t-statistics.

Definitions of variables:

e Effective exchange rate index as published by the Bank of England (scaled so that 1980 = 100 (NIESR) or 1975 = 1 (LBS)).

r Yield on UK Treasury bills (3 months), per cent.

r^* World short-term interest rate — averages of selected countries, per cent.

r_{US} Interest rate UK 3-month eurodollar deposits, per cent.

Table 13.1 *contd.*

Definition of variables:

P	UK producer price index (excluding food, drink and tobacco) 1980 = 100.
P*	World producer index, measured in foreign currency, 1980 = 100.
m	UK money supply, measured in £m.
m*	Index of world money supply, 1975 = 100.
GDP	UK real gross domestic product, measured in £m at 1975 prices.
GNP*	World real gross national product, index, 1975 = 1.
OR	Real value of UK's oil reserves (i.e. oil believed to remain under North Sea).
OIL	OPEC's sterling balances as a proportion of UK gdp.
OIL2	Value of UK's oil reserves as a proportion of UK gdp.
Q	Real value of UK's current account balance.
B	UK public sector borrowing requirement as a proportion of UK GDP.
TIME	Time trend

specified entirely in real terms. The dependent variable is the real effective exchange rate, rather than the effective exchange rate itself. The real exchange rate is the ratio of domestic wholesale prices expressed in foreign currency, eP, to world wholesale prices expressed in foreign currency, P^*; thus the real exchange rate is similar to a measure of competitiveness. If the price indices used related to traded goods and if commodity arbitrage ensured that prices for the same goods were identical in all countries, we would expect the real exchange rate to be constant. In practice, measurement difficulties and, more important, persistent market imperfections, mean that the real exchange rate can and does change. Furthermore, it is not in fact claimed that manufactures are traded on perfectly competitive markets so that the exercise of market power may lead to movements in the real exchange rate as defined.

The equation looks complicated to the unpractised eye, but it is easy enough to tease out its implications one by one. First, imagine that there is no inflation either in the UK or in the rest of the world (i.e. $\hat{P} = \hat{P}^* = 0$), that the current account is in balance ($Q = Q_2 = 0$), that the value of the UK's oil reserves is constant ($\Delta OR = 0$) and that domestic and foreign prices are equal ($P = P^*$). In these circumstances the equation reduces to

$$e - e_{-1} = 0.348 \, (r - r_{US}).$$

That is, if the UK interest rate exceeds the US interest rate by one percentage point, the exchange rate will appreciate by 0.348 points each quarter. In fact the exchange rate can only be constant if the interest rates are the same. An important implication of this equation is that it implicitly denies that the currency of denomination of an asset is an important attribute. If this were the case then, as we have discussed in Chapter 2, the level of the exchange rate would depend on the interest rate differential, that is

$$e = k(r - r_{US})$$

where k is some positive constant. The two formulations have completely different implications for forecasting. In the National Institute equation, a policy of maintaining an interest differential in the UK's favour would lead to a continuous rise in the exchange rate. In the alternative formulation an increase in the differential would lead to a once and for all rise in the exchange rate (which might take several periods to achieve).

Once we relax our diagnostic assumption that the UK price level is fixed, and repeat the argument in real terms, the conclusions are even more interesting. The equation is now:

$$\frac{eP}{P^*} - \frac{e_{-1}P_{-1}}{P^*_{-1}} = 0.348 \ [(r - 100\hat{P} - r\hat{P}) - (r_{US} - 100\hat{P}_{US} - r_{US}\hat{P}_{US})]$$

Consider the sequence of events following a rise in UK interest rates, starting from a position of zero inflation in the UK and in the rest of the world. An increase in the nominal rate of interest of 1 percentage point increases the real rate of exchange by 0.348. Without knowledge of the rest of the model, we cannot say how this is split between exchange rate changes and price level changes, but it seems likely that the exchange rate will be more flexible in the short run than prices. We may thus expect the exchange rate to rise. We know from earlier chapters that a rise in the exchange rate leads to a fall in the price level, thus the real interest differential is likely to become even greater in the short run, leading to renewed pressure on the real rate of exchange. Whether such a process is stable or not depends on the form of the whole model. Overall it seems likely that such an equation will make the transmission of interest rate shocks to the economy via the exchange rate a powerful tool of policy. (This is borne out by simulation results, see Brooks and Henry, 1983.)

We know from our previous work that an increase in the rate of inflation in the rest of the world will probably be associated with an increase in the UK's exchange rate. Assuming now that real interest rates are constant, but that inflation rates may vary, we can write the equation as

$$\frac{eP}{P^*} - \frac{e_{-1}P_{-1}}{P^*_{-1}} = -50.8 \; \Delta \; (\Delta \; (\frac{P^*}{P})) - 116.0 \; \Delta(\Delta(\frac{P^*_{-2}}{P_{-2}})).$$

If domestic and foreign rates of inflation are identical (P^*/P) will be constant, so that the real exchange rate will be constant. Suppose that the foreign rate of inflation is always 5 per cent faster than the UK rate, this means that[2]

$$\Delta \; (\frac{P^*}{P}) = \frac{P^*}{P} - \frac{P^*_{-1}}{P_{-1}} \cong 0.05.$$

But $\Delta(\Delta(P^*/P)) = \Delta(P^*/P) - \Delta(P^*_{-1}/P_{-1}) = 0$. The $\Delta\Delta$ terms are thus acceleration terms. So for a constant inflation differential, the real rate will be constant, thus

$$\frac{eP}{P^*} = \frac{e_{-1}P_{-1}}{P^*_{-1}}.$$

Given our previous calculations, this does indeed mean that, in equilibrium, the exchange rate will exactly offset the inflation differential. Only if the inflation differential changes do the acceleration terms become effective. It is easy to see that a speeding up of foreign inflation implies a depreciation of the real exchange rate. However, we cannot use this to form a forecast of the nominal exchange rate unless we can take a view of the effects on domestic prices. One easy case to work out supposes that domestic and foreign price levels have been equal and constant in the past, and that a change in foreign prices or the exchange rate takes at least one quarter to have any effect on domestic prices. In this case a sudden jump of one per cent in the foreign price level will reduce the nominal exchange rate by half a point immediately.

The term in $\Delta_2 Q$ shows that the real exchange rate depends positively on the real value of the currrent balance. Formally Hall argues for its inclusion as a measure of the out-flow on the capital account. The differenced way in which it appears is the result of a statistical search rather than a reflection of some deeply held *a priori* conviction. The positive sign on its coefficient is in accord with the conventional view that an improvement in the current balance will increase the exchange rate either directly by increasing the demand (relative to supply) for domestic currency or indirectly by increasing the confidence of asset holders in the sustainability of current exchange rate policies.

The final term, $+0.00162\Delta OR$, is the exogenous effect of the UK's reserves of crude oil under the North Sea. Oil price effects such as these can only be justified as *ad hoc* ways of measuring asset holders' confidence. They started to appear in econometric equations following the great appreciation of sterling in 1979 and 1980 which most equations then in existence completely failed to track. Over this period the world price of oil increased substantially, and econometric equations incorporating such effects attribute to oil prices most of the increase in the exchange rate. Much day-to-day discussion of oil prices and sterling is conducted in terms of the importance of oil prices for providing taxes to finance government expenditure. The fear is that without oil tax revenue, the government would resort to creating money to finance its plans and that such monetary creation would be inflationary. The foreign exchange market then anticipates the concomitant fall in the exchange rate. In practice this is the closest quarterly econometric models get to incorporating items of 'news'. For a review of the importance of these effects in current models of the exchange rate, see Vernon (1985).

In summary, the National Institute equation incorporates views about the effects of relative inflation rates, relative interest rates and the current balance on the exchange rate. Many of the important variables appear contemporaneously with the exchange rate so that its usefulness from a forecasting point of view pre-supposes the ability to forecast inflation rates, interest rates and oil prices as well as the current balance. While the equation was regularly used for forecasting, its within-sample standard error suggests an accuracy of plus or minus seven points, which at the time of writing means an error band of about plus or minus 10 per cent on a quarterly basis.

(ii) The London Business School Equation (1981). This equation, set out in Table 13.1, is not the exchange rate forecasting method currently in use at the London Business School. It has been chosen to contrast strongly with the National Institute model. The National Institute's real exchange rate equation emphasises the links between relative prices and the exchange rate; the exchange rate depends on the tendency of domestic and foreign price levels to be equalised when expressed in a common currency. Prices do not appear at all in the London Business School equation (LBS, 1981). Instead the driving force is the relative money supply variable, *RMG*. The effect of changes in the money supply were examined in Chapter 11. If the supply of domestic money increases with no change in the determinants of the private sector's demand for money, the exchange rate will have to fall to induce the private sector to hold the extra money. Any association between the exchange rate and the price level is the result of commodity arbitrage and the effects of asset market decisions. The equation can be re-written in a simplified form as:

$$\Delta\ln e = Z + 0.5453\Delta\ln(m/m^*) - 0.465\Delta\ln(m/m^*)_{-3}$$

$$-0.1968 \ln(e_{-2}m_{-3}/m^*_3) - 0.0182 \sum_{i=1}^{t-1} \ln(e_{-2}m_{-3}/m^*_3)_{-i}.$$

Here m and m^* are the UK and world money supply respectively. It has been assumed that world GNP and UK GDP are constant. All the other terms have been collected in the constant, Z. Unlike the National Institute equation, the LBS (1981) equation includes a definition of the *equilibrium* exchange rate. To examine this, suppose that both money supplies are constant. In the end the exchange rate will be constant too, so that the equation will be

$$0 = Z - 0.1968 \ln(e\ m/m^*) - 0.0182\ (t - 1)\ \ln(e\ m/m^*).$$

As e, m, m^* are all constant, the subscripts can be suppressed. Rearranging this slightly gives, setting Z to zero,

$$\ln e = -\ln(m/m^*)$$

or

$$e = m^*/m.$$

Thus an increase in domestic money supply, m, leads to an equi-proportionate fall in the exchange rate. This relationship holds in the long run, not instantaneously. The path of approach to the equilibrium is determined by all the terms in $\Delta\ln RMG$ and $\Delta\ln e$. It is straightforward to deduce the path of the exchange rate following a once-and-for-all change in the ratio of money supplies. This is shown in Figure 13.1. Although the exchange rate moves in the same proportion as relative money supplies in the end, the approach is rather erratic. It is always sensible to work out the responses of the exchange rate to changes in the determining variables in complicated equations as often short-run behaviour is found to be very different from the long-run relationship.

The role of interest rates in this model is again quite different from that in the National Institute model. Interest rates appear only in difference terms

$$0.939\Delta\ln R_{-1} + 0.666\Delta\ln R_{-3} = 0.939\ln R_{-1} - 0.939\ln R_{-2}$$
$$+ 0.666\ln R_{-3} - 0.666\ln R_{-4}.$$

As long as interest rates are constant, neither their level nor the differential between them has any effect at all on the level of the nominal exchange rate. How different this is from the effect in the National Institute model.

Figure 13.1: Percentage deviation of exchange rate from base values following a sustained 1 per cent increase in the domestic money supply

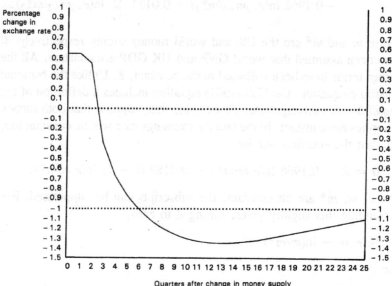

Quarters after change in money supply

Following a change in the interest rate nothing at all happens for one period because the first term in R is $0.939R_{-1}$; after one period, the exchange rate will rise by slightly less than the increase in R; in the next period it will fall back by the same amount; in the third period after the change, the exchange rate will rise by two-thirds of the rise in R and in the fourth period it will again fall back. The *direct* interest rate effects will be a set of mutually offsetting shocks with no net effect in the long run. The precise time path of the exchange rate will depend on the values of the coefficients on the lagged values of the exchange rate itself.

The interest rate is thus a short-run modifier of the exchange rate path. It is assumed that in the long run changes in relative interest rates are fully reflected in changes in the demands for money. As the exchange rate is supposed to adjust to keep the demands for domestic and foreign money in line, there is no extra role for the interest rate. Similarly, the PSBR, roughly speaking the government's financial deficit, also appears as a short-run disturbance factor because in the short run changes in the government deficit affect the supply of money as they are not typically matched exactly by changes in sales of government debt to the (non-bank) private sector.

One feature that this equation has in common with that of the National Institute is an effect from oil prices. In fact the LBS (1981) equation identifies two. The first is related to the composition of outstanding sterling-denominated liabilities by area of holder:

$$+1.7065 \ OIL.$$

This says that if the sterling balances of the oil exporting countries increase, then the exchange rate will be higher. Historically, the oil exporting countries have held a disproportionately large share of their official foreign exchange reserves in the form of UK government securities. One can understand why an increase in the oil exporters' current account surplus, that is a redistribution of world wealth in favour of oil exporters, might be expected to increase demand for sterling-denominated assets and thus increase sterling's exchange rate. The use of OPEC's sterling balances is more problematical and has to be justified by assuming that the share of OPEC balances going into sterling assets is independent of the level of the exchange rate. It is the case, however, that data on oil-exporting countries' official holdings of sterling-denominated assets is fairly easy to obtain, while there is much less information about their reserves in total.

The other variable, *OIL2*, which appears in the term

$$+0.0143 \Delta OIL2_{-1} + 0.0089 \ OIL2_{-3}$$

may be justified in the same way as the similar term ΔOR in the National Institute equation. Here we may merely note that as *OIL2* does not appear only in the form of differences, changes in the value of oil reserves affect the exchange rate in both the short and the long run.

To sum up, the LBS (1981) equation is based on a particular view of the long-run relationship between money supplies and the exchange rate which determines the equilibrium. Various modifying terms have been added to improve the explanation of short-run behaviour. Like the National Institute equation, the use of the LBS equation for forecasting requires information on the right hand side variables.

The Predictive Accuracy of Econometric Forecasting Equations

At the end of the day a forecasting team's ability to predict the exchange rate depends not only on its use of an appropriate forecasting equation but also on its ability to forecast the rest of the economy correctly so that the right hand side variables are set at their correct levels. Because of some of these variables depend on the value set for the exchange rate, the process is essentially simultaneous. While the modelling teams publish from time to time analyses of their own forecasting performance these are best viewed as evaluations of overall performance rather than as assessments of the equation's ability to forecast the exchange rate itself. This question has been investigated by Meese and Rogoff (1983).

Meese and Rogoff (M&R) compared the forecasting performance of econometric equations of the type considered above with that of certain rules. They considered, for example, the *random walk model* which states that the exchange rate now is the same as the exchange rate last period plus or minus some random disturbance, that is

$$e_t = e_{t-1} + u_t$$

where u is the random disturbance. A second rule they considered is the *forward rate rule* that next period's spot exchange rate is equal to the appropriate current forward exchange rate, that is

$$e_t = {}_{t-1}f_t$$

where ${}_{t-1}f_t$ is the forward rate in period $t - 1$ for period t.

The third model they considered was the *univariate autoregressive model*[3] in which it is assumed that the exchange rate can be explained by reference to its past values alone, that is

$$e_t = a_1 e_{t-1} + a_2 e_{t-2} + \ldots a_n e_{t-n}.$$

If such a rule turned out to be very accurate, it would be very useful for forecasting as it includes no other variables which have to be forecast so that given the past values of the exchange rate any number of forecasts can be computed using the chain rule of forecasting. For example, if the model were

$$e = a_1 e_{t-1} + a_2 e_{t-2}$$

then given values for, say, 1984 Q3 and 1984 Q4 we can form a forecast of 1985 Q1 and 1985 Q2 as

$$e^e_{85,1} = a_1 e_{84,4} + a_2 e_{84,3}$$
$$e^e_{85,2} = a_1 e^e_{85,1} + a_2 e_{84,4}$$

and so on. The random walk model is of course a special case of this more general model.

Choosing the appropriate econometric models for comparison presents a problem as there is no 'consensus' model as the differences between the National Institute and LBS (1981) equations indicate. M & R considered three variants of a basic model which is (with all variables expressed in logarithms except r and r^*)

$$e = a_0 + a_1 (m - m^*) + a_2 (y - y^*) + a_3 (r - r^*) + a_4 (\hat{P} - \hat{P}^*) + a_5 TB + a_6 TB^*$$

where in addition to our existing notation, *TB* is the cumulated current balance. The variants considered were (after their originators) Hooper-Morton (the basic model), Dornbusch-Frankel ($a_5 = a_6 = 0$) and Frenkel-Bilson ($a_4 = a_5 = a_6 = 0$). Strictly speaking then, M & R's conclusions hold only for these equations. While the equations have some common features with the National Institute and LBS (1981) equations, they omit the oil variables which UK forecasters have come to rely on. M & R estimate their equations on monthly data using as alternate dependent variables the \$/DM, \$/Yen and \$/£ exchange rates. While we may feel then that their model is not appropriate for the \$/£ case, it is not clear that the other cases are invalidated by such considerations.

M & R generated forecasts over the period November 1976 to June 1981, using only information available at the time that the forecast was supposed to have been made: thus, for example, forecasts 'made' in September 1978 used estimation periods ending in September 1978. They compared the relative accuracy of their equations according to the root mean square error criterion which is defined as

$$RMSE = \sqrt{\sum_{i=1}^{N} \frac{(FE)^2}{N}}$$

where *FE* is the forecast error and *N* is the number of forecasts. Thus the larger the *RMSE*, the less accurate the forecast method. The results of the study are shown in Table 13.2. In the cases of the \$/£ rate and the \$/Yen rate, the random walk model is the most accurate over all horizons considered; in second place is the forward rate model. Only in the \$/DM case do the econometric models out-perform the random walk model, and then only at the one-month horizon. It is important to note that the experiment is conducted in a way favourable to the econometric equations as actual values of the explanatory variables are used, thus eliminating errors in predicting right hand side variables as a source of forecast error. M & R also estimated equations with relative price levels substituted for relative money supplies (thus rendering the specifications more similar to the National Institute model) but the amendment did not upset the dominance of the random walk model.

The implications of the M & R study are depressing: given the choice of a single econometric equation or assuming that the exchange rate will take the same value in the next period as it has taken in the current period, using the equation leads to greater errors on average. In the next section we consider some of the inadequacies perceived by model builders and consider their efforts to overcome them.

Table 13.2: The Performance of Econometric Equations
Root Mean Square Forecast

	Dollar: Deutschmark rate			Dollar: yen rate			Dollar: sterling rate		
Horizon (months)	1	6	12	1	6	12	1	6	12
(a) Econometric models									
F-B[a]	3.17	9.64	16.12	4.11	13.38	18.55	2.82	8.90	14.62
D-F[a]	3.65	12.03	18.87	4.40	13.94	20.41	2.90	8.88	13.66
H-M[a]	3.50	9.95	15.69	4.20	11.94	19.20	3.03	9.08	14.57
(b) Other models									
Random walk	3.72	8.71	12.98	3.68	11.58	18.31	2.56	6.45	9.96
Forward rate	3.20	9.03	12.60	3.72	11.93	18.95	2.67	7.23	11.62
Time series	3.51	12.40	22.53	4.46	22.04	52.18	2.79	7.27	13.35

Source: Adapted from Meese & Rogoff (1983), p. 13.

Note: a: F-B = Frenkel-Bilson; D-F = Dornbusch-Frankel; H-M = Hooper-Morton.

Figure 13.2

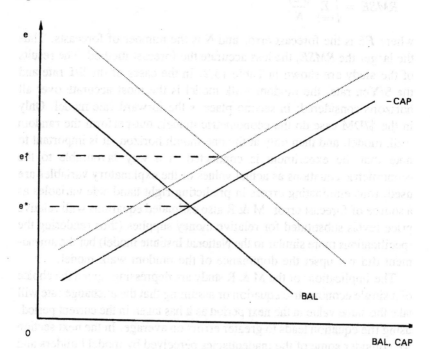

Why do Econometric Models Fail?

Nobody is sure. Two suggestions have been followed up which put the blame on inadequate modelling. The first of these denies that modellers should be seeking an exchange rate equation at all; the second considers that expectations are inadequately measured.

(a) Modelling the Capital Account. The single equation approach discussed above attempts to relate the exchange rate to influences on asset holders. It does not seem to work very well. One alternative is to model the capital account directly and obtain the exchange rate as the price of foreign exchange that clears the market.

The earliest instance of this technique in a UK macro-model is HM Treasury's capital flows model. This model was originally written up in Lomax and Denham (henceforth L & D) (1978) although it has subsequently been amended and extended, see HM Treasury (1982) and Barber (1984). The approach is based on the balance of payments identity which states that the current account surplus equals the net accumulation of foreign assets by residents, what we have referred to as 'hoarding'.

We have previously distinguished government and private sector hoarding, but for present purposes it is more convenient to consider discretionary changes in the government's accumulation of foreign assets from market-determined asset flows. In UK parlance the government's deliberate accumulation of assets is called the balance of official financing (BOF); we may call the market-determined flows CAP. The accounts are arranged so that

$$BAL + BOF + CAP = 0$$

where BAL is, as always, the current balance.

The relationship between the current balance and the exchange rate is described by the rest of the macro-model — export equations, import functions, price equations and so on. In many of these equations the exchange rate appears as an explanatory variable. We may summarise the relationship between the current balance and the exchange rate by writing

$$BAL = BAL(e).$$

Normally we would expect an increase in the exchange rate to worsen the current balance, although, in the short run, rigidities in prices may make the effect small or even perverse.

Economists normally believe they know quite a lot about the relationship of the current balance to the exchange rate, compared with what they know about the relationship between capital flows and the exchange rate. If we could find the analogous relationship between capital flows and the exchange rate, we could write

$$CAP = CAP(e).$$

Two possible relationships are sketched in Figure 13.2. In a floating exchange rate system, BOF is zero so that the market clearing exchange rate occurs where $BAL = -CAP$, that is when the exchange rate is $e*$. Changes in economic circumstances will shift the position of the curves and change the equilibrium exchange rate. For example, an increase in domestic interest rates will probably lead to an increase in the current balance at the existing exchange rate by depressing demand and thus reducing imports. So the BAL curve shifts to the right (broken line). Similarly, an increase in the interest rate makes domestic assets more attractive, leading asset holders to re-arrange their stocks and to a capital in-flow. This leads to a leftward shift in the $-CAP$ schedule and a new equilibrium exchange rate at e_1^*.

The argument that it is necessary to estimate a capital flows model to predict exchange rate movements rests in part on the assumption that the underlying structure at the single equation level has not been stable so that single equation estimation is not valid. It is hoped that stability reappears at a more disaggregated level or at least that the source of the instability may be isolated and given special treatment. The estimation of a capital flows model is a considerable undertaking, not helped by the fact that the capital flows data themselves are known to be of poor quality. Thus the search for structural stability brings with it new problems.

The model of capital flows described by L & D is based on the standard portfolio model of asset demand, which we have discussed extensively. The demand for each asset depends on the relative rates of return of competing assets. A flow is the result of a decision to redistribute the portfolios in the light of changes in these relative rates of return. Thus

$$CAP_i = CAP_i(\Delta r_1, \Delta r_2, \ldots, \Delta r_n)$$

where CAP_i is the in-flow of the ith asset and Δr_i is the change in the rate of return on the ith asset. The Treasury model includes estimates of such equations for the several types of asset, including long-term capital flows, trade credit and short-term capital flows, which add up to the total capital flow.

The rates of return include of course expected exchange rate changes. L & D face this issue head on, and have an elaborate structure for determining these expectations. This is best explained using an example. Their equation for short-term capital flows is (ignoring quarterly dummies and the scaling variables in world wealth)

$$SHT = 100 + 500 \, \Delta(r - r^* - c) + 150 \, \Delta(r - r^* + e^e)$$

where SHT is the capital in-flow (measured in millions of pounds) and the other variables have their usual interpretations. The new variable, c, is the cost of forward cover. This is the percentage difference between the spot exchange rate and the forward exchange rate. The first term then is the covered interest differential which measures the difference in the yields of domestic and foreign assets free of exchange risk. In the second term, $-c$ is replaced by $+e^e$, the expected exchange rate appreciation, which is the uncertain profit of investing in foreign assets. The relative risk in the relative rates of return is reflected in the much larger coefficient on the risk-free measure.

L & D distinguish long-run exchange expectations from expectations about the exchange rate in the next quarter. Asset holders' expectations of the long-term equilibrium exchange rate, e^*, depend on the ratio of domestic and foreign money supplies to real income ratios. Thus

$$e^* = a \, \frac{m^*/Y^*}{m/Y}$$

where a is constant. But, they argue, asset holders do not anticipate that the exchange rate will adjust to its equilibrium level instantaneously: rather there will be a path of adjustment that depends on previous departures from equilibrium. Thus

$$e^e = e^* + \Sigma\lambda_i \, (e - e^*)_{-i} \qquad \Sigma\lambda_i = 0.$$

The condition that the lag weights sum to zero ensures that if the exchange rate has always been equal to the equilibrium rate, it is expected to be so next period, even if the equilibrium rate itself changes.

Overall, the system of equations can be seen as fleshing out the single equation approaches discussed earlier. Neither the National Institute nor the LBS (1981) equations distinguished expectations from other influences, although the asset demand model assigns expectations a pivotal role. The apportionment of effects is quite clear in the Treasury model, which separates long-run determinants of the exchange rate (relative money supplies) from short-run determinants like interest rates and oil prices. The resulting equations are structural in the sense that each one claims to model a specific flow. The cost of using this method is considerable. Instead of a single unreliable equation, the model now contains several equations which depend on very doubtful data.

It is interesting to note that in more recent work the Treasury model has shifted back to an explicit exchange rate equation and omitted one of the capital flows equations (see Barber, 1984; HM Treasury, 1982), although this seems to be viewed simply as an inversion of the short-term capital flows equation.

(b) Modelling Expectations. The elaborateness of the Treasury's system is not worth a row of beans unless it works. To its credit, the Treasury model makes explicit the role of expectations and its own assumptions about how expectations are formed. In previous chapters (especially Chapter 4) we have stressed that equilibrium in markets in general and in the financial markets in particular depends to a large extent on what market agents think will happen in the future. In particular, the realised rate of return on foreign currency denominated assets will depend on what the exchange rate will turn out to be. Bearing in mind that the current value of the exchange rate depends on current values of other variables, like the oil price, any reasonable expectation of the future exchange rate is going to require expectations of these variables as well. Moreover, by induction, any reasonable expectation of next period's exchange rate must be based on a view of what is going to happen in the period after that. Thus it seems that to predict the exchange rate we are going to have to take a view on the entire future paths of all the determining variables.

When at each stage the expectation is consistent with what the model itself would predict, given that expectation, the method of forming reasonable expectations is known as 'rational expectations' and its use can be illustrated by a simple example. Suppose that the exchange rate is determined by the open arbitrage condition. That means that, given the expected value of the exchange rate next period and current interest rates, the current exchange rate is determined by the condition that investment at home and abroad should be equally profitable. £1 invested in the UK will yield $£(1 + r)$ at the end of the period; £1 converted into dollars on the spot market yields $\$e$, which, when invested, will yield $\$e(1 + r^*)$ at the end of the period which, when converted back into sterling at the expected rate of exchange next period, will be worth $£e(1 + r^*)/e_{+1}^e$ where e_{+1}^e is the exchange rate that is expected to rule one period hence. If each project is equally profitable,

$$(1 + r) = e(1 + r^*)/e_{+1}^e$$

or, after re-arrangement and taking logs,

$$\log e = \log e^e_{+1} + \log(1 + r) - \log(1 + r^*).$$

If the interest rates are small, this can be approximated by

$$\log e = \log e^e_{+1} + ID$$

where $ID = r - r^*$. The rational method of finding the unknown e^e_{+1} is to use the equation, thus

$$\log e = ID + \log e^e_{+2} + ID^e_{+1}$$

$$= ID + \sum_{i=1}^{n} ID^e_{+i} + e^e_{+(n+1)}.$$

By continuous substitution, we can push the unknown e^e further and further into the future and substitute the series of interest differentials ID^e. If interest rates are taken to be fixed by government policy, this may be more convenient.

This simple example illustrates the way in which future variables get into the formula for the current value of the exchange rate and also that there is always likely to be a problem of left-over far-off expectations, in this case $e^e_{+(n+1)}$. In the simple case examined the current value of the exchange rate depends on expectations of future interest differentials and on the value taken by the exchange rate in the long run. This far-off value of the exchange rate has to be supplied by the so-called terminal condition. Sometimes this might be that the long-run exchange rate is some given number but usually it will be a requirement that the nominal exchange rate is such that some more general condition is fulfilled — for instance, it might be required that the real exchange rate $P/(P^*/e)$ is some given value. Since the domestic price level depends on the path of the exchange rate, the computation of the terminal condition depends on current value of the exchange rate. In practice, the entire sequence of exchange rates must be determined at once. This is not a trivial task. Because in practice the terminal condition is unknown and the horizon at which it obtains is unknown, an element of extreme arbitrariness is introduced into the procedure.

If instead of this method of successive substitution we were prepared to accept the view that next period's exchange rate is expected to be some weighted average of past exchange rates, this problem does not arise. Suppose, for example, that

$$\log e^e_{+1} = \sum_{i=0}^{k} a_i \log e_{-i}$$

In this case we can substitute for e^e_{+1} directly to get

$$\log e = \sum_{i=1}^{k} a_i \log e_{-i} + ID = \frac{1}{1-a_0} \sum_{i=1}^{k} a_i \log e_{-i} + \frac{ID}{1-a_0}.$$

In other words, the exchange rate can be explained wholly on the basis of past realised and known values of e and the current known value of ID. This second type of model may naturally be called backward looking; the rational expectations model can be called forward looking.

The problem with backward-looking models is that they imply that expectations are nearly always falsified. In our example the difference between the actual exchange rate at time t and the expectation of that exchange rate formed one period earlier is given by

$$\sum_{i=1}^{k+1} \left[\frac{a_i}{1-a_0} - a_{-1} \right] \log e_{-i} + \frac{ID}{1-a_0}$$

which is not normally zero.

(c) The State of the Art? The logical cumulation of these two approaches to the exchange rate is an asset flows model to be solved under rational expectations. The only large example of this in the UK is the current LBS model described in Budd *et al.* (1984), and Keating (1984). In this model, nine sectors are distinguished, including the public and foreign sectors. Each sector has a portfolio of up to 19 assets. As the assets of one sector are the liabilities of another this multi-sectoral approach in principle makes explicit the separate supply and demand influences for each asset. The LBS model is certainly the most elaborate and theoretically satisfying: whether it will deliver the goods in terms of more accurate forecasts is, at the time of writing, an open question.

For each asset in each sector's portfolio the demand is given by an equation of the form

$$A_i = \Sigma a_{ij} r_j + b_i W + \Sigma c_{ij} A_j(-1)$$

where A_i is the stock of asset i, r_j is the expected rate of return on asset j, W is wealth and the a's, b's and c's are coefficients. The form of the equation is similar to the L & D formulation, except for the inclusion of the terms $\Sigma c_{ij} A_j(-1)$ which allows for the slow adjustment of asset holdings because of costs of adjustment. When the security in question is a liability of the sector rather than an asset, A_i will of course be negative. Because the model is a complete description of the sector's asset holdings, it must be the case that the b_i's sum to one for any sector. This is because all wealth must be held in some asset. Similarly, for any rate of return the sum of the coefficients associated with it in different equations must be zero to ensure that if a rate of return changes with no change in wealth, the new quantities of assets held are consistent with wealth constraint. Other, less immediately transparent, conditions are that the sum of the coefficients on the rates of return in each equation should be zero and that the coefficient on rate of return j in equation i must equal that of rate of return i in equation j for all i and j $(i \neq j)$.

The general strategy is then the same as in the former Treasury model, although the coverage of sectors and assets is much wider. Like the system described in L & D there is no explicit exchange rate equation, rather the exchange rate appears as part of the expected rate of return for foreign currency assets. Unlike the L & D model, the expected value of the future exchange rate is given by the assumption of rational expectations. This means that forecasts depend on what is assumed about the terminal condition and how far away the horizon at which the terminal condition is. More interesting from our point of view is that the assumption introduces an element of indeterminacy into forecasts because they now depend on what is assumed about the knowledge of participants in the market. If agents anticipate some future event that will have repercussions on the exchange market, their actions will mean that the repercussions will occur before the event actually takes place. Keating illustrates the problem by conducting a number of simulations of exogenous shocks, first on the assumption that the shock comes as a complete surprise to the markets, and secondly on the assumption that the market anticipates the change a year in advance. Figure 13.3 shows Keating's results of the effects of a bill-financed expansion in government spending and of a one percentage point increase in world interest rates. When the change is anticipated the exchange rate moves at the time the expectation is formed rather than when the event occurs; also the exchange rate shifts by rather less in the short run.

In practice, if the exchange rate moves on expectations of future events rather than on realisation, it may move on the expectation of something that in the end does not occur. This is going to make the discovery of causal links difficult, even if we assume that expectations are borne out on average. Furthermore, in practice it is unlikely that all market participants will form their expectations at the same time. Your forecast of the short-run behaviour of the exchange rate then depends on your expectations of future variables — possibly far distant — on your beliefs about what everybody else believes or will come to believe and on your judgement about whether the exchange rate has already adjusted. This is not really very helpful. It amounts to saying that in the end the path

Figure 13.3

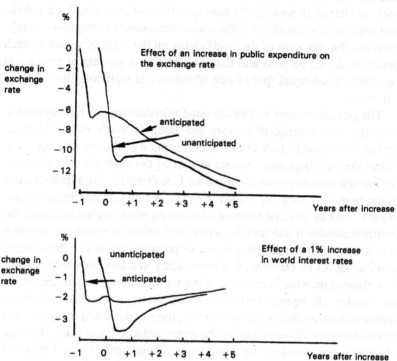

Source: Keating (1984).

of the exchange rate is determined by 'fundamentals', but the short-run behaviour is essentially unpredictable using information about the past. Whether this integrated approach to forecasting pays off, only time will tell.

Non-econometric Methods

Economists are drawn to econometric methods because by placing exchange rate forecasting in the context of theoretical argument — however loosely drawn in practice — they increase their own confidence in their forecast by checking that the whole picture looks right. The estimated equation is in practice the starting point of the exercise which summarises the average effects of explanatory variables in the past. In practice the data are not available to estimate the implications of the theories exactly and forecasters have to make do with rather crude approximations which, as the Meese & Rogoff study shows, may not be much use. In the circumstances, it may make sense to search for simpler methods which although even cruder from a theoretical point of view nevertheless contribute positively to the forecasting exercise. Such methods may be the best available over very short-run periods for which the data required by econometric analysis are not available. Alternatively they may be seen as a 'hi-tech' cloak to cover what is in fact a guess. There is nothing wrong of course with an educated guess based on the information to hand — this is after all just what an econometric equation is. What is at issue is whether *statistical* analysis is of much help in this area.

We have already considered one particular alternative, namely time series analysis, which resembles econometric methods in that an estimated equation is used but differs importantly because only lagged values of the exchange rate itself may appear as right hand side variables. Thus the equation has the form

$$e_t = a_1 e_{t-1} + a_2 e_{t-2} + \ldots + a_n e_{t-n} + u_t$$

where u_t is an error term. Time series analysis pays great attention to the proper specification of this error term after using the methods made popular by Box and Jenkins (1975).

The great advantage of the method is extreme economy of information. If we wish to obtain forecasts of the future for which our best guess about the unsystematic errors is that they will all be zero we can use the '*chain rule of forecasting*'. Suppose at time T we know enough past values to forecast period T_1 using the formula

$$e^e_{T+1} = a_1 e_T + a_2 e_{T-1} + \ldots + a_n e_{T-(n-1)}$$

where e^e_{T+1} is the value expected for period $T + 1$. The forecast for the next period is computed by advancing the formula using the previously computed forecast for period $T + 1$ to fill in the missing data:

$$e^e_{T+2} = a_1 e^e_{T+1} + a_2 e_T + \ldots + a_n e_{T-(n-2)}$$

Once the parameters (the a_i's) have been estimated such a formula is very easy to use. However it does not inspire much confidence as it appears to use so little of the available data. Perhaps the method is best suited to the identification of regular patterns in the exchange rate over very short periods for which the information required by full-blown econometric analysis is not available. Would anyone be prepared to justify a forecast merely on the basis that it was produced by an autoregressive equation, with no reference to other economic phenomena?

Time series analysis is the most statistical form of technical analysis, the most popular manifestation of which is 'chartism'. Chartists examine plots of exchange rates or exchange rate movements to try to identify recurring patterns. It has in common with time series analysis the advantage that historical data on the exchange rate alone is required and shares with time series analysis the difficulties inherent in a theory free approach. At its simplest the method assumes that the underlying movement of the exchange rate is a series of peaks and troughs, but that the picture is obscured by small erratic disturbances around this path. The trick is to spot the turning points. Suppose that the exchange rate has fallen below some previous peak by some pre-designated percentage. This may be considered too large to be explained by erratic movements and therefore identifies a new trend. Conversely at troughs significant upward movements may indicate the start of a new upswing. Such a *filter method* of prediction is shown in Figure 13.4.

One problem with this simple method is that, however well it may perform in detecting movement *away* from previous peaks or troughs, it does not help to predict these turning points. To capture these, an alternative method is based on the observation that, in the vicinity of a peak, the rate of increase of the exchange rate slows down, then becomes zero, and finally as the exchange rate falls becomes negative. If peaks tend to be similar, then an indicator of the approach of a peak can be found by constructing an index of momentum. In practice, the momentum can be measured by dividing the current exchange rate, e_t, by a previously observed exchange rate, e_{t-n}. The interval between the two observations should be short enough so that the ratio is a good indication of the rate of change of the exchange rate, but long enough so that the ratio is not dominated by random fluctuations. As the exchange rate approaches a peak, the ratio will be above unity but falling. When the peak is reached, the exchange rates e_t and e_{t-n} are equal so that the ratio will be unity. On the descent from the peak e_t will be less than e_{t-n} so that the ratio is less than unity. The relationship between the two approaches is shown in Figure 13.5. The main problem with using a measure of momentum is that it is easily fooled if instead of reaching a peak the rise in the exchange rate is merely checked temporarily as is shown in the figure.

Figure 13.4

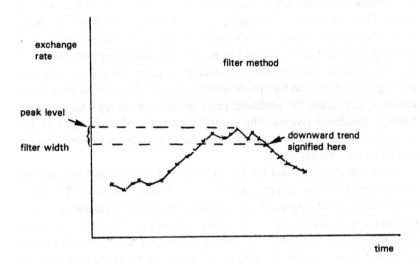

Figure 13.5

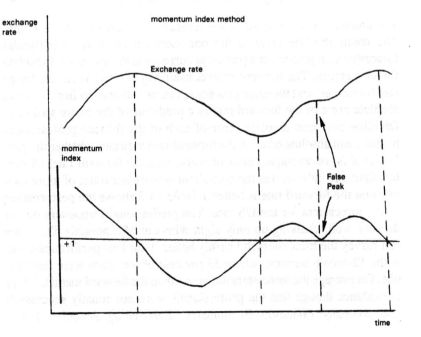

How Well do Professional Forecasters Forecast?

Professional economists provide forecasts because there is a demand for them. They have to use, normally in combination, whatever methods they judge to be most sensible. Given their training, economists will seek the help of economic theory and econometrics. But no-one would claim an unblemished track record in exchange rate forecasting. It is worth finding out whether in fact professionally supplied forecasts have been useful. If in practice the exchange rate cannot be predicted with any confidence, prudence requires the careful avoidance of exchange risk by using forward cover where available and such practices as matching assets and liabilities by currency.

In one study published by *Euromoney* in 1981 the performance of thirteen professional commercial forecasters was evaluated. The thirteen were those who agreed to participate although 30 organisations were originally approached. The forecasters supplied data on their forecasts over the period 1977–80. The forecasts covered up to nine bilateral exchange rates with the US dollar and were for horizons of from one month ahead to one year ahead. There is thus a maximum of 48 forecasts to consider. The forecast error is defined by

$$\text{forecast error} = \text{(predicted value of exchange rate)} - \text{(actual value of exchange rate)}.$$

The absolute forecast error is the forecast error disregarding its sign. The mean absolute error at the one month horizon for a particular forecaster's projections of a particular currency is the mean of 48 absolute forecast errors. The forward market itself can be used as an 'exchange rate forecaster' and the same procedure can be followed to find the mean absolute error of the forward rate as a predictor of the future spot rate. Dividing the mean absolute error of each of the thirteen professionals by the mean absolute error of the forward rate indicates whether the professional is, on average, better or worse than the forward rate. (Ratios less than one indicate that the consultant is more accurate; of more than one that the forward rate is better.) Table 13.3 shows the performance of the forecasters for the £/$ rate. The professional forecasters do not do very well, chalking up only eight wins out of a possible 52. In the full survey the forecasters did hardly better: their best performance was at the 12-month horizon, where 33 per cent of the ratios were less than one. On average the forecasters did worse than the forward market. There is evidence though that the professionals were not equally successful: one company (Wharton Econometric Forecasting Associates) out-

Table 13.3: Professionals Forecasts of the Sterling–Dollar Rate Performances Compared with the Forward Market

Organisation Horizon	1	2	3	4	5	6	7	8	9	10	11	12	13
1 month	1.01	1.11	1.15	1.44	**0.89**	**0.95**	1.03	1.05	1.09	1.30	**0.99**	1.11	1.13
3 months	1.11	1.24	**0.91**	1.44	1.09	**0.98**	1.05	1.09	1.27	1.69	1.03	1.22	1.01
6 months	1.38	1.33	1.28	1.56	1.02	1.04	1.20	**0.99**	1.36	1.28	1.02	1.39	**0.97**
12 months	1.59	1.27	1.28	1.62	1.23	1.16	1.40	**0.89**	1.31	1.05	**0.85**	1.03	1.44

Table shows for each organisation the mean absolute error of each forecast divided by the mean absolute error of the forward market. Cases in which forecasters are on average more accurate than forward market are underlined.

Source: Euromonecs.

performed the forward market in six out of nine currencies at the one month horizon, in seven at the three month horizon, in eight at six months and seven at 12 months.

Why is the Exchange Rate so Hard to Forecast? Conclusions

So far we have established that exchange rate forecasts do not have a very encouraging track record; our examination of econometric methods, with their dependence on forecasts of associated variables, has suggested that exchange rate forecasting may well be a very difficult task in principle. The M & R conclusion that the random walk model has a better track record than other methods can be given another interpretation: namely that the foreign exchange market is efficient. We considered the concept of efficiency in Chapter 4. In the current context, the market can be said to be efficient if all possibilities for profitable speculation have been exhausted. This means in particular that it is not possible consistently to make profits by following any rule, whether based on econometrics or technical analysis. If this were true we would expect exchange rate movements to be random — that is, to follow the random walk model.

Whatever the reason, from the investor's point of view the maintenance of an open position, so that his future wealth depends on the value of the exchange rate in the future, must be viewed as essentially risky. It is worth considering those mechanisms by which such positions can be closed and exchange risk eliminated. It is our view that those involved in foreign exchange transactions should not indulge in speculation by accident. Two mechanisms are described — the forward market and the matching of assets and liabilities. The forward market has already been extensively discussed (Chapter 3). Although this chapter is about forecasting, it must be emphasised that the forward market is an institution for avoiding risk — it does not in the least matter, from this point of view, whether the market is particularly accurate when looked at from a forecasting point of view. Suppose a firm incurs £100 of costs now and will receive $200 revenue from sales in three months. Without a forward market it would be impossible to know in advance whether the deal was going to be profitable. After three months the profitability will be known: it depends of course on whether the exchange rate is less than or greater than $2 = £1[4]. If a forward market exists, with a forward rate of $1.50 = £1, the proceeds can be sold *now* for £133.33 so that the deal is known to be profitable. Exchange risk can be eliminated. At the end of the day the firm may wish it had not covered, with the wisdom of hindsight. If the firm wishes to gamble on whether the future spot rate will be less than £1.50 and therefore maintain an open position, by not using the forward market, then that is an explicit decision to speculate.

It is sometimes argued that the existence of forward markets does not avoid the necessity of exchange rate forecasting because forward contracts are in practice available only a year ahead at most. If the $200 of the previous example is going to arrive in five years rather than three months, long-range exchange rate forecasting is still going to be needed however reluctant the firm is to speculate. However, as long as the firm has access to negotiable securities, it can still avoid risk by borrowing and lending in different currencies. In the example the firm should borrow dollars so that the $200 when it is received will pay off the principal and accumulated interest. The firm should borrow $200 $\div (1 + r_5)^5$ where r_5 is the annual rate of interest available now on five-year securities. If this were 10 per cent, the firm would borrow $124. This can be traded at once on the spot market. Assuming that the firm's costs are still £100, the deal will be profitable overall as long as the exchange rate is below 1.24. Thus markets for securities can be used instead of forward markets to eliminate exchange rate risk. It is worth noting that the break-even exchange rate depends on how long the firm has to wait before receiving $200. This is quite appropriate as the interval between costs incurred and the receipt of payment has elements of a forced loan.

While various strategies are available for minimising the effects of unanticipated exchange rate changes, exchange rate risk is, at the end of the day, just one more uncertainty facing those doing business in the international economy in the 1980s — whether they be individuals deciding where to go on holiday or giant multinational firms tendering for enormous development contracts. Under the current international institutional arrangements, and given the current low degree of policy co-ordination, exchange rate fluctuations are not going to disappear. Nor do we think forecasts of nominal exchange rates will magically improve. Exchange rate movements are needed to enforce accounting consistency on the disparate plans of private agents and national governments. While individual regional arrangements like the EMS may develop further, and while there may be sporadic outbreaks of international co-operation, we see no prospect of a return to a significantly more managed system in the near future.

Notes

1. For a review of current practice in UK macro-models see Wallis *et al.* 1985, Chapter 4. This exposition requires a good deal of prior knowledge.
2. Strictly speaking, this is an approximation valid for low rates of inflation and when the domestic and foreign price levels are initially equal.
3. See also section on Non-econometric Methods below.
4. Ignoring interest charges.

REFERENCES

Aliber, R.Z. (1973), 'The Interest Parity Theorem: A Reinterpretation', *Journal of Political Economy*, vol. 81, pp. 1451–59.

Argy, V., and Hodjera, Z. (1973), 'Financial Integration and Interest Rate Linkages in Industrial Countries, 1957–71', *IMF Staff Papers*, vol. 20, pp. 1–77.

Argy, V. (1981), *Post War International Money Crisis; An Analysis*, London, Allen and Unwin.

Artus, J.R., and Young, J.H. (1979), 'Fixed and Flexible Exchange Rates A Renewal of the Debate', *IMF Staff Papers* (December).

Atkinson, F.J., Brooks, S., and Hall, S.G.F. (1983), 'The Economic Effects of North Sea Oil', *National Institute Economic Review*, no. 104, pp. 38–44.

Attfield, C.L.F., Demery, D., and Duck, N. (1985), *Rational Expectations in Macroeconomics*, Oxford, Basil Blackwell.

Baillie, R.T., and McMahon, P.C. (1982), 'Expectations, Risk and the Foreign Exchange Market', discussion paper, University of Birmingham.

Ballie, R.T., Lippens, R.E., and McMahon, P.C. (1983), 'Testing Rational Expectations and Efficiency in the Foreign Exchange Market', *Econometrica*, vol. 51, pp. 553–64.

Bank of England (1982), 'The Supplementary Special Deposits Scheme', *Bank of England Quarterly Bulletin*, March, reprinted in *The Development and Operation of Monetary Policy 1960–83*, Bank of England, Oxford, pp. 117–27.

Barber, J. (ed.) (1984), *HM Treasury Technical Manual*, Supplement to the 1982 Technical Manual, London, HM Treasury.

Beenstock, M. (1978), *The Foreign Exchanges: Theory, Modelling and Policy'*, London, Macmillan.

Beenstock, M., and Bell, S. (1979), 'A Quarterly Econometric Model of the Capital Account in the UK Balance of Payments', *Manchester School*, 47, pp. 33–62.

Bilson, J.F.O. (1978), 'The Monetary Approach to the Exchange Rate: Some Empirical Evidence', *IMF Staff Papers*, vol. 25, pp. 48–75.

Bilson, J.F.O. (1981), 'The Speculative Efficiency Hypothesis', *Journal of Business*, vol. 54, pp. 435–51.

Box, G.E.P., and Jenkins, G.M. (1975), *Time Series Analysis*, San Fransisco, Holden Day.

Branson, W.H., and Hill, R.D. (1971), 'Capital Movements in the OECD Area', Paris, OECD.

Brooks, S. (1983), 'Exports and Imports', in Britton, A.J.C. (ed.), *Employment, Output and Inflation*, London, Heinemann.

Brooks, S., and Henry, S.G.B. (1983a), 'Re-estimation of the National Institute Model', *National Institute Economic Review*, no. 103, pp. 62–70.

Brooks, S., and Henry, S.G.B. (1983b), 'Simulation Exercises with the Whole Model', in Britton, A.J.C. (ed.), *Employment, Output and Inflation*, London, Heinmann.

Budd, A., Dicks, G., Holly, S., Keating, G., and Robinson, B. (1984), 'The London Business School Econometric Model', London Business School Centre for Economic Forecasting, discussion paper, no. 124.

Buiter, W.H., and Miller, M. (1981), 'Monetary Policy and International Competitiveness: The Problems of Adjustment', *Oxford Economic Papers*, vol. 33, pp. 143–75.

Byatt, I., Hartley, N., Lomax, R., Powell, S., and Spencer, P. (1982), 'North Sea Oil and Structural Adjustment', Treasury Working Paper, no. 22, London.

Carlson, J.A., and Parkin, J.M. (1975), 'Inflation Expectations', *Economica*, vol. 42, pp. 123–38.

Caves, R.E., and Jones, R.W. (1974), *World Trade and Payments*, Boston, Little Brown & Co.

Cornell, B. (1977), 'Spot Rates, Forward Rates and Exchange Market Efficiency', *Journal of Financial Economics*, vol. 5, pp. 55–66.

Cosander, P.A., and Laing, B.R. (1981), 'Interest Rate Parity Tests: Switzerland and Some Major Western Countries', *Journal of Banking and Finance*, vol. 5, pp. 187–200.

Cossett, J.C. (1984), 'On the Presence of Risk Premiums in Foreign Exchange Markets', *Journal of International Economics*, vol. 16, pp. 139–54.

Cumby, R.E., and Obstfeld, M. (1981), 'Exchange Rate Expectations and Nominal Interest Differentials: A Test of the Fisher Hypotheses', *Journal of Finance*, vol. 36, pp. 697–703.

Currie, D. (1984), 'Monetary Overshooting and the Exchange Rate', *Manchester School*, vol. 102, pp. 28–48.

Cuthbertson, K. (1982), 'The Measurement and Behaviour of the UK Saving Ratio', *National Institute Economic Review*, no. 99, pp. 75–93.

Davidson, J. (1982), 'Econometric Modelling of the Sterling Effective Exchange Rate', London School of Economics, mimeo.

Dornbusch, R. (1973a), 'Currency Depreciation, Hoarding and Relative Prices', *Journal of Political Economy*, vol. 81, no. 4, pp. 893–915.

Dornbusch, R. (1973b), 'Devaluation, Money and Non Traded Goods', *American Economic Review*, vol. 62, no. 5, pp. 871–80.

Dornbusch, R. (1976), 'Expectations and Exchange Rate Dynamics', *Journal of Political Economy*, vol. 84, pp. 1161–76.

Dornbusch, R. (1978), 'Monetary Policy under Exchange Rate Flexibility', in *Managed Exchange Rate Flexibility: The Recent Experience*, Federal Reserve Bank of Boston Conference Series, 20, pp. 90–122.

Dornbusch, R. (1980), 'Exchange Rate Economics: Where Do We Stand', *Brookings Papers on Economic Activity*, vol. 1, pp. 143–85.

Dornbusch, R. (1980a), *Open Economy Macroeconomics*, New York, Basic Books.

Durbin, J. (1954), 'Errors in Variables', *Review of the International Statistical Institute*, vol. 1, pp. 23–32.

Eastwood, R.K., and Venables, A.J. (1982), 'The Macroeconomic Implications of a Resource Discovery in an Open Economy', *Economic Journal*, vol. 92, pp. 285–99.

Forsyth, P.J., and Kay, J.A. (1980), 'The Economic Implications of North Sea Oil Revenues', *Fiscal Studies*.

Frankel, J.A. (1979a), 'A Test of the Existence of the Risk Premium in the Foreign Exchange Market Versus the Hypothesis of Perfect Substitutability', *International Finance Discussion Paper 149*, Federal Reserve System, Washington DC.

Frankel, J.A. (1979b), 'On the Mark: A Theory of Floating Exchange Rates Based on Real Interest Differentials', *American Economic Review*, vol. 69, pp. 610–22.

Frankel, J.A. (1980), 'Tests of Rational Expectations in the Forward Exchange Market', *Southern Economic Journal*, vol. 46, pp. 1083–101.

Frenkel, J.A. (1976), 'A Monetary Approach to the Exchange Rate: Doctrinal Aspects and Empirical Evidence', *Scandinavian Journal of Economics*, vol. 78, pp. 255–76.

Frenkel, J.A. (1981), 'The Collapse of Purchasing Power Parities During the 1970s', *European Economic Review*, vol. 16, pp. 145–65.

Frenkel, J.A. (1982), 'Flexible Exchange Rates, Prices and the Role of 'News', Lessons from the 1970's', in R. Batchelor and G. Wood (eds), *Exchange Rate Policy*, London, Macmillan.

Frenkel, J.A., and Johnson, H.G. (1976), 'Essential Concepts and Historical Origins', in Frenkel, J.A. and Johnson, H.G. (eds), *The Monetary Approach to the Balance of Payments*, London, Allen and Unwin.

Frenkel, J.A., and Levich, R.M. (1975), 'Covered Interest Arbitrage: Unexploited Profits?', *Journal of Political Economy*, vol. 83, pp. 325–38.

Frenkel, J.A., and Levich, R.M. (1977), 'Transactions Costs and Interest Arbitrage: Tranquil Versus Turbulent Periods', *Journal of Political Economy*, vol. 85, no. 6, pp. 665–705.

Frenkel, J.A., and Mussa, M.L. (1980), 'The Efficiency of Foreign Exchange Markets and Measures of Turbulence', *American Economic Review*, 70, pp. 374–81.

Frenkel, J.A., and Rodriguez, C.A. (1982), 'Exchange Rate Dynamics and the Overshooting Hypothesis', *IMF Staff Papers*, vol. 9, pp. 369–79.

Friedman, B.M. (1979), 'Optimal Expectations and the Extreme Informational Assumptions of Rational Expectations Macromodels', *Journal of Monetary Economics*, vol. 5, pp. 23–41.

Friedman, B.M. (1980), 'Survey Evidence on the "Rationality" of Interest Rate Expectations data', *Journal of Monetary Economics*, vol. 6, pp. 453–65.

Goodhart, C.A.E. (1975), *Money, Information and Uncertainty*, London, Macmillan.

Goodhart, C.A.E. (1984), *Monetary Theory and Practice: The UK Experience*, London, Macmillan.

de Grauwe, P., and Peters, T. (1979), 'The EMS, Europe and the Dollar', *The Banker* (April), pp. 39–45.

Grossman, S.J., and Stiglitz, J.E. (1980), 'The Impossibility of Informationally Efficient Markets', *American Economic Review*, vol. 70, pp. 393–408.

Grubel, H.G. (1970), 'The Theory of Optimum Currency Areas', *Canadian Journal of Economics* (May).

Haache, G., and Townend, J. (1981), 'Exchange Rates and Monetary Policy: Modelling Sterling's Effective Exchange Rate 1972–80', *Oxford Economic Papers*, vol. 33, supplement, pp. 201–47.

Hakkio, C.S. (1984), 'A Re-examination of Purchasing Power Parity: A Multi-Country and Multi Period Study', *Journal of International Economics*, vol. 17, pp. 265–78.

Hall, S. (1983), 'The Exchange Rate' in Britton, A.J.C. (ed.), *Employment, Output and Inflation*, London, Heinemann.

Hansen, L.P., and Hodrick, R. (1980), 'Forward Exchange Rates as Optimal Predictors of Future Spot Rates: An Econometric Analysis', *Journal of Political Economy*, vol. 88, pp. 829–53.

Hausman, J.A. (1978), 'Specification Tests in Econometrics', *Econometrica*, vol. 46, pp. 1251–72.

Hendry, D., and Mizon, G. (1978), 'Serial Correlation as a Convenient Simplification, Not a Nuisance: A Comment on a Study of the Demand for Money by the Bank of England', *Economic Journal*, vol. 88, pp. 549–63.

Heywood, J. (1981), *Foreign Exchange and the Corporate Treasurer*, 3rd edition, London, Black.

Hodjera, Z. (1971), 'Short Term Capital Movements of the United Kingdom', *Journal of Political Economy*, vol. 79, pp. 739–75.

Holden, K., Peel, D.A., and Thompson, J.L. (1985), 'Expectations, Theory and Evidence', London, Macmillan.

Hooper, P., and Morton, J. (1980), 'Fluctuations in the Dollar: A Model of Nominal and Real Exchange Rate Determination', *International Finance Discussion Paper*, 168, Board of Governors, Federal Reserve System, Washington DC.

House of Lords Committee on Overseas Trade (1985), *Report*, 3 vols., HL 238(I–III), HMSO.

Hughes, M. (1983), 'The Consequences of the Removal of Exchange Controls on Portfolios and the Flow of Funds in the UK', chapter 9 in D.C. Corner and D.G. Mayes (eds), *Modern Portfolio Theory and Financial Institutions*, London, Macmillan.

Hutton, J. (1977), 'A Model of Short-term Capital Movements, the Foreign Exchange Market and Official Intervention in the UK, 1963–70', *Review of Economic Studies*, vol. XLIV (1), pp. 31–41.

Ingram, J.C. (1973), 'The Case for European Monetary Integration', *Princeton Essays in International Finance*, no. 98.

Ishimaya, Y. (1975), 'The Theory of Optimum Currency Areas: A Survey', *IMF Staff Papers* (July).

Jacobs, R.L. (1982), 'The Effect of Errors in Variables or Tests for a Risk Premium in Forward Exchange Rates', *Journal of Finance*, vol. 37, pp. 667–77.

Johnston, R.B. (1983), *The Economics of the Euro-Market*, London, Macmillan.

Jones, R.W. (1974), 'The Small Country in a Many Commodity World', Rochester discussion paper, 73–14..

Journal of International Economics (1978), 'Purchasing Power Parity: A Symposium', vol. 8, no. 2, May.

Keating, G. (1984), 'The Financial Sector of the London School Model', London Business School Centre for Economic Forecasting, discussion paper, no. 115.

Keynon, A.K. (1981), *Currency Risk Management*, London, Wiley.

Krause, L.B., and Salant, W.S. (1973), *European Monetary Integration and Its Meaning for the United States*, Washington, Brookings.

Krugman, P.R. (1978), 'Purchasing Power Parity and Exchange Rates', *Journal of International Economics*, vol. 8, pp. 397–407.

Llewllyn, D.T. (1980), *International Financial Integration*, London, Macmillan.

Lomax, R., and Denham, M. (1978), 'A Financial Sector for the Treasury Model. Part Two. The Model of External Capital Flows', Treasury Working Paper, no. 8, London.

London Business School (1981), 'The London Business School Quarterly Econometric Model of the UK Economy: Relationships in the Basic Model as at June 1981', London Business School Econometric Forecasting Unit.

Macdonald, R. (1983), 'Some Tests of the Rational Expectations Hypothesis in the Foreign Exchange Market', *Scottish Journal of Political Economy*, vol. 3, pp. 235–50.

McCallum, B.T. (1976), 'Rational Expectations and the Estimation of Econometric Models: An Alternative Procedure', *International Economic Review*, vol. 17, pp. 484–90.

McCormick, F. (1979), 'Covered Interest Arbitrage: Unexploited Profits? Comment', *Journal of Political Economy*, vol. 87, April, pp. 418–22.

MacKinnon, S. (1980), 'The European Monetary System: A Review', *Irish Banking Review* (March).

McKinnon, R.I. (1963), 'Optimum Currency Areas', *American Economic Review* (September).

McKinnon, R.I. (1979), *Money in International Exchange*, Oxford, Oxford University Press.

Marston, R.L. (1976), 'Interest Arbitrage in the Euro-currency Markets', *European Economic Review*, vol. 17, pp. 1–13.

Mayes, David, G. (1984), 'Factor Mobility', chapter 16, in A.M. El Agraa (ed.), *The Economics of the European Community*, 2nd edition, Oxford, Philip Allan.

Meese, R.A., and Rogoff, K. (1983), 'Empirical Exchange Rate Models of the Seventies Do They Fit out of Sample?', *Journal of International Economics*, vol. 14, pp. 3–24.

Minford, P. (1978), *Substitution Effects, Speculation and Exchange Rate Stability*, Amsterdam, North Holland.

Minford, P., and Peel, D. (1983), *Rational Expectations and the New Macroeconomics*, Oxford, Martin Robertson.

Mullineaux, D.J. (1978), 'On Testing for Rationality: Another Look at the Livingston Price Expectations Data', *Journal of Political Economy*, vol. 86, pp. 329–36.

Mundell, R. (1961), 'A Theory of Optimum Currency Areas', *American Economic Review*, (September).

Mussa, M. (1979a), 'Empirical Regularities in the Behaviour of Exchange Rates and Theories of the Foreign Exchange Market', in K. Brunner and A.H. Meltzer (eds), *Policies for Employment, Prices and Exchange Rates*, Supplement to the *Journal of Monetary Economics*, vol. 11.

Mussa, M. (1979b), 'Macroeconomic Interdependence and the Exchange Rate Regime', in R. Dornbusch and J.A. Frenkel (eds), *International Economic Policy, Theory and*

Evidence, Baltimore, Johns Hopkins.

Neary, J.P., and Van Wijnbergen, S. (1984), 'Can an oil discovery lead to a recession? Comment on Eastwood and Venables', *Economic Journal*, vol. 94, pp. 390-5.

von Neumann Whitman, M. (1970), 'Policies for Internal and External Balance', Princeton Special Papers in International Economics, no. 9.

Niehans, J. (1984), *International Monetary Economics*, Oxford, Philip Allen.

Ormerod, P. (1980), 'The Forward Exchange Rate for Sterling and the Efficiency of Expectations', *Weltwirtshaftliches Archiv*, vol. 116, pp. 205-224.

Oxford Economic Papers (1981), 'Exchange Rates and the Money Supply', vol. 33, special supplement.

Pesaran, M.H. (1984), 'Expectations Formation and Macroeconomic Modelling', in P. Malagrange and P.A. Muet (eds), *Contemporary Macroeconomic Modelling*, Oxford, Basil Blackwell.

Richardson, G. (1980), 'The North Sea and the United Kingdom Economy: Some Long Term Perspectives and Implications, *Bank of England Quarterly Bulletin*, pp. 449-54.

Salter, W.E.G. (1959), 'Internal and External Balance: The Role of Price and Expenditure Effects', *Economic Record*, vol. 35.

Scandinavian Journal of Economics (1976), vol. 78, no. 2.

Solomon, R. (1982), *The International Monetary System, 1945-1981*, New York, Harper and Row.

Stern, R.M. (1973), *The Balance of Payments: Theory and Economic Policy*, London, Macmillan.

Strange, S. (1976), *International Monetary Relations*, Oxford, Oxford University Press.

HM Treasury (1982), *Macroeconomic Model Technical Manual 1982*, London, HM Treasury.

Tresize, P.H. (ed.) (1979), *The European Monetary System: Its Promises and Prospects*, Washington, Brookings.

Turnovsky, S.J. (1977), *Macroeconomic Analysis and Stabilization Policies*, Cambridge University Press.

Vernon, K. (1985), 'Oil Prices and the Exchange Rate', Annex to Powell, S. and Horton, G., 'The Economic Effects of Lower Oil Prices', Treasury Working Paper, no. 34, London, HM Treasury.

Wallis, K.F., Andrews, M.J., Bell, D.N.F., Fisher, P.G., and Whitley, J.D. (1985), *Models of the UK Economy*, Oxford, Oxford University Press.

Wickens, M., and Smith, P. (1984), 'The Sterling Effective Exchange Rate', University of Southampton, Dept. of Economics Discussion Paper.

Williams, D. (1978), 'Estimating in Levels or First Differences: A Defence of the Method used for Certain Demand for Money Studies', *Economic Journal*, vol. 88, pp. 564-8.

Yeager, L.B. (1976), *International Monetary Relations: Theory, History and Policy*, 2nd edition, New York, Harper and Row.

Zellner, A. (1962), 'An efficient method of estimating seemingly unrelated regressions and tests for aggregation bias', *Journal of the American Statistical Association*, vol. 57, pp. 348-68.

INDEX

For Product Safety Concerns and Information please contact our
EU representative GPSR@taylorandfrancis.com Taylor & Francis
Verlag GmbH, Kaufingerstraße 24, 80331 München, Germany